P9-CCJ-916

Gourmet

GONE WILD

Planning and Preparing Complete Menus for Game, Fish, and Fowl

LORELIE SCORZAFAVA

STACKPOLE
BOOKS

Published by
STACKPOLE BOOKS
5067 Ritter Road
Mechanicsburg, PA 17055
www.stackpolebooks.com

Printed in the United States of America

First edition

10 9 8 7 6 5 4 3 2 1

Library of Congress Cataloging-in-Publication Data

Scorzafava, Lorelie.
    Gourmet gone wild: planning and preparing complete menus for game, fish, and fowl / Lorelie Scorzafava.
        p. cm.
    Includes index.
    ISBN-13: 978-0-8117-3463-9
    ISBN-10: 0-8117-3463-3
    1. Cookery (Game) 2. Cookery (Fish) 3. Cookery (Poultry) I. Title.

TX751.S3496 2008
641.6'91—dc22

                                                                2007021504

CONTENTS

Part 3: WILD FISH

Part 4: OTHER GAME RECIPES

INTRODUCTION

I always thought that someday I would write a book, but I never thought it would be a cookbook. I do love to cook and I do love to eat, though, so I guess nature just took its course.

I grew up with folks who hunted and fished. One of my earliest recollections is hunting for night crawlers to use as fish bait. If we wanted to go fishing after supper, we had to find the worms. And that wasn't an easy task when you had only a tiny, tired backyard that had been beaten to death by a passel of kids playing ball and riding bikes on it. But we dutifully rolled rocks and lifted the bricks in my grandmother's flowerbeds to uncover worms. We couldn't wait to go fishing with Grandpa, who was the most avid fisherman I ever met. Of course, we'd bring home bluegills and sunnies or a trout or two, and Gramps would clean them and then we'd fry them up.

My uncle Junior used to hunt the Maine woods every year during deer season. He'd load up his provisions and his hunting buddies, which included my father, and make the pilgrimage to Maine. My dad never harvested a deer—I don't think he ever got a shot at one—but Uncle Junior always came home with a deer, which meant venison for dinner. One year my aunt Natalie harvested a deer at deer camp. I think that one was the best I ever tasted.

When I met my husband, I wasn't quite prepared for marriage to a guy who hunts, as he puts it, "365 days a year." Granted, most of them are from his easy chair, but he does bring home a deer the first day of hunting season year after year. Nor was I ready to have a freezer stocked with bear, caribou, elk, geese, ducks, arctic char, salmon, and the like. So I figured I'd better start cooking this wild game meat to make room for the frozen corn and ice cream.

I have always been a cook, and my love affair with food has been a long one. I was inspired by the women in my family. My grandmother was an excellent cook, and I learned many of the basics at an early age, right by her side. We'd get supper ready, with her telling me what to do. My mother, too, was a demon in the kitchen. She liked nothing better than a houseful of people packed into her kitchen or backyard sharing a meal and good times—the more the merrier. When I lived at home, I was her sous-chef. Not happy with just the standard meat and potatoes, we tried cooking new and exotic things, we went to Chinese cooking school, we made homemade pasta, and we canned, pickled, and preserved. Above all, I learned that cooking and eating are about more than just the food. They are about sharing and about loving and nurturing those we love.

My cooking experiences have been part of my life's journey. When I married, I experimented with Mexican food, which wasn't readily available—there was no Taco Bell in those days. I learned how to make Greek food from one college friend and Polish food from another. Of course, I had to expand my Italian cuisine when I married an Italian. I tried bread making one day when I was snowed in and wanted some pita bread. As for game meat, although I now use it in many traditional and classic recipes, I started out with just a lump of game meat and two cans of mushroom soup.

This book is for those who find themselves with wild meat, fowl, or fish but aren't quite sure what to do with it. Many people ask not only "How should I cook it?" but also "What goes with it?" The recipes in this book provide the answers.

A gourmet is a person with a discriminating palate and a knowledge of food. I hope that this book inspires you to expand your repertoire of cooking techniques and recipes as you include the bounty of nature's wild offerings of meat, fish, and fowl. You too can be a "gourmet gone wild," cooking the fruits of your excursions into the wilderness.

part 1

GAME MEAT

For some hunters, the reward of the hunt is a trophy rack or a glossy fur rug. They may eat a steak or the fresh liver at deer camp, but they don't know what to do with the meat after they get it home. Some hunters have the animal butchered, dump the meat in the freezer, and never really get a chance to enjoy it. Many home chefs don't know how to cook game meat, which, if prepared like domestic meat, may be disappointing.

The true prize of the hunt is the game meat you can bring to your table. Wild game meat is a limited commodity, and it can't be found at the local supermarket. Even the finest restaurants that boast venison or buffalo are serving a domesticated version of the meat, not true wild game. So if you are a hunter, or if you cook for one, that meat is a special treat, and it deserves to be treated as such.

Long before it lands in your kitchen, many variables have already affected the quality of your game meat. Most obvious is the animal's age and sex and the time of year it was taken. Certainly, a young animal is different from an old bruiser. And whitetails taken during the rut may have a stronger flavor than those taken at the beginning of the season. The adage "you are what you eat" is true when it comes to game meat. What an animal has been eating greatly affects its taste. For instance, a bear eating agricultural crops tastes very different from one foraging; venison from a deer eating corn has a different flavor from one eating bark and acorns.

Perhaps the biggest factor affecting the taste of wild meat, however, is one that is within the hunter's control: meat handling. Hunters are often so fixated on the trophy antlers or the pelt that the meat becomes an afterthought. Yet the care game meat receives is a critical aspect of its taste. For

GAME MEAT TEMPERATURE CHART

Degree of Doneness	Internal Temperature (degrees F)
Rare: red center, cool	120
Medium rare: red center, warm	130
Medium: pink center, warm	140
Medium well: light pink center, hot	150
Well-done: no pink, hot center	160–170

many years, hunters hung their deer for days before butchering it—partly, I'm sure, to show off their trophies, partly out of a misguided sense of tradition, and perhaps out of necessity, while waiting for a butcher. This may be acceptable in cold weather, but hanging a deer in a tree when the temperature is too warm is an invitation for trouble. Often, the "gamy" taste that people refer to is actually a sign of spoilage. It is imperative to get the animal butchered and the meat cleaned, wrapped, sealed, and refrigerated or, better yet, frozen as soon as possible. Then you can let the meat age in the freezer. If your treasured game meat is improperly handled in the field, it may have an "off" taste no matter how you prepare it.

Given that game meat is not easy to come by, you should use only the freshest and finest ingredients when cooking it. Use fresh herbs whenever possible. If you're using wine, remember this rule of thumb: if you wouldn't drink it in a glass, don't cook with it. Because game meat is generally low in fat, it should be cooked using a moist method, such as braising or stewing, and served on the rare side. The only exception is bear meat, which (like pork) needs to be cooked thoroughly until it is well-done—no pink. Marinades can add or lock in moisture and flavor for steaks or chops that will be grilled or broiled. You can also tenderize game meat by marinating it in an oil and acid-based sauce such as wine, vinegar, or even fruit juice. Slow cookers are a good way to prepare game meat. Alternatively, roasting in an oven bag or covered roasting pan, or adding fat such as bacon, lard, or butter, can keep your meat moist and succulent. When cooking game meat, it is critical to avoid overcooking, so always use a thermometer. Meat can be removed from the heat source when the internal temperature reaches 165 degrees; if it is allowed to stand for 10 to 15 minutes, the temperature will increase to about 170 degrees.

Many of the recipes in this book are interchangeable, depending on what you have on hand. Most of the venison recipes also work with antelope, moose, elk, or caribou. Personally, I find that caribou meat is the closest to beef, but others say elk. Bear meat is stronger and has a coarser grain.

Don't be afraid to substitute ingredients or experiment with these recipes. If you like a certain ingredient, add it; if you don't like something (ginger, for me), decrease the amount or leave it out. If you don't have enough of one kind of meat or fowl, try adding a similar type of meat or a domestic version. Not enough deer burger? Add some ground beef, veal, or pork. Not enough wild turkey to go around? Cook a ham or a domestic bird to accompany it. Also remember the trick of serving substantial side dishes or a hearty first course if your game meat supply is running low. You can also use game meat as a starter or in a soup to give everyone a taste and then serve a domestic main course. Be creative and enjoy your cooking experiences. After all, what you cook and how you cook it are not only expressions of yourself but also expressions of your feelings for family and friends.

ANTELOPE

Antelope Steak in Mushroom Sauce

Braising the steaks in a mushroom sauce makes for a tender and tasty dinner, so don't be afraid to bring an antelope home to your range.

menu

Appetizer:	*Cheese Soufflés*
Entrée:	*Antelope Steak in Mushroom Sauce*
Sides:	*Mashed Buttermilk and Chive Potatoes; Acorn Squash Rings*
Dessert:	*Cran-Orange Loaf Cake*

Cheese Soufflés

These cheesy little soufflés are a great appetizer and salad rolled into one. They can be prepared in advance and reheated just before serving.

> 2 tablespoons butter
> 3 tablespoons flour
> 1 ¼ cups hot milk
> 1 teaspoon lemon juice
> 1 splash red pepper sauce, or to taste
> 1 splash Worcestershire sauce
> ¼ teaspoon salt
> ⅛ teaspoon ground white pepper
> 4 ounces cheddar cheese, shredded (or a semihard
>   goat cheese, crumbled)
> ¼ cup dried bread crumbs
> ¼ cup ground walnuts
> melted butter
> 2 eggs, separated, plus 2 egg whites
> 4 cups salad greens with vinaigrette dressing

Preheat oven to 375 degrees. In a saucepan, make a roux by melting the butter and stirring in the flour. Cook for 1 minute until thick; then gradually whisk in the milk to make a thick white sauce. Cook until the mixture thickens and boils for 2 minutes. Add the lemon juice, red pepper sauce, Worcestershire sauce, salt, and pepper. Remove the pan from the heat and stir in the cheese until melted. Let the mixture cool.

Mix the bread crumbs and walnuts together. While the sauce is cooling, brush the insides of 6 ramekins or custard cups with melted butter. Coat the inside of the ramekins with the crumb–nut mixture, tapping the edge of the cup on the counter to remove any excess.

Beat the 2 egg yolks into the cooled cheese mixture. In a separate bowl, beat the 4 egg whites until they form soft peaks; then fold them into the cheese mixture. Spoon the mixture into the ramekins. Place the soufflés in a shallow roasting pan and pour boiling water into the pan until it reaches halfway up the sides of the ramekins. (It's best to set the roasting pan on the oven rack and then add the water from a kettle, to avoid sloshing the boiling water about.) Bake for about 12 to 15 minutes until the soufflés have risen and are golden brown. Serve immediately on a bed of dressed salad greens.

To serve later, cool and refrigerate the soufflés. Before serving, run a knife around the inside of each ramekin and carefully turn out each little soufflé.

Place them on a baking sheet and reheat at 375 degrees for 12 minutes until puffed and hot. Serve as above.

Antelope Steak in Mushroom Sauce

4 tablespoons butter
2 tablespoons flour
½ cup flour, seasoned with salt and pepper
2 to 3 pounds antelope steak, about 1 inch thick
2 ½ to 3 cups chicken stock
½ cup sliced celery
½ cup sliced onions
1 pound sliced fresh mushrooms
salt and pepper to taste

Melt 2 tablespoons of butter in a small skillet; stir in enough flour to form a thick paste (roux). Cook for 1 to 2 minutes. Set aside. Melt the remaining butter in a large skillet. Dredge the steaks in the seasoned flour, and cut into serving pieces. Brown the meat in the melted butter. Add 2 cups of stock and simmer for 30 minutes. Add the remaining ingredients, including some of the remaining stock if needed. Season with salt and pepper. Cover and simmer on low heat for 1 hour, until the vegetables are soft and the meat is fork tender. Heat the roux until bubbly, add to the meat and vegetables, and mix in well. Continue cooking until the sauce thickens—about 3 to 5 minutes. Add more stock if the gravy is too thick.

Mashed Buttermilk and Chive Potatoes

4 pounds potatoes, peeled and quartered
1 teaspoon salt
1 cup buttermilk
½ stick butter
¼ cup chopped fresh chives
salt and pepper

Place the potatoes in cold, salted water and boil until tender. Mash or rice the cooked potatoes until no chunks or lumps remain. Stir in buttermilk and butter. Mix well; add more buttermilk to reach desired consistency. Adjust seasoning. Gently mix in chives, reserving 1 teaspoon for garnish. Transfer to a serving bowl, and sprinkle chives on top.

Acorn Squash Rings

2 acorn squash
salt and pepper
2 tablespoons water
½ stick butter, melted
brown sugar

Preheat oven to 400 degrees. Cut the squash crosswise into rings 1 inch thick. Remove seeds and any stringy membranes. Arrange overlapping slices in a baking dish, sprinkle with salt and pepper, add water, and cover tightly with foil. Bake until squash is soft. Remove the foil, drizzle the squash with butter, and sprinkle with brown sugar. Turn the broiler on, place the dish on the middle rack, and broil until the sugar has dissolved and is bubbly and golden brown—about 2 to 3 minutes. Be careful not to burn it. Remove to a serving dish, and spoon pan juices over the squash.

Cran-Orange Loaf Cake

1 large navel orange with bright, blemish-free skin
3 eggs plus 2 egg whites
1 cup sugar
¼ cup cornstarch
1 cup flour
1 teaspoon baking soda
¼ teaspoon salt
½ cup dried cranberries
confectioners' sugar (optional)

Preheat oven to 350 degrees. Grease and flour a 9- by 5-inch loaf pan. Quarter the orange and remove any seeds, then finely chop it in a food processor or by hand, or pass it through the medium blade of a meat grinder. Set aside. Beat the eggs and whites with an electric mixer until well blended and foamy (use a whisk attachment, if possible). Continue beating while slowly adding the sugar. Beat until thick and light colored, at least 5 minutes. Combine the cornstarch, flour, baking soda, and salt. Fold in the dry ingredients using the lowest speed, very briefly. Check the sides of the bowl for any flour mixture, and gently fold it in by hand. Fold in the chopped orange and cranberries. Spread the batter in the pan. Bake for about 45 minutes, but start checking for doneness after 35 minutes, using a toothpick inserted in the center. Cool in the pan for 10 minutes; then invert onto a rack to continue cooling. Dust with confectioners' sugar if desired. Serve. (This cake is even better the next day!)

Roasted Antelope Tenderloin

Antelope tenderloin is similar to deer (venison) but smaller, usually about half the size. The sweetness of Vidalia onions complements the red meat. Don't overcook this roast. Use a thermometer and remove the meat while it's still rare, because it will continue to cook after it leaves the oven.

---

menu

Salad: Green Salad with Creamy Vinaigrette

Entrée: Roast Antelope with Vidalia Onion Sauce

Sides: Creamy Cottage Potatoes; Peas with Lettuce

Dessert: Chocolate Lava Cakes

Green Salad with Creamy Vinaigrette

6 cups assorted salad greens
1 tomato, sliced
1 red onion, cut into rings

Dressing
3 ounces cream cheese, softened
1 shallot, minced
1 clove garlic, finely minced
1 teaspoon minced onion
1 teaspoon chopped fresh dill leaves or chopped fresh parsley
1 teaspoon sugar
½ teaspoon spicy brown mustard
¼ cup vegetable oil
3 tablespoons vinegar

For the dressing: Use a blender to mix all ingredients until smooth. Serve over salad greens topped with tomato and onion slices. Store remaining dressing in the refrigerator.

Roast Antelope with Vidalia Onion Sauce

3- to 4-pound boneless loin of antelope or other boneless roast
2 tablespoons butter
2 tablespoons oil
salt and pepper
2 large Vidalia onions, sliced
2 carrots, chopped
2 ribs of celery, chopped
1 tablespoon minced garlic
1 cup dry red wine (Merlot or Cabernet Sauvignon)
2 cups stock (game or beef)
½ stick butter

Preheat oven to 400 degrees. Heat butter and oil in a heavy roasting pan large enough to accommodate the roast. Salt and pepper the roast, and brown on all sides on the stove top. Remove the roast and add onions, carrots, celery, and garlic to the pan; stir to loosen any browned bits from the bottom of the pan while the vegetables are sweating, about 4 or 5 minutes. Return the antelope roast to the pan and continue cooking in the oven until the desired degree of doneness is reached; do not overcook. Tenderloin should be medium rare in 10 to 12 minutes. Check the thermometer and remove the meat from the oven when it's 5 degrees below the desired temperature. Tent with foil to keep warm. Add wine to the roasting pan on the stove top and deglaze over high heat, stirring constantly. Add stock and reduce by half. Remove vegetables by straining sauce into a saucepan, and reduce further if needed. Remove from heat and whisk in butter 1 tablespoon at a time. Salt and pepper to taste. Serve sauce over antelope slices.

Creamy Cottage Potatoes

4 large Idaho or russet potatoes
½ stick butter
salt and pepper
1 cup cottage cheese
½ cup Vidalia onions, finely chopped
paprika

Preheat oven to 350 degrees. Peel and quarter potatoes and boil in salted water until tender, about 20 minutes. Mash with butter, salt, and pepper. Add cottage cheese and onions. Stir well but gently. Spoon into a casserole dish, dot with additional butter, and sprinkle with paprika. Bake until the cheese has melted and the potatoes are browned on top, about 30 minutes. The casserole can be prepared ahead of time and refrigerated overnight; adjust the baking time as needed.

Peas with Lettuce

6 outer lettuce leaves
1 small shallot, minced
4 tablespoons butter, melted
1 pound frozen peas
salt and pepper
2 tablespoons milk
grated fresh nutmeg (optional)

Wash the lettuce leaves and slice into ½-inch strips. In a heavy saucepan with a tight-fitting lid, sauté the shallot in 1 tablespoon of butter for 1 minute. Stir in lettuce and cook for 1 or 2 minutes. Remove about half the lettuce; set aside. Layer peas over the remaining lettuce, sprinkle with salt and pepper, and add remaining butter and milk. Top with reserved lettuce shreds. Cover tightly and simmer until peas are heated through and tender. Stir and check for seasoning. Add nutmeg to taste. Strain or serve slightly juicy.

Chocolate Lava Cakes

6 ounces semisweet chocolate chips
½ stick butter
½ cup sugar
3 eggs
1 teaspoon vanilla extract
⅓ cup flour

Preheat oven to 350 degrees. Butter 4 ramekins, or spray a large muffin pan with cooking spray. Melt the chocolate and butter over low heat or in the microwave, stirring several times. Set aside and let cool. In a mixing bowl, beat the sugar and eggs until the sugar has dissolved and the mixture is light in color. Stir in the chocolate and vanilla; then stir in the flour. Pour batter into individual ramekins and place on a baking sheet. Bake for about 10 to 12 minutes. Cakes should be puffed and set but not too firm in the center. Tip the ramekin upside down on a dessert plate and serve with a dollop of whipped cream or vanilla ice cream.

These cakes can be prepared ahead of time and then baked just before serving, while the table is being cleared and the coffee is brewing.

BEAR

Belgian Bear Roast

A hearty dark beer and brown sugar give this roast its flavor. If you prefer not to cook with alcohol, substitute beef stock. Slow braising tenderizes this bear roast, which can be a sumptuous addition to your holiday table.

---

menu

Appetizer:	*Baked Brie with Broccoli and Bacon*
Entrée:	*Belgian Bear Roast*
Sides:	*Baked Potato Boats; Steamed Carrots with Orange Sauce*
Dessert:	*Pumpkin Spice Bars*

Baked Brie with Broccoli and Bacon

A wedge of Brie wrapped in pastry is an impressive start to your meal—sure to please family and friends.

   1 cup broccoli florets
   2 strips bacon, sliced
   8-inch wheel Brie cheese
   1 package frozen puff pastry dough (2 sheets)
   1 egg yolk beaten with 1 tablespoon water

Steam or boil fresh broccoli in salted water until just tender; drain completely. If using frozen broccoli, thaw and thoroughly drain excess water. Fry bacon pieces in a skillet until crisp; remove from pan. Cut the wheel of cheese in half horizontally.

Roll each sheet of puff pastry dough into a 12-inch square. Center one sheet in a 9-inch pie pan. Place the bottom piece of Brie on the pastry. Sprinkle with broccoli and bacon. Top with the second piece of cheese. Fold pastry up the sides and over the top of the cheese leaving a 1-inch overlap; trim and save the excess dough. Use the top of the cheese box as a guide and cut out a circle of pastry from the second sheet of puff pastry dough. Set the pastry on top of the Brie. Gently roll or press the edges of pastry together and crimp to seal. Make decorations from the extra dough pieces, and attach them to the top with an egg yolk wash.

Refrigerate for 30 minutes or up to 24 hours. Preheat oven to 400 degrees. Brush pastry with egg wash. Bake for 10 minutes, then reduce heat to 350 degrees. Bake until puffy and golden. Let stand 30 minutes. Remove to a serving platter. Serve with slices of French bread or your favorite crackers.

Belgian Bear Roast

½ cup flour
salt and pepper
1 bear roast (any cut), large enough to feed your
    guests
olive oil
½ pound salt pork or bacon, diced
2 tablespoons butter
2 shallots, minced
2 cloves garlic, minced
2 medium onions, thinly sliced
3 tablespoons brown sugar
12-ounce bottle dark beer, ale, or lager
fresh parsley for garnish

Preheat oven to 325 degrees. In a large plastic or paper bag, combine flour, salt, and pepper. Shake to mix. Add meat and shake to coat evenly. On the stove top, in an ovenproof casserole or Dutch oven, brown meat on all sides in hot olive oil. Remove meat; add salt pork to the pan and cook over medium heat, stirring frequently, until the fat has been rendered and the chunks are golden brown. Remove salt port with a slotted spoon and save. Add butter to the pan and let it melt. Add shallot, garlic, and onion. Cook over medium heat until soft. Add 1 tablespoon of brown sugar and cook until the onions have browned. Add beer and the remaining brown sugar, scraping any bits stuck on the bottom of the pan. Return the salt pork and the bear roast to the Dutch oven. Cover tightly and bake until meat is tender and well-done, 2 to 4 hours, depending on the size of the roast. Remove to a platter, slice, garnish with parsley, and serve with pan drippings.

Baked Potato Boats

4 large Idaho or russet potatoes
¼ stick butter
1 cup sour cream
salt and pepper to taste
milk (if needed)
1 tablespoon chives or parsley
1 tablespoon butter, melted

Bake potatoes in a 350-degree oven until cooked. Slice off the top third of the potatoes. Scoop out the insides, leaving ¼ inch of pulp inside the skin; also remove any potato flesh from the top pieces, and then discard the top skins. Mash the potato pulp with butter, sour cream, salt, pepper, and a bit of milk if necessary until the potatoes are smooth and fluffy. Add parsley or chives at the last minute, mix, and mound the potato mixture in the potato shells. Brush with additional melted butter, and return to a 350-degree oven until piping hot and tops are golden brown. Garnish with additional parsley or chives before serving if desired.

Steamed Carrots with Orange Sauce

2 pounds peeled baby carrots
2 tablespoons butter
¼ cup orange marmalade
1 tablespoon lemon juice
1 tablespoon sweet sherry
lemon or orange zest

Steam carrots using a steaming basket or in the microwave until just tender, 4 to 5 minutes. While the carrots are cooking, melt butter and marmalade in a large skillet. Add lemon juice and sherry, and stir until smooth. Add the cooked carrots to the pan, and stir to coat. Let simmer for 1 minute. Remove to a serving dish and garnish with a sprinkle of lemon or orange zest.

Pumpkin Spice Bars

2 eggs
1 cup sugar
½ cup vegetable oil
2 tablespoons molasses
1 cup fresh or canned pumpkin puree
1 cup flour
1 teaspoon baking powder
½ teaspoon baking soda
1 teaspoon cinnamon
¼ teaspoon ground ginger
⅛ teaspoon ground cloves
¼ teaspoon salt
½ cup raisins
¼ cup chopped walnuts and additional walnuts for
   garnish (optional)

Cream Cheese Frosting
   3 ounces cream cheese, softened
   1 teaspoon vanilla extract
   3 cups sifted confectioners' sugar
   1 tablespoon water

Preheat oven to 350 degrees. Grease and flour the bottom and sides of a 9-by 13-inch pan. In a large bowl, combine eggs, sugar, oil, molasses, and pumpkin. Beat until smooth. Stir in flour, baking powder, baking soda, cinnamon, ginger, cloves, and salt. Stir in raisins and nuts if desired. Spread batter into prepared pan. Bake for 30 minutes or until a toothpick inserted in the center comes out clean. Cool completely. Frost with cream cheese frosting and sprinkle the top with nuts, if desired.

For the frosting: Beat cream cheese and vanilla until softened. Gradually beat in confectioners' sugar, until smooth. Add water to achieve desired spreading consistency. If frosting is too thin, add more sugar; if it's too thick, add water a drop at a time.

Braised Bear Steaks

Thick, meaty steaks are slowly simmered in a wine and tomato sauce that bubbles away until the meat melts in your mouth. A slow cooker can also be used; just follow the cooking time directions based on your heat setting.

menu

Appetizer:	*Creamy Italian Sausage and Bean Soup*
Salad:	*Spinach Salad with Bacon Dressing*
Entrée:	*Braised Bear Steaks*
Sides:	*Onion Potatoes; Cheese-Crusted Zucchini Coins*
Dessert:	*Fruity Pizza*

Creamy Italian Sausage and Bean Soup

2 tablespoons olive oil
1 pound hot or sweet Italian sausage links
2 ounces pancetta or bacon, finely diced
1 onion, chopped
2 ribs celery, sliced
2 carrots, cut in ¼-inch cubes
2 cloves garlic, minced
2 16-ounce cans cannelini beans
1 quart chicken stock or broth
2 cups water
salt and pepper
1 teaspoon lemon juice
Parmesan cheese for garnish

In a large saucepan, heat the oil. Fry the sausages, browning on all sides until firm. Remove the sausages from the pan and let cool. In the same pan, cook the pancetta until browned, and remove from the pan. Sauté onion, celery, and carrots in the drippings until soft. Remove from heat and add garlic; cook for 30 seconds while stirring. When the sausages are cool enough to handle, slice them in ¼-inch slices. Mash one can of beans with a fork and add them along with the remaining can of beans, sausage, chicken broth, water, salt, and pepper to the pot. Return to heat and bring to a boil. Reduce heat and simmer for 20 minutes. Stir in lemon juice. Serve with thin, freshly planed slices or grated Parmesan cheese.

Spinach Salad with Bacon Dressing

½ pound bacon, cut in ¼-inch slices
**1 pound baby spinach leaves, washed and dried
    (or spinach torn into bite-size pieces, stems
    removed)**
1 cup fresh mushrooms, sliced
2 hard-cooked eggs, coarsely chopped
¼ cup finely shredded Swiss cheese

Dressing
    reserved bacon drippings
    vegetable oil if needed
    ¼ cup cider vinegar
    2 tablespoons sugar
    2 tablespoons water
    1 shallot, finely minced

Cut bacon in thin strips and fry until golden brown and crispy in a skillet. Set aside. For dressing: Pour bacon drippings into a measuring cup and add oil to measure ½ cup. Pour into a jar with a lid, add remaining dressing ingredients, and shake well. If you have to hold the dressing before serving, keep the jar in a pan of hot water until needed, and shake vigorously just before serving.

In a large salad bowl, place the spinach, mushrooms, and bacon pieces. Toss gently. Sprinkle chopped eggs and cheese on top. Pour hot bacon dressing over the salad and serve immediately.

Braised Bear Steaks

3 tablespoons vegetable oil
1 tablespoon seasoned salt
4 bear steaks, 1 inch thick (about 3 to 4 pounds
  total)
2 onions, finely chopped
4 shallots, minced
2 celery stalks, thinly sliced
4 carrots, sliced
2 cups fresh white button mushrooms, left whole
  (if small) or sliced
2 cloves garlic, minced
1 large or 2 small bay leaves
4 sprigs fresh thyme
2 cups dry red wine
3 tablespoons tomato paste
1 15-ounce can stewed tomatoes
2 cups beef stock
¼ cup chopped fresh basil
¼ cup chopped parsley
⅛ to ¼ teaspoon crushed red pepper flakes
salt and pepper to taste

Heat oil in a large Dutch oven or covered casserole until hot. Sprinkle seasoned salt on steaks and brown meat on both sides, taking care not to crowd the pan. Do several batches if necessary. Remove meat and set aside. Add onions, shallots, celery, carrots, and mushrooms to the Dutch oven and cook, stirring occasionally, until vegetables are soft and beginning to caramelize, about 6 to 8 minutes. Add the garlic, bay leaves, and thyme, and cook for 1 minute. Add red wine and stir well with a spoon, scraping browned bits from the bottom of the pan. Stir in tomato paste, coarsely chopped stewed tomatoes and their juice, beef stock, basil, parsley, crushed red pepper, salt, and pepper. Return the steaks to the pan and bring the mixture to a boil. Cover the Dutch oven, lower heat to a simmer, and cook for 2 to 3 hours, stirring occasionally, or until the meat is tender. The covered pan can also be placed in a slow 300-degree oven and cooked until the meat is tender. Add more stock if needed to keep the meat covered. Adjust seasoning if necessary.

Onion Potatoes

6 to 8 medium-sized russet potatoes
1 teaspoon salt
½ stick butter
½ cup milk
1 8-ounce container whipped cream cheese with
**   chives**
salt and pepper to taste
¼ cup minced onion

Peel and quarter potatoes. Rinse, put in a pan, cover with cold water, and add salt. Bring to a boil, reduce heat, and cook until potatoes are tender, 20 to 30 minutes. Strain potatoes. Add butter and milk to a saucepan and heat until butter is melted. Add potatoes and cream cheese with chives to the saucepan, and mash with a potato masher until the desired smoothness is achieved. For lighter potatoes, whip with an electric beater for 15 to 20 seconds. Do not overbeat, or potatoes will become shiny and starchy. Salt and pepper to taste. Stir in minced onion and serve immediately.

Cheese-Crusted Zucchini Coins

4 medium or 6 small zucchini squash
2 tablespoons butter
2 tablespoons olive oil
¼ cup grated Parmesan cheese

Zucchini should be tender, without large seeds. Slice squash into ¼-inch round slices—the "coins." Melt butter and oil in a large skillet. Arrange squash slices in the pan, cover, and sauté over medium heat, turning once to bring the bottom slices to the top, until all are just tender. Do not overcook. Remove from heat, sprinkle cheese over the top, and cover the pan until the cheese melts.

Fruity Pizza

The crust for this pizza is really a giant sugar cookie formed on a round pizza pan. You can use a package of refrigerator cookie dough or a mix to save time, but I prefer to make my own.

Crust
>   2 ¾ cups all-purpose flour
>   1 teaspoon baking soda
>   ½ teaspoon baking powder
>   1 cup butter, softened
>   1 ½ cups white sugar
>   1 egg
>   1 teaspoon vanilla extract

Topping
>   8-ounce package cream cheese, softened
>   2 tablespoons confectioners' sugar
>   ½ teaspoon vanilla extract
>   ½ cup peach preserves
>   ripe fresh fruit of your choice, including but not
>   limited to the following: 1 to 2 peaches, peeled,
>   halved, and sliced; 1 pint fresh strawberries,
>   sliced; 2 kiwis, peeled and sliced; 1 star fruit,
>   sliced; fresh blueberries or raspberries
>   ¼ cup chopped walnuts
>   whipped cream or whipped topping

Preheat oven to 375 degrees. For the crust: In a small bowl or paper bag, mix the flour, baking soda, and baking powder. Set aside. In a mixing bowl, cream the butter and sugar until smooth. Beat in the egg and vanilla. Gradually add the dry ingredients, blending well. Press the dough onto a pizza pan to a thickness of ¼ inch. Prick the surface with a fork. Bake 18 to 20 minutes, or until light golden brown. To avoid breakage, cool the crust completely on a rack; then build your pizza right in the pan.

For the topping: Mix cream cheese, confectioners' sugar, and vanilla until smooth. Spread the cheese mixture over the cookie crust. Spread the peach preserves over the cream cheese layer. Arrange fruit over the preserves in concentric circles. Sprinkle with chopped walnuts. Chill until serving time. Serve with a dollop of whipped cream or whipped topping.

Bear Shoulder Roast

This bear roast, simmered with the incredible flavors of bacon, apples, and balsamic vinegar, will have your family and friends begging for more.

---

menu

Appetizer: *Tangy Coleslaw*

Entrée: *Bear Shoulder Roast*

Sides: *Spaetzle; Beets and Apple Slices*

Dessert: *Wacky Cake*

Tangy Coleslaw

**1 head cabbage, finely shredded (or 1-pound bag
precut slaw mix)**
½ cup mayonnaise
2 tablespoons cider vinegar
½ teaspoon dry mustard or Dijon-style mustard
½ teaspoon celery seed
salt and pepper

In a large bowl, toss the cabbage with the remaining ingredients. Check for taste: the dressing should be tangy, but not too sour from the vinegar. If it's too sour, add a bit more mayonnaise, a splash of milk, or water.

Bear Shoulder Roast

1 bear shoulder roast
2 to 3 cloves garlic, sliced
1 teaspoon Dijon mustard
olive oil
salt and pepper
1 onion, sliced, plus 2 onions, chopped
5 to 6 slices bacon (optional)
3 Granny Smith apples, peeled and quartered
2 16-ounce cans stewed tomatoes
1 cup beef stock, red wine, or water
3 tablespoons Worcestershire sauce
2 tablespoons balsamic vinegar
minced parsley for garnish

Preheat oven to 350 degrees. Trim any fat off the bear roast. Make deep slits in the top of the roast and insert garlic slices. Mix mustard with olive oil, salt, and pepper; spread over roast. Cut 1 onion into ¼-inch slices, and lay them on the bottom of a Dutch oven to keep the roast from sitting on the bottom of the pan. Place the roast on top of the onion slices; cover with several strips of bacon if desired. Roast for 1 hour, then add the apples and chopped onions. Mix the remaining ingredients, and pour over the roast. Cover with a lid or foil, and continue to cook for about 2 hours or until very tender. Add more stock, wine, or water as needed to make a thick sauce. Garnish with minced parsley.

Spaetzle

4 quarts water
1 teaspoon salt
2 cups flour
3 eggs
½ cup water
½ teaspoon salt
1 tablespoon butter
1 tablespoon seasoned bread crumbs or grated
    cheese (optional for garnish)

In a 6-quart pot, bring 4 quarts water and 1 teaspoon salt to boiling over high heat. Reduce heat and let simmer while making the dumplings. Beat flour, eggs, water, and salt in a medium bowl with a wire whisk or spoon until batter is smooth. Adjust heat to medium. Using a rubber spatula, press the batter through a large-holed colander or spaetzle maker into the boiling water. Stir the water gently to keep the spaetzle from sticking together. Boil 3 to 5 minutes, depending on size. Dumplings will float to the surface when done. Cook until just tender but firm (al dente); drain. Garnish with butter and seasoned bread crumbs or grated cheese if desired.

Beets and Apple Slices

A twist on Harvard beets, this version repeats the apple flavor of the roast.

1 can sliced beets, drained, with liquid reserved
2 teaspoons lemon juice
2 teaspoons sugar
1 teaspoon cornstarch mixed with ½ cup reserved
    beet juice
1 Granny Smith apple, peeled, cored, and sliced the
    same thickness as the beets
1 teaspoon butter
pinch cinnamon

Mix lemon juice, sugar, cinnamon, and cornstarch–beet juice mixture together in a saucepan. Bring to a boil over medium heat. Cook, stirring constantly, until thick and clear. Add apple slices, reduce heat, and simmer slowly until apples are just tender. Add beets and butter and cook until heated through.

Wacky Cake

This moist chocolate cake was served in my school cafeteria, and when I was a teenager, I got the recipe from the cafeteria cook and rushed home to try it. I must have made an error somewhere along the way and ended up with a pan that looked like it had fallen into the La Brea tar pits. I threw the pan away and started over, much to my mother's horror (fearing the loss of another pan). But this time, the quick and easy, no-mess cake came out perfectly. There are no eggs in this cake, and mixing is done right in the baking pan. I topped it with chocolate icing, although at school they served it with a sprinkling of powdered sugar. Either way is great.

1 ½ cups flour
1 cup sugar
3 tablespoons unsweetened cocoa
1 teaspoon baking soda
½ teaspoon salt
1 teaspoon vanilla extract
1 teaspoon vinegar
5 tablespoons vegetable oil
1 cup cold water

In a 9-inch-square pan, mix flour, sugar, cocoa, baking soda, and salt. Make three wells in the flour mixture: one for the vanilla, one for the vinegar, and one for the oil. Pour the cold water over the mixture and stir until moistened. Bake at 350 degrees for 25 to 30 minutes, or until the cake springs back when touched lightly. (You can also mix the batter in a bowl and pour it into a prepared pan, but then there's an extra bowl to wash.)

Backyard Barbecued Bear

This brisket gets its start on the stove top, where it simmers until tender. It then goes out to the grill to get a smoky barbecue flavor.

menu

Appetizer: Salmon-Stuffed Cherry Tomatoes

Salad: Italian Pasta Salad

Entrée: Bear Brisket for the Barbecue

Sides: Grilled Squash; BBQ Butter Beans

Dessert: Whoopee Pies

Salmon-Stuffed Cherry Tomatoes

Stuffed tomato appetizers are a real crowd-pleaser, and they can be prepared in advance. This is a great way to use up a glut of cherry tomatoes if you grow your own. For individually plated appetizers, use a larger tomato and serve on a bed of lettuce.

½ cup salmon (leftover or canned, smoked or not)
¼ cup mayonnaise
1 tablespoon cream cheese
1 teaspoon lemon juice
¼ cup black olives, chopped
½ stalk celery, chopped to fine dice
½ teaspoon prepared horseradish
cherry tomatoes (or larger Campari tomatoes)
chives

If using canned salmon, drain it and remove the bones. Flake the fish and blend with mayonnaise, cream cheese, lemon juice, olives, celery, and horseradish. Slice tops from cherry tomatoes and scoop or squeeze out pulp. Stuff with salmon mixture, and sprinkle with chives. Refrigerate until serving time.

Italian Pasta Salad .

1 pound tricolor pasta spirals
1 7½-ounce jar roasted red pepper strips
1 4-ounce can black olive slices
4 or 5 pepperoncini, sliced in rings
1 cup small cherry or grape tomatoes
4 ounces pepperoni slices, cut into thin strips
1 6½-ounce jar marinated artichoke hearts and juice
8-ounce can sliced mushrooms, drained
2 tablespoons grated Parmesan cheese
½ teaspoon garlic powder
½ teaspoon oregano
salt and pepper

Dressing

This dressing may be a bit too intense for lettuce, but it holds up to the task of flavoring the pasta so it won't be bland.

> ½ **cup red wine vinegar**
> ¼ **cup water**
> 1 **cup olive oil**
> 1 **teaspoon minced fresh garlic, or ½ teaspoon dry**
>   **or ground**
> 1 **tablespoon minced fresh onion, or 1 teaspoon dry**
>   **flakes**
> 1 **teaspoon dry oregano**
> 1 **teaspoon dry Italian seasoning**

Boil the pasta in salted water until it reaches the desired degree of firmness. Strain and rinse with cold water. Drain well. In a large bowl, mix the pasta with all the remaining ingredients. Toss with homemade dressing or an 8-ounce bottle of your favorite oil and vinegar Italian-type dressing. For best results, make this salad a day in advance and refrigerate to let the flavors blend. Before serving, stir once or twice to redistribute dressing. Check the seasoning and make sure the salad isn't too dry. Add more dressing if needed. Remove to a serving dish garnished with a sprinkle of grated cheese.

Bear Brisket for the Barbecue

> 5 **pounds bear brisket or other roast**
> 2 **10½-ounce cans French onion soup diluted with**
>   **2 cans water, or 4 cups homemade beef stock**
> 2 **bay leaves**
> 3 **cloves garlic**
> 1 **tablespoon Liquid Smoke (optional)**
> **salt and pepper**

Place all ingredients in a Dutch oven, cover, and cook over medium to medium-low heat until nearly tender, at least 2 hours. Remove from pan and finish cooking over a medium-hot grill, basting with your favorite barbecue sauce and turning often. (Pan drippings can be thickened and used as a gravy.) Use leftovers for hearty sandwiches made by piling slices of carved meat topped with barbecue sauce on your favorite kaiser-type roll.

Grilled Squash

While the grill is hot, you can cook small zucchini or summer squash at the same time.

>**4 to 8 small squash**
>**olive oil**
>**1 teaspoon garlic powder**
>**1 teaspoon oregano**
>**salt and pepper**

Slice squash in half lengthwise. Put in a plastic bag, add the remaining ingredients, and toss to coat. Let the squash marinate for 10 to 15 minutes; save the marinade. Grill the squash until browned; turn and cook the other side. When the squash is just tender, brush with the remaining marinade and turn twice more until cooked.

BBQ Butter Beans

Tired of the same old baked beans? Try this recipe using canned butter beans. Oven time is minimal, and they make a tasty addition to any cookout. If your family likes them sweeter or spicier, add more sugar or a dash of cayenne pepper.

>**2 15-ounce cans butter beans, drained, with liquid**
>   **reserved**
>**½ cup brown sugar**
>**¼ cup ketchup or bottled barbecue sauce**
>**½ cup thinly sliced onions**
>**4 strips bacon, 2 diced, 2 left whole**

Preheat oven to 350 degrees. Place beans in a greased 1 ½- to 2-quart glass casserole dish. Mix beans with all the remaining ingredients except the 2 whole strips of bacon, which are cut into halves and arranged on top of the beans. Cover and bake for 30 minutes. Check to make sure that the beans are still saucy but not soupy, and that the bacon and onion have cooked. Remove the cover and continue baking until browned on top. Add some reserved bean liquid or a bit of water if necessary to prevent the beans from drying out.

Whoopee Pies

These hand-held desserts are not a pie at all but two little cakes held together with filling. They can be made days in advance and keep well if wrapped individually. One word of caution: if you put them out on the table too early, they may become an appetizer!

Cakes
> ½ **cup shortening**
> 1 **cup sugar**
> 2 **eggs**
> 2 **cups flour**
> 4 **tablespoons unsweetened cocoa**
> 1 **teaspoon baking soda**
> ½ **teaspoon baking powder**
> 1 **cup milk**

Filling
> 3 **tablespoons flour**
> ¾ **cup milk**
> ¾ **cup sugar**
> 1 **tablespoon vanilla extract**
> ¾ **cup shortening**

Preheat oven to 425 degrees. For the cakes: Cream shortening and sugar together until well mixed. Beat in eggs until light and fluffy. Sift together dry ingredients and add to creamed mixture alternating with the milk, beginning and ending with milk. Drop batter from a tablespoon on a cookie sheet that has been lined with waxed paper or parchment sprayed with cooking spray. Bake for about 8 minutes, until risen and firm to the touch. Check for doneness with a toothpick. Cool.

For the filling: Combine flour and milk in a small saucepan, and cook until a thick, smooth paste is formed. Let cool. In a mixing bowl, beat together sugar, vanilla, and shortening. Add the flour mixture, and continue beating until light and fluffy, like whipped cream.

Put two cakes together with a generous spoonful of filling in between. For a grab-and-go treat, wrap them individually in plastic wrap. For a more festive dessert, split in half on a plate, add a scoop of vanilla ice cream, and top with hot fudge sauce.

Marinated and Grilled Bear Steaks

There are few meals that I enjoy more than a grilled steak. It's simple and delicious, and since I'm one of those people who doesn't mind a well-done steak, bear on the grill works for me.

---

menu

Appetizer:	*Bacon and Scallop Wraps*
Salad:	*Pea Salad*
Entrée:	*Grilled Bear Steaks*
Sides:	*Spicy Potato Wedges;* *Spinach-Stuffed Tomatoes*
Dessert:	*Piña Colada Cheesecake Squares*

Bacon and Scallop Wraps

½ pound bacon
½ pound small scallops
¼ cup white wine
¼ cup olive oil
1 tablespoon Dijon mustard
1 tablespoon chopped fresh parsley
1 clove garlic, minced
salt and pepper
salad greens
lemon juice

Cut bacon slices in half. Mix wine, oil, mustard, parsley, garlic, salt, and pepper; toss scallops in this marinade, and refrigerate at least 2 hours. Remove scallops from marinade, wrap one piece of bacon around each scallop, and fasten with a toothpick. Arrange scallops on a broiler tray and broil about

4 inches from the heat for 7 to 10 minutes, until bacon is brown. Turn and cook the other side until the scallops are cooked through. Remove toothpicks before serving. Arrange over salad greens, and sprinkle with lemon juice.

Pea Salad

This crunchy salad is a great starter when served in a lettuce cup, or it can double as a side dish with the main course.

> **1-pound bag frozen baby peas**
> **2 strips bacon, sliced thin**
> **1 8-ounce can sliced water chestnuts**
> **2 cups sour cream**
> **1 tablespoon sugar**
> **splash lemon juice**

Thaw and drain peas. Cook bacon until crisp, and drain on paper towels. Combine peas and bacon with the remaining ingredients. Stir to coat evenly. Refrigerate until serving time.

Grilled Bear Steaks

> **1-inch bear steaks (1 per person)**
> **½ cup olive oil**
> **¼ cup wine or cider vinegar**
> **¼ cup water**
> **1 beaten egg**
> **1 teaspoon garlic powder**
> **1 teaspoon onion powder**
> **1 teaspoon sage**
> **1 teaspoon dried oregano**
> **salt and pepper to taste**

Mix all ingredients and marinate steaks for several hours or overnight in the refrigerator. Use a plastic zipper-lock bag or a glass or plastic bowl for marinating; avoid metal bowls. Use the excess marinade to baste the steaks often as you grill them. Bear meat must be cooked until well-done: 170 degrees. To avoid dried-out steaks, test the meat with a thermometer and remove the steaks as soon as they reach 165 degrees. Let the meat stand for 10 minutes—during which time it continues to cook a bit—before slicing and serving.

Spicy Potato Wedges

8 large baking potatoes
½ cup oil
1 teaspoon salt
½ teaspoon garlic powder
½ teaspoon paprika
**¼ teaspoon pepper (for a spicier version, use
      cayenne pepper)**
2 tablespoons grated Parmesan cheese

Use unpeeled potatoes, washed and cut into wedges. Mix oil and spices well.
Roll potatoes in oil mixture, and arrange in a single layer in a shallow baking.
pan. Sprinkle on cheese. Bake at 375 degrees for 45 minutes, or until wedges
are tender.

Spinach-Stuffed Tomatoes

6 to 8 very ripe medium-sized tomatoes
1 cup cooked spinach, drained
2 cloves garlic, minced
4 tablespoons olive oil or butter
½ cup dry bread crumbs
¼ cup plus 1 teaspoon grated Parmesan cheese
¼ teaspoon thyme

Preheat oven to 350 degrees. Cut the top quarter off the tomatoes, and
squeeze out the seeds and pulp into a mixing bowl. Chop the spinach and
add it to the tomato pulp. Sauté garlic for 1 minute in 1 tablespoon olive oil
in a small skillet. Add garlic and oil to spinach mixture. Mix in bread crumbs
and ¼ cup cheese. Moisten the crumb mixture with the remaining olive oil
or melted butter or a combination of both. Stir in thyme. Mix well. Spoon
stuffing mixture into tomatoes, making sure to press it into the spaces and
mounding slightly. Arrange the tomatoes on a baking sheet. Drizzle tops
with a bit more olive oil or butter, and sprinkle with a teaspoon of grated
Parmesan. Bake for about 30 minutes. If tops brown too quickly, cover
loosely with foil and continue baking until tomatoes are soft and stuffing is
heated through.

Piña Colada Cheesecake Squares

2 cups graham cracker crumbs
½ cup finely chopped macadamia nuts
½ cup butter, melted
3 8-ounce bars cream cheese, softened
¾ cup sugar
1 teaspoon vanilla extract
3 eggs
1 cup crushed pineapple, well drained
1 cup flaked coconut
1 cup sour cream
½ cup flaked coconut, lightly toasted★

Preheat oven to 350 degrees. Mix graham cracker crumbs, nuts, and butter together and press into the bottom of a 9- by 13-inch glass baking pan. In a mixing bowl, beat cream cheese until soft. Add sugar and vanilla. Beat with electric mixer on medium speed until well combined. Add eggs one at a time, beating after each addition. Stir in pineapple and 1 cup coconut. Bake 30 minutes until set. Remove from oven, spread sour cream on top, and return to oven for 5 minutes. Sprinkle with toasted coconut. Let cool, then refrigerate. Cut into squares when cold.

★To toast coconut in the microwave, spread it on a microwave-safe plate and microwave on high in 30-second intervals. Toss lightly and continue microwaving until coconut is lightly browned, with some white parts still visible.

CARIBOU

Mexican Fiesta with Caribou Fajitas

These caribou fajitas have a bit more sophisticated flavor than traditional fajitas. They work well as a lunch entrée or as a starter for a meal with a Mexican flair.

menu

Appetizer: *Spicy Gazpacho*

Entrée: *Caribou Fajitas with Portobello Mushrooms and Red Onion*

Sides: *Arepas (Cheesy Corn Cakes); Quick Spanish Rice*

Dessert: *Mexican Bananas and Cream*

Spicy Gazpacho

Gazpacho is sometimes called liquid salad. This thick and chunky soup, served cold, goes down easily on a hot day. It's also a great way to use up some vegetables when your garden is at its peak. In our house, we like our gazpacho spicy, but you can adjust the heat level to your own taste. Don't worry about a bowl and spoon. Serve gazpacho in a mug, topped with a drop of sour cream.

1 onion
1 green pepper
1 cucumber, peeled
2 ripe tomatoes
1 jalapeño pepper (pickled or fresh)
1 clove garlic, finely minced
2 cups tomato juice cocktail or vegetable juice cocktail
¼ cup cider vinegar
¼ cup water
½ cup olive oil
⅛ teaspoon each garlic powder, oregano, sugar, cilantro, cayenne pepper
salt and pepper
bottled hot sauce to taste
sour cream, tortilla strips, or shredded cheese for garnish

Chop vegetables in bite-size pieces (omit the jalapeño if you prefer less heat). Put all ingredients in a blender or food processor, and pulse to blend. Don't puree; there should be some chunks of vegetables. Serve well chilled with your choice of garnish. Pass more hot sauce for those who like it extra spicy.

Caribou Fajitas with Portobello Mushrooms and Red Onion

1 to 2 pounds caribou steak
2 tablespoons fresh lime juice
2 tablespoons Worcestershire sauce
2 tablespoons balsamic vinegar
4 cups sliced portobello mushrooms
2 cups red onion, sliced vertically
3 cloves garlic, finely minced
1 jalapeño or serrano chili pepper, minced (adjust
    heat to taste)
2 tablespoons fresh cilantro
4 to 6 flour tortillas
1 cup queso fresco (or substitute a mild feta cheese)
salsa verde (see recipe below) or bottled salsa of
    your choice
sour cream (optional)

Marinate the caribou steak in the lime juice, Worcestershire sauce, and balsamic vinegar for about 10 minutes, or while slicing the mushrooms and onions. Remove steak from marinade, reserving liquid, and slice on the diagonal. Quickly sear meat in a hot skillet to the desired degree of doneness; remove meat from the pan. Add mushrooms and onions and sauté until they just begin to soften. Add garlic, chili pepper, and reserved marinade, and sauté 1 minute longer. Return meat to the pan; mix. At the last moment, sprinkle with fresh cilantro. To serve, place a portion of the fajita filling in a warm flour tortilla, sprinkle with queso fresco, top with salsa verde and sour cream if desired, and fold the fajita in half.

Salsa Verde
> 1 pound tomatillos
> 2 Anaheim chilies, roasted, peeled, and cut into large
>   pieces
> 2 fresh serrano chilies
> 1 small onion, cut into quarters
> 2 cloves garlic
> ½ cup fresh cilantro leaves
> 2 tablespoons olive oil
> salt and pepper

Remove the papery skins from the tomatillos by rubbing them on a dry dish towel. Cut into large chunks. In a food processor, coarsely chop the tomatillos, chilies, onion, garlic, and cilantro. Don't overprocess; the salsa should be chunky, not liquefied. Pour into a bowl and add olive oil, salt, and pepper to taste. Adjust the heat with green pepper sauce if desired.

Arepas (Cheesy Corn Cakes)

In the late summer, when the country fairs are hopping, I always find myself drawn to the Latin food concessions. These cheesy little corn cakes are one of my favorites. I've tried to capture the traditional taste of Venezuelan arepas using ingredients that are readily found in your pantry or freezer. Arepas are used much like hamburger buns and can be filled in a variety of ways. I prefer two thin arepas with queso blanco in the middle to create something like a grilled-cheese sandwich—only better.

> 1½ pounds corn kernels (thawed, if frozen)
> 4 tablespoons butter, melted
> 1 egg
> 1 tablespoon milk
> 1 cup masa harina (corn flour found in the Spanish
>   section of your grocery store), or use yellow
>   cornmeal ground in a food processor to make
>   finer
> 2 tablespoons sugar
> ½ teaspoon salt
> ⅓ cup Monterey Jack cheese, grated
> 2 tablespoons butter
> 2 tablespoons oil
> queso blanco for filling (optional)
> sour cream for garnish

In a food processor or blender, puree the corn, melted butter, egg, salt, and milk. Strain out solids, and return the mixture to the food processor or blender (or, if it's nearly full, place the ingredients in a large mixing bowl). Pulse or mix in the masa harina and sugar, and let this batter stand for 15 to 20 minutes. Stir in the cheese. In a large skillet or griddle over medium heat, melt together 1 tablespoon each of butter and oil for frying. When hot, drop heaping tablespoons of batter into the pan, spreading in a circle with the back of the spoon. Cook for 3 or 4 minutes per side, until light golden brown. If you're making the grilled-cheese version, top half the arepas with some queso blanco, cover with another arepa, and cook for a minute or two until the cheese melts. If you're serving them plain, garnish with sour cream.

Quick Spanish Rice

Cook 2 cups white rice according to package directions. Just before serving, add 1 cup of your favorite salsa, ½ teaspoon chili powder, and ½ teaspoon cumin. Let the rice absorb the juice from the salsa, and serve when the mixture is heated through.

Mexican Bananas and Cream

4 firm bananas or 2 ripe medium plantains
4 tablespoons butter
¼ cup packed brown sugar
1 teaspoon vanilla extract
¼ teaspoon ground cinnamon
1 ounce Kahlúa liqueur (optional)
2 tablespoons toasted pecans or walnuts, chopped
whipped cream or vanilla ice cream for
**   accompaniment**

Peel bananas or plantains and cut into ½-inch-thick slices on a diagonal. Melt butter in a large, heavy skillet. Add the bananas or plantains. Heat until the fruit is warm and tender—about 2 to 3 minutes for bananas, and a minute or two longer if you're using plantains—gently stirring occasionally. Sprinkle with brown sugar, and stir gently until sugar melts. Carefully stir in vanilla, cinnamon, and Kahlúa if desired. Sprinkle with nuts. Simmer 1 minute more. Serve immediately over vanilla ice cream or with whipped cream dusted with cinnamon.

Caribou Steaks

Caribou is my personal favorite when it comes to game meat. It is best showcased with a simple marinade and a quick broiling or grilling. A wet marinade can tenderize the meat as well as impart flavor. A dry rub offers more intense flavors, can seal in juices, and is great for those who like their meat rare, to avoid losing moistness.

---

menu

Appetizer:	*Cream Cheese–Stuffed Mushrooms*
Salad:	*Arugula, Apple, Orange, Pomegranate, and Fennel Salad*
Entrée:	*Caribou Steaks*
Sides:	*Lyonnaise Potatoes; Green Beans with Hot Dressing*
Dessert:	*Coconut Custard Pie*

Cream Cheese–Stuffed Mushrooms

Stuffed mushrooms are always a crowd-pleaser. These make a great appetizer, and they can also double as a side dish with the main course; they are especially fabulous paired with steak.

1 pound medium mushrooms
2 slices bacon, cut into thin strips
½ stick butter
1 small onion, finely chopped
3 ounces cream cheese, cut into chunks
¼ to ½ cup seasoned bread crumbs

Preheat oven to 400 degrees. Clean mushrooms and remove stems. Trim off bottoms, and finely chop the stems. Fry bacon in a skillet until crisp.

Remove from pan and set aside. Remove all but 1 tablespoon of drippings; add butter and melt over medium heat. Sauté mushroom stems and onion until soft. Reduce heat and add creamed cheese. Stir until smooth. Add enough bread crumbs to give body to the mixture, being careful to keep it moist. Stir in bacon. Mound stuffing mixture in mushroom caps. Place in a buttered baking dish, and bake until mushrooms are tender and tops are golden.

Arugula, Apple, Orange, Pomegranate, and Fennel Salad

Pomegranate is a gem of a fruit, rich in antioxidants. But even better, it has a zippy, sweet-tart flavor, and the little ruby-colored arils look magnificent garnishing any food. Pomegranates can be a trial to remove from their skins, however, and unless you are wearing a red shirt, you should try the tip for harvesting the arils under water.*

> 2 navel oranges, peeled and cut crosswise into 4
>   slices
> 1 firm red apple, cored and thinly sliced
> 1 fennel bulb, cut in half and shaved into very thin
>   slices
> 6 cups arugula leaves, washed and spun dry
> ½ cup pomegranate arils (seeds)

> *Dressing*
> ½ cup olive oil
> ¼ cup fresh lemon juice
> ¼ cup orange juice (from oranges used in the salad)
> 1 shallot, minced
> ½ teaspoon grated lemon peel
> salt and pepper

For the dressing: Reserve 2 orange slices for each salad; squeeze the remainder and mix together with the other dressing ingredients in a small bowl.

In a large bowl, mix the apple slices, fennel, and arugula. Arrange a serving-size portion on a salad plate. Drizzle with some dressing (or pass it tableside); top with 2 orange slices and one-quarter of the pomegranate seeds.

*To open and clean a pomegranate without squirting red juice all over yourself and your kitchen, cut off the top, and then cut the pomegranate into quarters. While holding each piece under water in a deep bowl, gently rub out the arils. The membranes, pith, and skin will float to the top; the little red arils will sink to the bottom. Simply skim off anything floating in the water, and then pour the water and seeds into a strainer.

Caribou Steaks

Start the grill, pick a wet or dry marinade, and let the steaks sizzle.

4 caribou steaks, 1 inch thick

Wet Marinade
- **2 shallots, minced**
- **1 clove garlic, minced**
- **1 tablespoon brown sugar**
- **¼ cup soy sauce**
- **3 tablespoons Worcestershire sauce**
- **2 tablespoons balsamic vinegar**
- **⅓ cup vegetable oil**

Dry Rub
- **2 tablespoons paprika**
- **2 tablespoons crushed black pepper or coarsely ground black pepper**
- **2 tablespoons kosher salt**
- **1 tablespoon garlic powder**
- **1 tablespoon onion powder**
- **1 tablespoon ground sage**
- **1 tablespoon crushed coriander**
- **1 tablespoon dill weed**
- **1 tablespoon crushed red pepper flakes**

For the dry rub: Mix all ingredients, and sprinkle on both sides of steak. Rub some oil on both sides to help keep the meat moist. Store remaining rub in a container with a tight-fitting lid.

For the wet marinade: Mix all ingredients. Marinate caribou steaks for several hours.

Grill or broil steaks to desired doneness—4 or 5 minutes per side for rare.

Lyonnaise Potatoes

4 cups cooked, sliced potatoes
6 tablespoons butter
1 cup chopped onion
salt and pepper
¼ cup chopped fresh parsley

Peel potatoes and cut into ¼-inch slices. Boil in salted water until just tender. Drain and set aside. In a large, heavy skillet, heat butter over low heat; add onion and sauté until golden brown. Add the potatoes to the browned onions and cook for 4 to 5 minutes, turning frequently (a spatula works better than a spoon). Add salt, pepper, and parsley. Toss gently to mix. Serve.

Green Beans with Hot Dressing

1 pound green beans
2 strips bacon
2 tablespoons bacon drippings or melted butter
¼ cup red wine vinegar
1 tablespoon sugar

Clean green beans and remove tough strings. Boil or steam beans until just tender. Place in serving bowl and keep warm. Cut bacon into thin strips and fry in a small skillet until crispy. Pour off all but 2 tablespoons of the drippings (or discard drippings and melt 2 tablespoons butter in the same pan). Add vinegar and sugar, and stir until sugar is dissolved. Toss beans with dressing and serve hot.

Coconut Custard Pie

Coconut custard pie was a favorite of my grandmother's, and I would often surprise her with a piece from the neighborhood luncheonette. Years later, after I learned to bake it myself, it was a special treat we shared. Whenever I bake a coconut custard pie, I think of her with fond memories and love.

pastry for 1-crust pie; or
ready-made, unbaked 9-inch pie shell

Filling
> **4 eggs**
> **½ cup sugar**
> **2 ½ cups milk**
> **1 teaspoon vanilla extract**
> **¼ teaspoon salt**
> **1 cup sweetened shredded coconut**

Preheat oven to 425 degrees. Put the pastry in deep-dish pie plate, and flute the edges. Line with aluminum foil, and weigh down with pie weights or dry beans. Bake for 5 minutes, remove weights, and set aside. Reduce oven temperature to 325 degrees.

In a mixing bowl, beat eggs; add sugar, milk, vanilla, and salt. Stir in coconut. Pour filling into prebaked shell. Bake at 325 degrees for 50 to 60 minutes. Check for doneness by inserting a knife in the center; the pie is done when the knife comes out clean. Cool on a rack.

Braised Caribou Strips in Wine

Slowly braised in the oven, this caribou will melt in your mouth. Be careful not to overseason the meat; you want to enhance its natural flavor, not overpower it. This meal makes for easy entertaining because much of it can be prepared in advance or does not require close watching.

menu

Appetizer:	*Chinese Chicken Wings*
Salad:	*Balsamic Onion and Blue Cheese Salad*
Entrée:	*Braised Caribou Strips in Wine*
Sides:	*Cheesy Baked Orzo with Olives; Baked Stuffed Tomatoes*
Dessert:	*Chocolate Crepes with Banana Cream Filling*

Chinese Chicken Wings

These chicken wings have been a family favorite ever since my mom and I took a Chinese cooking class. I always use a wok, but if you don't have one, a deep skillet will do. Just be sure that you crisp the wings before adding the sauce. You might want to make a double batch, because they disappear quickly.

> **12 whole chicken wings, or 2 pounds wing and
>   drummette sections**
> **2 tablespoons peanut oil**
> **2 slices fresh ginger root (about the size of a dime)**
> **1 large clove garlic, crushed**
> **½ cup dark soy sauce**
> **½ cup water**
> **1 tablespoon sugar**
> **1 tablespoon rice wine or sherry**
> **1 scallion, cut in half**
> **1 star anise**
> **1 teaspoon red hot peppercorns, crushed**
> **½ teaspoon sesame oil (optional)**

Sauté chicken in a wok or large skillet in peanut oil over medium-high heat until wings are lightly browned and crispy. Reduce heat, push chicken wings to the side, and cook ginger root and garlic until very light brown, about 1 minute. Add soy sauce, water, sugar, wine, scallion, star anise, and hot peppercorns, and return heat to medium-high. If you use a large amount of chicken or a skillet instead of a wok, you may need to double the sauce or keep turning the wings. Cover and cook 15 to 20 minutes, until chicken is cooked thoroughly. Stir often to keep the sauce from getting too thick and syrupy, and check the heat to avoid scorching the sauce. Remove the wings to a serving platter (the sauce is not served), and drizzle with sesame oil if desired. The wings can be kept warm in a 300-degree oven if made in advance, or they can be served cold.

Balsamic Onion and Blue Cheese Salad

1 large or 2 small heads red leaf lettuce
3 small red onions, sliced thinly
¼ cup balsamic vinegar
¼ cup olive oil
salt and pepper
4 ounces blue cheese, crumbled

Dressing
1 teaspoon Dijon mustard
¼ cup olive oil
¼ cup red wine vinegar
1 shallot, minced

Preheat oven to 375 degrees. Wash, spin, and tear lettuce into bite-sized pieces. Set aside. Toss onions with balsamic vinegar and olive oil, season with salt and pepper, and bake for 10 to 15 minutes. Let cool.

For the dressing: Stir oil, vinegar, and shallot into Dijon mustard. Mix well.

In a large bowl, layer salad greens on bottom, followed by red onions and blue cheese. Add dressing and serve.

Braised Caribou Strips in Wine

2 pounds caribou, cut into 2- by ½-inch strips
¼ cup flour seasoned with salt and pepper
oil
⅛ to ¼ teaspoon each thyme, rosemary, and sage
1 cup red wine
1 cup homemade beef stock
1 onion, cut in vertical strips
1 shallot, minced
1 garlic clove, crushed
1 bay leaf

Preheat oven to 325 degrees. Dredge caribou strips in seasoned flour. Cover the bottom of a hot skillet with oil, and brown the meat strips in several batches. Don't crowd the pan. Place browned meat and remaining ingredients in a Dutch oven. Bake covered for 1 ½ to 2 hours, until meat is fork tender. Add more stock or wine if necessary to keep the meat covered.

Cheesy Baked Orzo with Olives

½ pound orzo (rice-shaped pasta)
4 tablespoons olive oil
1 onion, finely chopped
2 stalks celery, sliced
2 cloves garlic, minced
1 cup chicken stock
1 15-ounce can plum tomatoes in juice, chopped
    and drained (if in puree, rinsed and drained)
2 tablespoons chopped parsley, plus extra for garnish
1 tablespoon fresh basil, cut chiffonade style (in thin
    strips)
½ cup black olives, pitted and thinly sliced
1 cup grated mozzarella, divided
1 cup grated pecorino Romano cheese (or
    Parmesan), divided
salt and pepper

Cook the orzo in salted water until very firm. To test for doneness, split one piece in half; you should see a white center line. Drain well, and transfer to a large baking dish that has been oiled or coated with cooking spray or butter.

In a large skillet, heat the olive oil over medium heat and cook the onion, celery, and garlic until softened, about 5 minutes. Add the chicken stock, chopped tomatoes, parsley, and basil. Simmer and stir for 5 minutes. Stir the tomato mixture into the orzo along with the olives, ½ cup mozzarella cheese, and ¾ cup Romano cheese, and season with salt and pepper. Sprinkle the remaining mozzarella and Romano cheeses over the top. The dish can be prepared up to this point 1 day in advance and kept covered and refrigerated. Bake the orzo in a preheated, 400-degree oven for 30 minutes or until it is heated through, the cheese has melted, and the top is golden and crispy.

Baked Stuffed Tomatoes

6 ripe tomatoes, cored and halved
½ cup flavored bread crumbs
¼ cup grated Parmesan cheese
¼ cup minced shallots
¼ cup olive oil
2 cloves garlic, minced
¼ cup fresh parsley leaves, minced
½ teaspoon oregano
salt and pepper

Preheat oven to 375 degrees. Cut tomatoes in half crosswise and gently squeeze out seeds and juice. Arrange tomatoes in an oiled shallow baking dish. In a bowl, mix the remaining ingredients, and moisten with additional olive oil if necessary. Press mixture into each tomato half, mounding the filling on top. Bake the tomatoes, uncovered, for about 20 minutes, until they are sizzling and the filling is golden. Don't overcook, or the tomatoes won't hold their shape.

Chocolate Crepes with Banana Cream Filling

You can make the crepes and pudding in advance and assemble the dessert at the last minute, while the coffee is brewing. Extra crepes can be frozen between layers of waxed paper and sealed tightly in plastic.

Crepes
>   1 cup flour
>   3 tablespoons unsweetened cocoa
>   ¼ teaspoon salt
>   1 ¼ cups milk
>   3 eggs
>   1 teaspoon vanilla extract
>   ¼ cup sugar
>   ¼ cup melted butter

Filling
>   1 3.4-ounce package vanilla pudding (instant or
>   cooked style)
>   2 bananas
>   1 12-ounce jar hot fudge or chocolate sauce
>   whipped cream for garnish

For the crepes: Place all ingredients in a blender, and blend for 30 seconds. Scrape down sides. Blend for 30 seconds more. Cover and let sit for 30 minutes (this helps the flour absorb more of the liquids).

Heat a nonstick 8-inch skillet or crepe pan over medium heat and brush lightly with melted butter, or spray with cooking spray. Pour about ¼ cup batter into the pan (use a measuring cup), tilt the pan, and swirl to form a very thin disk. Cook for about 2 minutes; flip, and cook about 1 minute more. Stack crepes between layers of waxed paper, and continue until all the batter is cooked.

For the filling: Mix the vanilla pudding according to package directions and chill.

To assemble: Place an open crepe on a plate. On top of the crepe, add ½ cup vanilla pudding and half of a sliced banana. Fold the crepe, pour hot fudge or chocolate sauce on top, and garnish with a dollop of whipped cream.

ELK

Melt-in-Your-Mouth Swiss-Style Elk Steak

In this version of Swiss steak, the elk meat is slowly braised with tomatoes, onion, and celery. This creates not only an incredibly tender and tasty meat but also a rich sauce to serve over mashed potatoes. This dish is high up on my list of comfort foods.

---

menu

Appetizer:	*Cream of Mushroom Soup*
Salad:	*Broccoli Salad*
Entrée:	*Swiss Elk Steak*
Sides:	*Garlicky Mashed Potatoes; Julienned Carrots and Parsnips*
Dessert:	*Apple Crisp*

Cream of Mushroom Soup

This soup is so easy to make, you may never eat the canned type again. If you want to use it in a recipe in place of condensed soup, just add enough broth or cream to get that thick consistency. One day, my friend Donna served this creamy soup with a salad when she had us girls over for lunch. We all demanded the recipe, and it has always gotten rave reviews. Thanks, Donna.

1 pound fresh white mushrooms, sliced
1 medium onion, chopped finely
6 tablespoons butter
⅓ cup flour
1 teaspoon salt
3 cups chicken broth
2 cups half-and-half
salt and pepper to taste

Sauté mushrooms and onion in butter over medium-low heat, 10 minutes or until tender. Add flour, stirring until smooth. Add salt. Cook 1 minute, stirring constantly. Gradually add chicken broth, and continue to cook and stir until thickened and bubbling. Reduce heat. Stir in half-and-half. Heat gently; do not boil. Check for seasoning, and add salt and pepper to taste.

Broccoli Salad

5 to 6 cups fresh broccoli florets (about 1 pound)
1 teaspoon salt
4 slices cooked bacon
½ cup toasted sunflower seeds
¼ cup red onion, sliced lengthwise
1 cup mayonnaise
4 tablespoons apple cider vinegar
¼ cup honey
salt and pepper to taste

Blanch broccoli in boiling salted water for 1 minute to lock in the bright green color. Drain and immediately put the broccoli in a bowl of ice water to stop the cooking. Let it cool, and drain very well. Meanwhile, cook the bacon until crispy. Reserve drippings. Combine broccoli florets, bacon, sunflower seeds, and onion in a large serving bowl. In a separate bowl, whisk together mayonnaise, 1 tablespoon bacon drippings, cider vinegar, honey, salt, and pepper. Add dressing to the salad, and toss to mix well. Chill thoroughly before serving.

Swiss Elk Steak

3 to 4 pounds boneless elk steaks, about 1 inch thick
    (in serving-size pieces)
1 cup flour seasoned with salt and pepper
oil
4 or 5 cloves garlic, minced
3 large onions, thickly sliced vertically
1 bunch celery, cut into ½-inch slices
2 28-ounce cans crushed or whole tomatoes, cut up,
    including juice (not puree)
2 bay leaves
1 teaspoon thyme or marjoram

Dredge steaks in flour, and pound with a meat tenderizer or the bottom of a bottle until steaks are about ½-inch thick. As you pound, add a bit more flour if needed. Brown steaks a few at a time in hot oil in a skillet. Transfer the steaks to ovenware large enough to accommodate them in a double layer and to hold all the vegetables; a roasting pan or large Dutch oven works well. Sprinkle the steaks with garlic. Top with onions, celery, and finally the tomatoes. The meat should be covered by the tomatoes and their juice; add more tomatoes or some stock, if necessary. Add spices and bake tightly covered at 325 to 350 degrees until the sauce has thickened and the meat is fork tender—at least 2 to 3 hours. If the sauce is too thin, you can uncover it and continue cooking for another 30 minutes.

Garlicky Mashed Potatoes

4 pounds Yukon Gold potatoes, peeled and cut into
    chunks
6 cloves garlic, peeled
1 teaspoon salt
1 cup milk
salt and pepper
½ stick butter

Place the potatoes and garlic in a saucepan, cover with cold water, add 1 teaspoon salt, and bring to a boil. Decrease heat to medium and simmer for about 20 minutes, until the potatoes are tender. In a separate small saucepan, heat the milk over medium heat until small bubbles appear around the edges of the pan. Drain the potatoes and garlic and mash together, preferably using a ricer. Return the potatoes to the saucepan and add the hot milk, fluffing the potatoes with a fork. Season to taste with salt and pepper. Add the butter and serve at once.

Julienned Carrots and Parsnips

4 or 5 carrots
4 or 5 medium parsnips
1 shallot, chopped
½ stick butter
salt and pepper to taste
¼ teaspoon dried tarragon

Peel the carrots and parsnips and cut them into 4-inch lengths; then cut them into julienne strips (a food processor and julienne disk can be a real time-saver). Melt the butter in a pan over medium-low heat. Add the carrots, parsnips, shallot, salt and pepper to taste, and cook covered, stirring several times until just tender and glazed. Add an additional pat of butter or a few drops of water if necessary. Remove from pan and sprinkle tarragon on top.

Apple Crisp

10 medium apples—Cortland, Granny Smith,
  McIntosh, or a combination
½ cup sugar
1 teaspoon cinnamon
1 tablespoon flour or cornstarch

Topping
¾ cup brown sugar
¾ cup flour
¾ cup quick-cooking rolled oats
¾ teaspoon cinnamon
¼ teaspoon nutmeg
½ stick butter, softened

Hard Sauce
1 stick butter
1 cup confectioners' sugar
½ teaspoon vanilla or rum extract

Preheat oven to 375 degrees. Peel, core, and slice apples. Put them in a 9- by 13-inch baking pan. Toss with sugar, cinnamon, and flour. For the topping: Blend all ingredients until the mixture is crumbly, using a fork, pastry blender, or even your fingertips. Top the apples with the crumb mixture. Bake for 45 to 55 minutes, or until apples are tender and bubbly and the topping is golden brown. Cover loosely with foil if it browns too quickly. For the sauce: Beat the butter until very creamy and fluffy. Gradually beat in the powdered sugar. Add vanilla at the last minute. Spread in an 8-inch-square pan or a pie plate. Chill about 1 hour. Run a spoon along the bottom of pan to scoop out a large curl of hard sauce. Serve over warm apple crisp.

Stuffed Elk Roast with Port Wine Reduction

Flavors from the forest pair well with game meat. This stuffed elk roast is loaded with nuts and fruit and flavored with balsamic vinegar. The roast is glazed with currant jelly and served with a port reduction. It's a scrumptious dish that makes an impressive statement for an important occasion.

menu

Appetizer:	*Spinach and Roasted Red Pepper Cheesecake*
Salad:	*Mesclun Salad Greens with Honey Buttermilk Dressing*
Entrée:	*Glazed Fruit and Nut–Stuffed Elk Roast with Port Wine Reduction*
Sides:	*Boursin Cheese Potato Bake; Sweet and Sour Red Cabbage; Roasted Brussels Sprouts*
Dessert:	*Old-fashioned Grape Nuts Custard*

Spinach and Roasted Red Pepper Cheesecake

2 large red bell peppers, roasted and peeled; or 1 jar
    roasted red peppers
½ cup Italian-flavored bread crumbs
2 tablespoons butter, melted
3 8-ounce packages cream cheese, softened
15-ounce carton ricotta cheese
8 ounces feta cheese, crumbled
2 tablespoons flour
4 eggs
4 cups loosely packed fresh spinach leaves, washed,
    dried, and sliced (stems removed)
2 gloves garlic, minced
1 teaspoon fresh dill
½ teaspoon salt
½ teaspoon pepper
¼ cup toasted pine nuts or walnuts, chopped

Preheat oven to 350 degrees. Cut red peppers into strips and drain on paper towels while preparing the cheesecake. Mix bread crumbs with melted butter and press into the bottom of a 9-inch springform pan. Bake 10 minutes. Remove from oven, cool. Reduce temperature to 325 degrees.

Using an electric mixer, beat cream cheese until soft. Add ricotta and feta cheeses and flour, and beat until blended. Add eggs one at a time, beating after each addition. Stir in the spinach, garlic, dill, salt, and pepper by hand.

Pour the batter into the crumb-lined pan. Bake at 325 degrees for 15 minutes. Carefully remove the pan from the oven and arrange roasted red pepper strips around the outside of the cake. Bake another 30 to 40 minutes, or until set in the center. Turn the oven off, and leave the cheesecake in the oven for 15 minutes. Then remove and cool on a wire rack for 10 minutes. Carefully run a knife around the inside of the pan, and remove the sides of the pan. Garnish the outside edge with chopped nuts. Allow the cheesecake to cool another 15 minutes. Serve warm or chill and serve cold with crackers or baguette slices.

Mesclun Salad Greens with Honey Buttermilk Dressing

> 6 to 8 cups mesclun salad greens
> 4 ounces grape tomatoes
> 1 cucumber, peeled and thinly sliced

Dressing
> ¼ cup cider vinegar
> ¼ cup sour cream
> ¼ cup mayonnaise
> ¼ cup fresh buttermilk, or buttermilk powder
>   mixed according to package directions
> 2 tablespoons honey
> 1 teaspoon minced garlic
> 1 tablespoon chopped chives
> 1 tablespoon chopped parsley

For the dressing: Mix all ingredients together. Let sit for 1 to 2 hours before serving to allow flavors to blend. For the salad: Toss rinsed, dried salad greens with grape tomatoes and cucumber slices. Serve with dressing on the side.

Glazed Fruit and Nut–Stuffed Elk Roast

> 6 ounces mixed dried fruit bits
> 1 small onion, finely chopped
> 2 shallots, finely chopped
> 2 tablespoons balsamic vinegar
> ¼ cup fine plain bread crumbs
> ½ cup chopped walnuts
> 2 tablespoons melted butter
> ¼ teaspoon ground allspice
> 1 elk tenderloin roast or boneless roast, about 4
>   inches thick
> 1 tablespoon balsamic vinegar
> 2 tablespoons softened butter
> salt and pepper
> 6–8 bacon strips (enough to cover rolled roast)
> 1 12-ounce jar red currant jelly, melted

Preheat oven to 325 degrees. For the stuffing: Mix fruit, onion, shallots, and balsamic vinegar, and cover with boiling water. Let stand for 20 to 30 minutes; drain. Finish the stuffing by adding bread crumbs, nuts, melted butter, and allspice. Gently mix. Set aside.

Depending on the cut of meat, you will want to butterfly the elk roast and pound it to a relatively flat, even thickness in a rectangular shape, if possible. If the meat is in pieces, pound them flat and overlap the pieces about an inch to form a rectangular shape. Sprinkle with 1 tablespoon balsamic vinegar and smear with softened butter; season with salt and pepper. Spread stuffing mixture on meat. Starting from one long side, roll up jelly-roll style. Wrap bacon strips around the roast. Tie tightly with kitchen string in several places. Place the roast in a shallow pan and roast for 1 ½ to 2 ½ hours, depending on size. Brush with melted jelly and cook for the last 15 minutes. Remove the roast from the oven and pan, cover it with foil, and let it rest for 15 minutes before carving. Serve with a port wine reduction (recipe follows). The flavor is intense, so a little goes a long way.

Port Wine Reduction
4 cups ruby port wine
2 tablespoons butter, cut into 4 pieces

In a large saucepan, bring the wine to a heavy boil over high heat. Reduce heat and continue boiling until the wine reduces and thickens to about ½ cup of syrup. Remove from heat and add butter one piece at a time, gently swirling the pan until it is incorporated.

Boursin Cheese Potato Bake

3 pounds potatoes, peeled and cut into ¼-inch slices
2 cups heavy cream
5-ounce container Boursin or other garlic-flavored
  cheese spread
salt and pepper
1 tablespoon chopped fresh chives or parsley

Preheat oven to 350 degrees. Butter a 2-quart casserole dish with a tight-fitting lid (or use foil to cover). Warm cream and cheese together until cheese is melted and mixture is smooth, blending well. Layer half the sliced potatoes in the bottom of the casserole, sprinkle with salt and pepper, cover with half the cheese mixture, and repeat layers, ending with cheese. Cover and bake for 1 hour, or until potatoes are tender. Before serving, sprinkle with chives or parsley.

Sweet and Sour Red Cabbage

I grew up eating this wonderful accompaniment. My grandmother would make a big batch often using 5 or 6 heads of cabbage. If you are energetic, you can make a big pot and freeze the leftovers in meal-size containers. It complements virtually any game meat and is also great with pork.

**6 strips bacon or 3 tablespoons rendered bacon
    drippings**
1 head red cabbage, finely shredded
1 tart apple, peeled, cored, and chopped
½ teaspoon salt
¼ cup cider vinegar
¼ cup sugar

Brown bacon strips in a large pot until the fat has rendered. Remove bacon. Add cabbage, apple, and salt to the pot, and toss to coat. Cover and cook until the cabbage wilts and begins to soften. When the cabbage has cooked down and is soft, add vinegar and sugar. Let cook for several minutes, and taste. The cabbage should be sweet and sour; if you can't tell which, it's perfect. There should be some juice, but it shouldn't be too wet. Add more vinegar or sugar, as needed. Continue cooking until the apple disappears, the cabbage is soft, and most juice has been reduced. Serve warm or at room temperature.

Roasted Brussels Sprouts

1 pound brussels sprouts
3 tablespoons extra virgin olive oil
1 teaspoon kosher salt
ground black pepper

Trim ends off brussels sprouts and remove any yellowed leaves. Cut a cross in the stem with a knife. If any sprouts are overly large, cut them in half from tip to stem. Put all ingredients in a plastic bag and toss to coat. Place sprouts on a baking sheet and roast in a 400-degree oven for about 15 minutes; check for doneness. Stir and redistribute the sprouts so they brown evenly. Return them to the oven and continue cooking until done. Brussels sprouts should be browned and crisp on the outside and tender on the inside. Remove to a serving dish and add a dusting of salt and pepper. Serve hot or cold.

Old-fashioned Grape-Nuts Custard

2 cups milk
1 cup Grape-Nuts cereal
1 cup sugar
4 eggs, beaten
½ teaspoon salt
1 teaspoon vanilla extract

Preheat oven to 350 degrees. Scald milk. Add cereal to hot milk and cool. Add sugar, eggs, salt, and vanilla. Pour into a buttered custard dish. Place the dish in a pan with hot water. Bake until a knife inserted in the center comes out clean. Serve warm or cold with a drizzle of honey and a spoonful of whipped cream.

MOOSE

Baked BBQ Moose Steaks

When I think moose, I think Maine. That's where I saw my first moose in the wild. When my husband thinks moose, he thinks big. A moose is a large animal and provides a lot of meat. Don't be afraid to substitute moose in almost any beef or game meat recipe. These steaks require little attention and can even be served buffet style from a chafing dish—just make the pieces smaller.

menu

Appetizer:	*New England Clam Chowder*
Entrée:	*Baked BBQ Moose Steaks*
Sides:	*Four-Cheese Gemelli; Broccoli*
Dessert:	*Frozen Strawberry Dessert*

New England Clam Chowder

4 slices bacon or salt pork, finely diced
1 small onion, chopped
2 celery stalks, sliced
4 medium potatoes, peeled and diced
½ stick butter, divided
¼ cup flour
2 cups bottled clam juice
2 6½-ounce cans chopped clams and juice
2 cups whipping cream
1 teaspoon salt
½ teaspoon ground white pepper

In a large, heavy pan, sauté bacon or salt pork until the fat has been rendered and the pork is golden brown. Add onion, celery, and potatoes, and cook for 3 or 4 minutes. Add 2 tablespoons butter, and let it melt. Stir in flour, and cook 1 minute more. Stir in clam juice and chopped clams, and bring to a slow boil. Cook, stirring often, until potatoes and celery are tender. Add cream until desired thickness is reached; add salt and pepper, and check for seasoning. Just before serving, float 2 tablespoons of butter on top of the soup. If you like, you can substitute heavy cream for the whipping cream and omit the flour.

Baked BBQ Moose Steaks

This recipe is for those who just love a steak. And who doesn't? With this method of braising, the steaks cook slowly, allowing them to become moist and tender while ensuring thorough cooking.

2 to 3 pounds moose steak, 1 inch thick
½ cup flour
salt and pepper
¼ teaspoon cayenne pepper
¼ teaspoon garlic powder
2 tablespoons butter
4 tablespoons oil
1 18-ounce bottle barbecue sauce
1 teaspoon dehydrated onion flakes
½ cup beef stock or water

Preheat oven to 350 degrees. Cut meat into serving-size pieces and trim. Place flour, salt, pepper, cayenne, and garlic powder in a plastic bag; mix well.

Shake steaks one at a time until lightly coated with flour mixture. Heat butter and oil in a skillet over medium-high heat. Brown steaks on both sides in several batches. Arrange steaks in a roasting pan, and spoon barbecue sauce on top of each steak. Sprinkle with dehydrated onion flakes. Add beef stock to the skillet and cook for a minute, stirring to loosen any browned bits. Add the stock to the baking pan. Cover tightly with a lid or foil, and bake for about 30 minutes. Check meat and add more stock or water if necessary. Bake uncovered for another 15 minutes, or until done and lightly browned on top.

Four-Cheese Gemelli

1 pound gemelli pasta or other twisted or spiral pasta
2 tablespoons butter
½ cup heavy cream
2 ounces fontina cheese, cut in thin julienne strips
2 ounces mozzarella cheese, cut in thin julienne strips
2 ounces Gorgonzola cheese, crumbled
½ cup Parmesan cheese, shredded or grated
salt and pepper

Cook pasta in boiling salted water until firm (al dente). Rinse with hot water and drain well. Set aside. In a large pan, melt butter and add heavy cream. Add the four cheeses and melt over low heat, stirring to prevent sticking. When the sauce is smooth and thick, check for seasoning and adjust salt and pepper. Add the pasta to the pan, toss to coat, and reheat.

Broccoli

2 large heads broccoli, cut into spears
2 tablespoons olive oil
2 tablespoons butter
1 clove garlic, minced
pinch crushed red pepper flakes
salt and pepper to taste

Clean broccoli, trim tough ends, and scrape or peel any remaining stalks. Cut into spears by following the thick portion of the stem and dividing it up to the crown into several pieces. In a large skillet, sauté the garlic and pepper flakes in oil and butter. Add broccoli and toss to coat; sauté for 10 minutes or until crisp tender. Salt and pepper to taste. Serve hot.

Frozen Strawberry Dessert

2 cups strawberries
½ cup sugar
4 egg whites (Since freezing doesn't kill salmonella,
consider using powdered or pasteurized egg
whites.)
1 cup sugar
several berries for garnish
4 mint leaves for garnish

Wash and hull strawberries. Drain. Place berries in a small bowl and mash with a potato masher, or pulse several times in a food processor. Remove 1 cup and set aside. Sweeten remaining berries with ½ cup sugar. Refrigerate the berries while making the meringue. Beat egg whites with an electric mixer until soft peaks form. Add sugar gradually and continue beating until mixture is thick and glossy. Add reserved 1 cup of berries and beat until just blended. Transfer meringue mixture to a freezer container and cover. Freeze at least 1 hour until solid. To serve, spread crushed berries in the bottom of a clear glass dish or stem glass. Top with frozen berry meringue. Garnish with a sliced strawberry and a mint leaf.

VENISON

The word *venison* is derived from the Latin *venari,* which means "to hunt," so technically, any meat obtained while hunting could be called venison. Normally, however, we think of venison as primarily the edible flesh from a member of the deer family.

Grilled Venison Chops

Medium-rare venison cooked outdoors on a charcoal fire is a meal fit for royalty. Summertime meals like this one are quick, easy, and so delicious.

menu

Appetizer: Creamy Cucumber Salad

Entrée: Grilled Venison Chops

Sides: Seasoned Potato Wedges;
Asparagus with Orange
and Almonds

Dessert: Pear Bread Pudding

Creamy Cucumber Salad

When I was young, my mother always had a garden, and every season we'd come across a cucumber or two that had escaped being picked in a timely fashion. Whenever we found one of these monsters, she'd say, "There's one for the sour cream!" If the seeds were too woody, she'd scoop them out; otherwise, we'd peel and slice the cukes, cover them with dressing, and let them sit in the refrigerator for several hours or overnight.

> **2 to 3 medium cucumbers**
> **2 teaspoons salt**
> **⅔ cup sour cream**
> **1 tablespoon vinegar (or juice from dill pickles)**
> **1 teaspoon chopped dill weed**
> **salt and pepper to taste**
> **paprika and dill weed for garnish**

Peel and thinly slice the cucumbers. Sprinkle with 2 teaspoons salt, and let them stand and drain for 30 minutes. Rinse and pat dry. Mix with remaining ingredients. Chill for several hours to let the flavors marry. Check seasoning, and garnish with a sprinkle of dill weed and paprika.

Grilled Venison Chops

Venison chops are tender, tasty morsels. Sealing the chops with a paste-type marinade and cooking them quickly over a hot fire or under a hot broiler will ensure that the succulent juices are trapped inside. Soaking venison in evaporated milk overnight will remove any gaminess and keep the meat moist.

> 1 ½–2 pounds venison chops
> 2 tablespoons Dijon-style mustard
> ¼ teaspoon oregano
> ½ teaspoon minced garlic or ¼ teaspoon garlic powder
> 2 tablespoons olive oil
> 2 tablespoons cider vinegar
> salt and pepper

Mix together ingredients to form a paste. Brush both sides of each chop with the mixture. Grill over medium-high heat. Cooking time depends on the meat's thickness and your personal preference: for medium, cook ¾- to 1-inch chops 4 to 5 minutes per side. To avoid overcooking, use a meat thermometer.

Seasoned Potato Wedges

> 4 to 6 baking potatoes, such as Idaho or russet
> ¼ cup oil
> ¼ teaspoon paprika
> ¼ teaspoon garlic powder
> ½ teaspoon seasoned salt
> ¼ teaspoon pepper

Preheat oven to 375 degrees. Scrub potatoes and cut into quarters, lengthwise. Mix all other ingredients in a zipper-style plastic bag or a large bowl. Add potato wedges and toss to coat thoroughly. Place potatoes skin-side down on a baking pan. Roast until tender, about 45 minutes, depending on the size of the potatoes.

Asparagus with Orange and Almonds

1 pound asparagus spears
2 tablespoons butter
1 tablespoon olive oil
1 ½ teaspoon grated orange zest
juice of 1 orange
¼ cup sliced almonds

Clean asparagus and bend in an arc so that the woody end snaps off, leaving only the tender stem. Sauté spears in butter and olive oil until just tender. Add orange zest and juice and cook for 1 minute more. Remove to serving dish and top with almond slices.

Pear Bread Pudding

8 slices egg bread, crusts removed, cut into quarters
1 cup fresh pears, peeled and diced; or fruit from
        1 can sliced pears
4 eggs
¾ cup sugar
3 cups half-and-half or milk
¼ cup pear brandy (optional)
1 teaspoon vanilla extract
1 teaspoon cinnamon
3 tablespoons butter, melted
jar of caramel sauce

Butter an 8- by 8-inch pan. Layer two-thirds of the bread in the bottom of the pan. Cover with pear chunks. Top with remaining bread. Beat eggs, sugar, half-and-half, brandy, vanilla, cinnamon, and melted butter together. Pour over bread and pears, making sure that the mixture is absorbed by the bread. Cover and refrigerate overnight or for at least 4 hours. Bake for 40 minutes in a 350-degree oven, or until a knife inserted in the center comes out clean. To keep the bread pieces submerged, cover the pudding with a piece of buttered foil, weighted down with an ovenproof dish or a smaller pan. Remove the foil for the last 15 minutes to allow the pudding to brown. Remove from oven, drizzle with caramel sauce. Serve warm with cream or vanilla ice cream.

Hearty Venison Stew

The addition of pungent allspice and juniper berries imbues this rich stew with complex flavors. And this dish is cooked in the oven, which means you don't have to stand over the stove stirring the pot.

---

menu

Salad:	*Green Salad with Blue Cheese Dressing*
Entrée:	*Hearty Venison Stew*
Side:	*Crusty French Bread*
Dessert:	*Double Chocolate Pudding*

Green Salad with Blue Cheese Dressing

4 to 6 cups assorted salad greens, washed, spun dry, and torn into bite-size pieces
1 cup olive oil
4 ounces blue cheese
½ cup garlic-flavored croutons

Place salad greens in a large bowl. Add oil to the bowl of a food processor or blender. Break blue cheese into chunks and add to the oil. Puree until thick and creamy. Garnish salad with croutons, toss with dressing. Serve additional dressing on the side. Store leftover dressing in the refrigerator.

Hearty Venison Stew

2 pounds venison, cut into 1-inch pieces
½ cup flour seasoned with salt and pepper
2 tablespoons butter
2 tablespoons oil
2 onions, quartered
4 cloves garlic, minced
2 shallots, minced
2 cups fruity red wine (Beaujolais or Valpolicella)
2 tablespoons brown sugar
1 tablespoon sweet Hungarian paprika
½ to 1 teaspoon ground cayenne pepper (according
    to taste)
6 to 8 whole juniper berries
2 to 4 whole allspice berries
1 large or 2 small bay leaves
salt and pepper

Preheat oven to 300 degrees. Dredge venison pieces in seasoned flour. Melt butter in a Dutch oven over medium heat, adding the oil to prevent burning. Brown venison pieces on all sides, being careful not to crowd the meat. Cook in several batches if necessary. Remove the meat. Add the onions, garlic, and shallots to the pan and sauté for 1 minute. Add wine (or, if you don't like to cook with wine, use beef stock or half water and half wine), and deglaze the pan, making sure to scrape up the browned residue on the bottom of the pan. Return the meat to the pan. Add sugar, spices, berries, bay leaves, and salt and pepper to the cooking pot, and bring to a boil. (For easy removal, make a bouquet garni by placing the berries and bay leaves in a square of cheesecloth and tying it closed with string.) Remove the Dutch oven from the burner. Cover tightly and bake in the oven for about 3 hours, or until the venison is fork tender. Remove the berries and bay leaves before serving.

Crusty French Bread

1 package active dry yeast or 1 yeast cake
1 cup warm water (110 to 115 degrees)
3 cups flour
1 teaspoon salt
cornmeal
1 egg white
1 teaspoon water

Dissolve yeast in warm water and let it work for 5 to 10 minutes, until bubbly. By hand, add 1 ½ cups flour and salt, and beat until well blended. Add ½ cup flour at a time, incorporating as much of the remaining flour as possible to make a soft dough. Knead on a floured surface until dough is smooth and elastic, about 10 minutes (add more flour or a few drops of water if needed). Place dough in a greased bowl and turn once. Cover and let dough rise in a warm place until it has doubled in bulk—2 to 4 hours, depending on the room temperature.

Punch dough down and turn out onto a lightly floured surface. Cover and let rest for 10 minutes. Roll dough into a large rectangle measuring 12 by 6 inches. Starting with the long side, roll the dough tightly in jelly-roll fashion. Moisten edges and ends with water, and pinch to seal. Stretch and roll dough to shape. Grease a large baking sheet and sprinkle with cornmeal. Place loaf, seam side down, on the prepared sheet. Cover loaf with a damp towel and let rise 45 minutes to 1 hour. Beat egg white with 1 teaspoon water and brush on the loaf. Using a very sharp knife or razor, make several diagonal slashes across the top of the loaf. Bake in a preheated 425-degree oven for 20 to 30 minutes. Spray loaf with water several times during baking for a crispier crust. Check for doneness by tapping the loaf until it sounds hollow. Loosely cover with foil if the crust is browning too fast. Remove from pan and cool on a wire rack.

Double Chocolate Pudding

¼ cup cornstarch
pinch salt
3 cups milk
3 ounces unsweetened chocolate
½ cup sugar
2 ounces premium milk chocolate bar (e.g.,
    Ghirardelli, Lindt)
1 ounce crème de cacao or Kahlúa liqueur
    (optional)
1 teaspoon vanilla extract
whipped cream for topping

In a small bowl, mix cornstarch and pinch of salt with ¼ cup of the milk. In a saucepan over low heat, scald the remaining milk, add unsweetened chocolate and sugar, and stir until the chocolate is melted. Add cornstarch mixture to chocolate mixture and continue cooking over low heat, stirring constantly, until pudding is thick and smooth. Cook for 3 minutes to thoroughly cook cornstarch. Remove from heat, add 2 ounces chocolate and liqueur, if desired, and stir until chocolate is melted and blended in. Add vanilla. Pour into serving dishes. Chill. Top with whipped cream.

Chili Times Three

One of my all-time favorite dishes is chili. It's a rib-sticking comfort food that can be a main dish or a savory accompaniment to a sandwich. Everybody has their own preferred way of enjoying this spicy dish. I grew up with an Irish grandmother who was a potato person, and I still like my chili over mashed potatoes or topping a baked potato. My kids like it served in a bowl (with rice on the side), so they can dip tortilla chips in it. Sometimes I make it thick and chunky enough to fill a flour tortilla. Just sprinkle with cheese, and you have a kind of Tex-Mex sloppy joe. Venison or other game meat adds a real meaty flavor to the dish. Ground meat is the traditional favorite, but small meat chunks work well too. If you don't have venison, use any ground red game meat, or mix half beef and half venison. Whether you like your chili, mild, hot, or on fire, you can be creative with these recipes: add a new bean or even a vegetable or two. And don't forget a salad and perhaps a cerveza (beer) to quench the flames.

menu

Appetizer: *Avocado and Tomato Salad*

Entrées: *Hearty Venison Chili;*
Chili à la Natalie;
Chili and Cheese Enchiladas

Dessert: *Caramel Custard Flan*

Avocado and Tomato Salad

8 slices French bread
olive oil
2 avocados, cut into wedges
juice of 1 lemon
2 medium tomatoes, cut into wedges
1 small red onion, sliced thinly into rings
4 cups baby spinach leaves
2 ounces crumbled blue cheese

Dressing
½ cup red wine or cider vinegar
¾ cup vegetable or olive oil
2 cloves garlic, minced
1 teaspoon dried oregano
¼ teaspoon dried basil
1 tablespoon sugar

For the dressing: Mix all ingredients in a jar and shake well. For the salad: To make croutons from the French bread slices, brush both sides with olive oil and grill in a skillet until lightly browned. Cool and cut each slice into fourths. Set aside. Peel and pit the avocados, slice into wedges, and toss with lemon juice to prevent discoloration. Cut tomatoes into eighths, and slice the red onion. To assemble: Place 1 cup spinach on each salad plate; top with tomato, avocado wedges, and onion rings. Divide croutons and sprinkle on top of salad. Top with blue cheese crumbles. Drizzle each salad with dressing. Serve immediately.

Hearty Venison Chili

2 pounds ground venison
4 large onions, sliced vertically
1 green or red bell pepper, chopped finely
8 cloves fresh garlic, minced; or 3 tablespoons
    prepared minced garlic
2 28-ounce cans crushed tomatoes in juice
2 15.5-ounce cans red, pink, or white kidney beans
4 tablespoons chili powder
1 tablespoon cumin
1 teaspoon cayenne pepper (optional)
salt and pepper

Brown venison, onions, and pepper in a large, heavy stockpot or Dutch oven. Add all the remaining ingredients and simmer for about 45 minutes, until chili is thick and flavors have blended. Check seasoning, and add more cayenne pepper if you really like it hot. Simmer for an additional 15 minutes. Serve topped with shredded cheese or a dollop of sour cream.

Chili à la Natalie

This chili recipe, which comes from my aunt, may sound too bland and basic to be good, but don't let the simplicity fool you. This chili isn't as red or saucy colored as some, but its thick meaty goodness and peppery flavor make it a bang-up dish that's great with mashed potatoes.

4 large onions, chopped
2 tablespoons oil
2 pounds venison burger
1 28-ounce can peeled Italian tomatoes in juice
    (not puree)
2 15.5-ounce cans dark red kidney beans
1 tablespoon black pepper (or more to taste)

Cook onion in oil until soft. Add ground venison burger and cook until no longer pink. Break up tomatoes by hand or with a quick whiz in the blender or food processor; some chunks should remain. Add tomatoes and their juice, beans, and pepper to the meat mixture and simmer gently for about 1 hour. Make sure the chili is spicy enough; if not, add some more pepper just before serving.

Chili and Cheese Enchiladas

Here's a great way to stretch a little bit of leftover chili and get another easy meal for your family. This dish can be prepared ahead of time and popped into the oven just an hour before dinner.

> **8 corn tortillas**
> **2 cups shredded mild cheddar or Colby cheese**
> **1 cup shredded Monterey Jack cheese**
> **½ cup chopped onion**
> **3 tablespoons diced green chilies**
> **2 cups chili**
> **sour cream, salsa, or guacamole for garnish**
> **(optional)**

Preheat oven to 350 degrees. Wrap the tortillas in foil and put them in the oven for a few minutes to warm, until soft and pliable. Lightly grease a 12- by 7-inch baking dish. In a bowl, combine 1 cup cheddar cheese, Monterey Jack cheese, onion, and chilies. Place about ⅓ cup cheese filling in the center of each tortilla, roll up tightly, and place seam side down in the baking dish. Pour chili over the tortillas. Bake covered for 30 to 40 minutes, or until heated through and cheese has melted. Top with remaining cheddar cheese and return to oven for 5 minutes. Remove from oven and let stand for 10 minutes. Serve with condiments of your choice and a leafy green salad.

Caramel Custard Flan

> **¾ cup sugar**
> **4 cups whole milk**
> **½ cup sugar**
> **1- to 2-inch piece cinnamon stick**
> **4 eggs plus 4 egg yolks**

Heat ¾ cup sugar in a small skillet over low heat until it begins to dissolve. Continue cooking until sugar caramelizes. Do not burn. Pour the caramel into a 3-quart baking dish, and quickly tip the dish so that the caramel coats the sides. Set aside.

Preheat oven to 350 degrees. On the middle oven rack, place a pan or dish large enough to hold the baking dish and deep enough to make a water bath.

In a saucepan, mix the milk, ½ cup sugar, and cinnamon stick. Bring to a boil slowly, stirring until the sugar dissolves. Cook over medium heat until the mixture has reduced slightly. Set aside to cool.

In a large bowl, beat the eggs and egg yolks well. Remove the cinnamon stick and add the cooled milk mixture to the eggs. Beat well. Pour into the baking dish. Place the baking dish in the larger pan and add enough hot water to bring it halfway up the sides of the baking dish. Bake for approximately 1½ to 2 hours. Flan is done when a knife inserted in the center comes out clean. Remove from the pan, let cool, and refrigerate. To serve, invert on a large plate, spooning any remaining custard on top.

Pepper-Crusted Rack of Venison

This menu may be a little more involved than some of the others, but the end result is worth it. Save it for a special occasion, such as a romantic evening for two or a dinner party to impress the boss.

---

menu

Appetizer:	*Shrimp and Spinach Crepes*
Salad:	*Endive and Tomato Salad*
Entrée:	*Pepper-Crusted Rack of Venison*
Sides:	*Potato Fans; Apple-Stuffed Acorn Squash*
Dessert:	*Poached Pears with Amaretti*

Shrimp and Spinach Crepes

Crepes are always an excellent first course. The crepes themselves are easy to make—all you need are some simple ingredients and a small nonstick skillet—and they can be prepared well in advance. Just stack them between layers of waxed paper, cover tightly, and refrigerate for a day or two or freeze for even longer.

Crepes

    2 eggs
    ¼ teaspoon salt
    1 cup flour
    1 cup milk
    2 tablespoons melted butter

Filling

    1 10-ounce package frozen creamed spinach
    1 clove garlic, minced
    ½ small onion, minced
    8 ounces fresh mushrooms, sliced
    2 tablespoons butter
    8 ounces small cocktail shrimp, cooked, peeled, and
        deveined
    2 tablespoons lemon juice
    ¼ teaspoon tarragon
    salt and pepper
    1 cup shredded Swiss or Gruyère cheese

For the crepes: Whirl all ingredients in a blender and let sit for about 30 minutes. Melt 1 teaspoon butter in the bottom of an 8-inch nonstick skillet and wipe it out with a paper towel (you can reuse the paper towel to refilm the pan for the next crepe, because not much butter is needed). Heat the pan over medium heat and pour about ¼ cup batter into the pan, tilting and swirling quickly to thinly cover the bottom of the skillet. Cook the crepe for about 1 to 2 minutes, until it looks like it is beginning to dry. Run a spatula around the edges of the crepe and then under it to turn it over. Cook the second side for about 30 seconds. Continue until you have made 8 thin crepes.

For the filling: Thaw the creamed spinach. In a skillet, sauté garlic, onion, and mushrooms in butter until softened. Add creamed spinach, shrimp, lemon juice, tarragon, salt, and pepper. Check for seasonings and adjust if needed.

To assemble: Place about ½ cup filling in the center of each crepe and roll. Place seam side down in the baking dish. Cover with shredded cheese and bake at 375 degrees until hot in the center and cheese is melted. Serve 1 crepe per person for an appetizer.

Endive and Tomato Salad

1 head Belgian endive
2 ripe tomatoes, thinly sliced

Dressing
10 fresh basil leaves
2 tablespoons fresh parsley, chopped
¼ cup olive oil
1 tablespoon white wine vinegar
1 tablespoon balsamic vinegar
1 tablespoon water

Trim ends and wash and separate endive leaves. Arrange leaves on a small platter like the spokes of a wheel, radiating out from the center. Overlap tomato slices in the center on top of the endive. Mix dressing ingredients together and drizzle over salad.

Pepper-Crusted Rack of Venison

2 4-rib racks of venison, frenched★
2 cups sliced mushrooms
2 tablespoons butter
2 tablespoons Dijon mustard
1 tablespoon olive oil
3 tablespoons each cracked black, green, and red
    peppercorns
¼ cup chopped shallots
¾ cup burgundy wine
½ cup water or beef stock
1 tablespoon tomato paste
2 sprigs fresh thyme, oregano, or rosemary
salt to taste

★To french the rack of venison, scrape 1 to 2 inches of meat from the bone ends of the rib roast. Paper collars may be added after cooking for a fancy presentation.

Preheat oven to 375 degrees. Sauté mushrooms in butter until soft, and set aside. Mix mustard and oil together and brush on both sides of the meat. Put peppercorns on a large plate and press them into the meat, coating both sides. Roast the venison flesh side up until it is rare or medium rare (use a meat thermometer), about 20 to 25 minutes. Remove the roast from the hot pan and tent it with foil to keep it warm, allowing the racks to rest. Add shallots to the roasting pan and cook over medium heat until soft. Deglaze the pan with red wine and water or beef stock, and reduce by half over high heat. Stir in tomato paste and thyme, oregano, or rosemary, as preferred. Add mushrooms and cook for a minute or two. Check seasoning and add salt to taste. Cut racks into individual chops, and serve with pan sauce.

Potato Fans

4 medium-sized potatoes
1 tablespoon olive oil
¼ teaspoon garlic powder
¼ teaspoon paprika
salt and pepper
2 tablespoons grated Parmesan cheese

Preheat oven to 425 degrees. Peel the potatoes. To make fans, cut ⅛-inch slits 80 percent of the way through each potato from top to bottom. (Tip: Place the potato on a large serving spoon and cut downward; the edge of the spoon will stop the knife from going through to the bottom of the potato.) Place potatoes, oil, and seasonings in a bowl or plastic bag. Roll potatoes in mixture to coat. Bake about 45 minutes, or until potatoes are tender and fans have spread slightly. Sprinkle grated cheese on top, and bake for 5 minutes more.

Apple-Stuffed Acorn Squash

Fruits and nuts make a great filling for acorn squash. If you are short on time, you can prebake the empty squash the day before or precook the squash in the microwave until a fork pierces it easily. Then add the stuffing and bake until it is cooked and browned, saving about half the time.

2 acorn squash
½ cup maple syrup
3 tart apples, cored and cut into bite-size pieces
½ stick butter, melted
½ cup chopped walnuts or pecans
¼ cup chopped celery
¼ cup chopped onion

Preheat oven to 400 degrees. Wash squash, cut them in half, and scoop out the seeds. Mix remaining stuffing ingredients, and fill the cavity of each squash. Place in a baking pan and add about 1 inch of water. Cover with foil and bake for about 40 minutes. Remove foil and continue baking until squash is tender and stuffing is golden brown.

Poached Pears with Amaretti

6 ripe Bosc or Anjou pears
1 ½ cups dry white wine or champagne; or, for more
**   colorful pears, dry red wine**
½ cup water
¾ cup sugar
1 vanilla bean
1 cinnamon stick
2 strips lemon zest
2 strips orange zest
juice of 1 orange (about ¼ cup)

Amaretti (Cookies)
8 ounces canned almond paste
1 cup sugar
2 large egg whites

For the cookies: Preheat oven to 350 degrees. Beat all ingredients together. Pipe or spoon onto a cookie sheet lined with parchment paper. Bake for 20 minutes. Store extra cookies in an airtight container.

For the pears: Bring all ingredients except the pears to a slow simmer in a small but deep saucepan (the pan should be able to accommodate all the pears and keep them covered in the poaching liquid). Meanwhile, peel the pears and slice a little off the bottoms so that they will stand upright. With a melon baller or grapefruit knife, scoop out the seeds and core. Lower the pears into the poaching liquid and simmer very slowly for 15 to 30 minutes, depending on the ripeness, variety, and size of the fruit. When the pears are tender but not mushy, remove them and chill. Continue to simmer the liquid on medium-high heat until it has reduced to a thick syrup. To serve, pour syrup over pears and garnish with amaretti.

Charcoaled Venison Steaks with Horseradish Sauce

Gas grills are convenient, but sometimes you just can't beat the taste of meat cooked over a charcoal fire. Backyard eating doesn't get any better than this recipe.

---

menu

Appetizer:	*Mussels in Spicy Tomato Sauce*
Salad:	*Green Bean and Tomato Salad*
Entrée:	*Charcoaled Venison Steaks with Horseradish Sauce*
Side:	*Grandma's Potato Salad*
Dessert:	*Fresh Strawberry Pie*

Mussels in Spicy Tomato Sauce

4 pounds mussels
1 teaspoon black pepper
4 cloves garlic, finely minced, plus 1 whole clove
⅓ cup olive oil
1 cup red wine
2 28-ounce cans peeled Italian tomatoes, drained
    and chopped
pinch crushed red pepper flakes
2 tablespoons chopped flat-leaf parsley
8 slices Italian bread, toasted and rubbed with the
    whole garlic clove

Scrub mussels; remove beards. Discard any mussels whose shells are not closed tightly. Let soak for 15 minutes in cold water to which black pepper has been added. Place mussels in a large cooking pot with a tight-fitting lid. In a skillet, sauté the minced garlic for 1 or 2 minutes in 2 tablespoons olive oil. Add the rest of the olive oil, wine, tomatoes, and pepper flakes. Bring to a boil and simmer for 5 minutes. Pour over mussels, add parsley, cover, and bring to a boil. Cook for 5 to 10 minutes, until mussels have steamed open. Discard any mussels that remain closed. Check seasoning and add more red pepper flakes, if desired. Serve over two pieces of garlic toast.

Green Bean and Tomato Salad

This is a salad made for summer—garden-fresh green beans, ripe tomatoes, Parmesan cheese, and pancetta. You can substitute bacon for the pancetta, but if this unsmoked Italian bacon is available, use it. The flavor is marvelous in the salad.

> **2 medium-sized ripe tomatoes**
> **3 tablespoons red wine vinegar**
> **2 teaspoons white corn syrup**
> **¼ pound thinly sliced pancetta**
> **1 pound fresh green beans**
> **3 tablespoons olive oil**
> **salt and pepper**
> **½ cup Parmesan cheese, shaved**

Core the tomatoes, slice them in half horizontally, and gently squeeze out most of the pulp. Cut the tomatoes into 1-inch chunks. Set aside. In a small bowl, mix the vinegar and corn syrup. Set aside.

Heat a large sauté pan to medium heat. Cut the pancetta into 1- by ¼-inch strips. Cook the pancetta until golden and crisp. Drain on paper towels. Reserve 1 tablespoon drippings and remove excess from pan.

Bring a medium saucepan of salted water to a boil. Add the beans and cook until tender, about 10 minutes. Drain the beans and remove to a serving bowl. Add the tomatoes.

Add the olive oil to the pancetta drippings, heat, and stir in the vinegar and syrup mixture. Turn the heat up and continue to whisk as the mixture boils and blends. Pour the hot dressing over the green beans and tomatoes. Season with salt and pepper. Add the pancetta and Parmesan, and toss gently to mix.

Charcoaled Venison Steaks with Horseradish Sauce

1 ½ to 2 pounds venison steaks, cut about 1 inch
    thick
salt and pepper
½ cup bottled Italian salad dressing or homemade
    vinaigrette

Horseradish Dipping Sauce
¼ cup mayonnaise
¼ cup sour cream
2 tablespoons prepared horseradish
1 tablespoon snipped chives

For the dipping sauce: Stir the ingredients together in a small bowl. Top with
a sprinkle of chives. Chill covered until serving time.

Season steaks on both sides with salt and pepper. Place steaks in a large,
shallow dish or a zipper-style plastic bag. Pour dressing over venison, making
sure to coat all sides. Let marinate for 1 hour, turning once, in the refrigerator. Remove steaks from marinade, pour leftover marinade in a small bowl,
and set aside.

Preheat the grill. Grill venison steaks over medium-high heat, turning
once and basting once with reserved marinade. Grill steaks for 5 to 6 minutes per side for rare. Time depends on the position of the rack and the thickness of the meat; to eliminate guesswork, use a meat thermometer. Don't
overcook. Serve with horseradish dipping sauce.

Grandma's Potato Salad

4 pounds waxy potatoes (e.g., Red Bliss)
2 tablespoons vinegar
½ to ¾ cup mayonnaise
¼ cup cider vinegar
1 small onion, finely chopped
3 hard-boiled eggs
½ teaspoon dry mustard
salt and pepper
lettuce, parsley, and paprika for garnish

Wash potatoes. Boil in generously salted water until tender and a knife
inserted in the center comes out easily. Peel potatoes while still warm; cut into
quarters and then slice. Sprinkle 2 tablespoons vinegar over warm potatoes

and refrigerate until cold. Stir cider vinegar into mayonnaise and mix with potatoes and onion. Chop hard-boiled eggs and add them to the potato mixture. Mix in mustard. Add more mayonnaise if needed. Add salt and pepper to taste. Refrigerate for several hours or overnight to blend flavors. Before serving, adjust seasoning and add a bit more mayonnaise if the salad is too dry. Arrange on lettuce leaves; garnish with parsley, hard-boiled egg slices, and a sprinkle of paprika.

Fresh Strawberry Pie

1 heaping quart fresh ripe strawberries
1 prebaked 9-inch pie shell (store-bought or
**   homemade)**
2 teaspoons strawberry jam
1 cup water
¼ to ½ cup sugar (depending on the tartness of the
**   berries)**
2 teaspoons cornstarch
red food coloring

Wash, hull, and dry the strawberries. Reserve ½ cup berries. Cover the bottom of the pie crust with the strawberry jam. Arrange whole berries, cut side down, inside the shell. Mash the reserved berries in a small saucepan; add 1 cup water and sugar. Cook for 5 minutes. Strain through a fine sieve. Discard berry pulp and return juice to the saucepan. Mix cornstarch with a small amount of cold water (1 or 2 tablespoons). Add cornstarch mixture to berry juice. Stir well. Cook over medium-high heat, stirring constantly, until boiling; continue to boil until thick and clear. Tint with a few drops of red food coloring. Remove from heat and cool slightly. Stir and pour over berries in shell. Chill until firm, and keep cold until ready to serve. Top with whipped cream.

Italian Trattoria-Inspired Venison Casserole with Polenta

Try this recipe if you want to cook your venison with a taste of sunny Italy. Let the flavors blend and send your taste buds reeling.

menu

Appetizer:	*Olive-Studded Focaccia*
Salad:	*Tomato and Mozzarella Salad*
Entrée:	*Mediterranean Venison Casserole*
Sides:	*Creamy Polenta; Sautéed Escarole*
Dessert:	*Rice Torta*

Olive-Studded Focaccia (2 loaves)

Knead this bread by hand unless you are very familiar with making bread in a heavy-duty mixer or bread machine. Serve with extra virgin olive oil for dipping or butter for spreading.

4 teaspoons fresh, active dry yeast; or 2 packets
   granular, active dry yeast
2 cups warm water
1 tablespoon sugar
½ cup extra virgin olive oil
5 ½ to 6 cups unbleached white bread flour
2 teaspoons salt or 1 tablespoon kosher salt
¼ cup chopped kalamata olives, or 1 teaspon minced
   garlic and 1 tablespoon oregano
additional oil and kosher salt for prebake finish

Combine yeast, ½ cup warm water, and sugar in a large bowl. Let sit for about 10 minutes, until foamy. Add olive oil and remaining water. Set aside.

Mix flour and salt in a large bowl. Add to the yeast mixture 1 cup at a time; it may be necessary to knead the last cup of flour into the dough. Turn the dough onto a lightly floured surface and knead vigorously for 5 to 10 minutes. Add a little more flour if needed to keep dough from sticking. The dough will be very sticky at first but becomes smoother and more elastic as you knead it. Knead in chopped olives or garlic and oregano. Place the focaccia in an oiled bowl, turn to coat, and cover with plasic wrap and a kitchen towel. Allow to rise in a warm place for 1 ½ hours, until doubled in bulk. Tip: Put a bowl of hot water in the oven and let the bread rise there, free of drafts (but remember to take the dough out of the oven before you turn it on to preheat).

Preheat oven to 450 degrees. Lightly film 2 large baking sheets with oil. Press half the dough into each baking sheet. (If you want to make only 1 loaf, you can wrap and freeze the other half of dough.) Cover and let rise for 30 minutes. Dimple dough with the end of a wooden spoon or your finger, brush with oil, and sprinkle with coarse salt (or more chopped olives for variation). Place in the oven, reduce heat to 375 degrees, and bake for 20 to 25 minutes, until lightly golden. Transfer to a rack to cool.

Tomato and Mozzarella Salad

4 large ripe tomatoes, cut into ½-inch slices
12 ounces mozzarella cheese, cut into ¼-inch slices
½ cup fresh basil leaves, cut into thin slices
¼ cup extra virgin olive oil
salt and pepper to taste

Alternate slices of tomato and cheese in a spiral pattern on a flat serving plate. Lightly roll several basil leaves together and slice crosswise; repeat until all are cut into chiffonade. Sprinkle tomato and cheese slices with fresh basil leaves, and drizzle olive oil over all. Salt and pepper to taste. Serve with slices of Italian bread or focaccia.

Mediterranean Venison Casserole

1 pound Italian sausage (hot or sweet)
1 pound venison, cut into 1-inch chunks
3 to 4 tablespoons olive oil
5 to 6 cloves garlic, minced
1 eggplant, peeled and cut into 1-inch cubes
2 small zucchini, cut into bite-size pieces
1 large onion, sliced
1 pound fresh mushrooms, sliced
2 28-ounce cans plum tomatoes in juice, sliced
   (reserve juice)
1 teaspoon dried oregano or 1 tablespoon fresh
½ teaspoon anise seed
½ teaspoon fennel seed
salt and pepper to taste
2 cups red wine

Cook sausages and slice into ¼-inch pieces. Brown venison chunks in olive oil in a Dutch oven or deep casserole with a tight-fitting lid. Add garlic and cook for 1 minute, being careful not to brown. Layer sausage on top of venison and garlic, then add eggplant, zucchini, onion, mushrooms, and tomatoes. Sprinkle with herbs and salt and pepper, and pour reserved tomato juice and wine over the top. Bake covered at 325 degrees until meat is tender, vegetables are cooked, and sauce thickens.

Creamy Polenta

4 cups water
1 tablespoon salt
3 tablespoons butter
1 cup polenta
¾ cup whipping cream
½ cup freshly grated Parmesan cheese

In a large, heavy saucepan, bring salted water to a boil over high heat. Add 1 tablespoon butter and slowly whisk in polenta in a slow, steady stream, until the mixture is smooth. Cook, stirring constantly with a wooden spoon, for 10 to 15 minutes. Add cream and continue to cook and stir until mixture is very thick and creamy and tastes cooked, about 10 minutes more. Remove from heat and stir in remaining butter and cheese. Keep warm until ready to serve.

Sautéed Escarole

2 cloves garlic, minced
1 small onion, sliced
2 tablespoons olive oil
1 head escarole lettuce, cleaned, drained, and cut
    into bite-size pieces
salt and pepper
pinch hot red pepper flakes
1 15.5-ounce can cannelini beans (optional)
lemon wedges

In a large skillet, sauté garlic and onion in olive oil over medium heat until soft. Do not brown. Add escarole and turn to coat. Sprinkle with salt and pepper and crushed red pepper flakes. Cover and let cook for 2 to 3 minutes, until lettuce is wilted and softened. If desired, toss a can of cannelini beans with the escarole and cook for 1 more minute to heat the beans. Serve warm or cold with lemon wedges.

Rice Torta

This is a creamy rice pudding with a custard top. My husband's family makes it for Easter, when it's traditionally served with candied fruits and citron and no nuts.

3 cups milk
¾ cup Arborio rice
1 cup sugar
4 eggs, beaten
½ cup sugar
½ cup unsalted pistachio nuts, chopped
⅓ cup golden raisins
1 teaspoon vanilla extract
2 tablespoons butter
2 teaspoons grated lemon zest
2 tablespoons rum (optional)

In a saucepan over medium heat, bring the milk to a simmer. Add the rice and reduce heat to the lowest setting. Cook for about 30 minutes, until the rice has absorbed the milk. Lower heat to prevent sticking, but try to avoid stirring and breaking up the rice. Remove from heat; let cool.

Preheat oven to 350 degrees. Dip a pastry brush in water and run it around the inside of a 9- by 13-inch pan (this prevents crystals from forming). In a small saucepan, heat 1 cup sugar until it melts and turns an amber color. Quickly pour this syrup into the baking pan, tilting to cover the bottom. It will harden when it cools. Set aside.

Stir the beaten eggs into the rice. Add sugar, nuts, raisins, vanilla, butter, and lemon zest. Pour into the baking pan, over the hardened caramel. Bake for 1 hour, or until a toothpick inserted in the center comes out clean. Remove from the oven. If desired, pierce the top all over with a fork, and sprinkle rum over the cake. Cool and invert on a large cookie sheet. Cut into diamond-shaped pieces. Place on serving platter. Serve cold.

South-of-the-Border Venison Chops with Chilies

The flavors and textures of Mexican food always amaze me. These chops are flavored with cumin and chilies and slowly simmered to perfection.

menu

Appetizer:	*Chicken Tortilla Soup*
Salad:	*Salad Greens with Avocado Dressing*
Entrée:	*Venison Chops with Chilies*
Sides:	*Potato Bake; Green Beans in Tomato Sauce*
Dessert:	*Mexican Chocolate Cheesecake*

Chicken Tortilla Soup

1 whole chicken
1 teaspoon salt
1 tablespoon olive oil
1 onion, chopped
2 celery stalks, sliced
2 cloves garlic, minced
2 teaspoons chili powder
1 teaspoon dried oregano
28-ounce can crushed tomatoes
1 quart chicken broth (reserved from cooking
    chicken)
1 cup whole corn kernels
4-ounce can chopped green chilies
1 15.5-ounce can black or red beans, rinsed and
    drained
¼ cup chopped fresh cilantro
tortilla strips or crushed tortilla chips
sliced avocado, shredded Monterey Jack cheese, and
    chopped green onions for garnish

In a medium stockpot, cover the chicken with water, add 1 teaspoon salt, and simmer gently until chicken is cooked. Remove from broth and let cool. Reserve chicken stock for soup base. Remove chicken meat from bones and discard skin. Cut white meat into bite-size pieces, and reserve dark meat for another use.

In the stockpot, heat oil over medium heat. Sauté onion, celery, and garlic until soft. Stir in chili powder, oregano, tomatoes, and reserved broth. Bring to a boil; then simmer for 10 minutes until all vegetables are cooked. Stir in corn, chilies, beans, cilantro, and chicken. Simmer for 15 minutes longer. Ladle soup into individual bowls; top with tortilla strips or crushed tortilla chips, avocado slices, cheese, and chopped green onion.

Salad Greens with Avocado Dressing

4 to 6 cups romaine lettuce (or any salad greens),
   torn into bite-size pieces
½ small head red cabbage, shredded
2 beets, shredded
1 jicama, peeled and cut into matchsticks
1 cup croutons

Dressing
2 avocados
1 tablespoon lime juice
1 cup sour cream
1 cup cream
1 clove garlic
salt and pepper
⅛ teaspoon cayenne pepper or red pepper sauce
¼ teaspoon paprika
1 tablespoon chives
1 tablespoon fresh cilantro or parsley

For the dressing: Peel, pit, and mash avocados with lime juice. Place in the bowl of a food processor and combine with remaining ingredients, except chives and cilantro. Process until smooth. Remove to serving bowl and stir in chives and cilantro.

Combine salad vegetables, pour dressing over salad, add croutons, toss to mix, and serve immediately.

Venison Chops with Chilies

1 large or 2 small venison chops per person
1 cup flour seasoned with:
   ½ teaspoon salt
   ¼ teaspoon pepper
   ¼ teaspoon ground cumin
1 4-ounce can chopped green chilies
1 or 2 jalapeño peppers, finely minced
2 onions, sliced
1 28-ounce can crushed tomatoes in juice

Heat oil in a large skillet. Dredge chops in seasoned flour and brown on both sides in the hot skillet, cooking in batches. Return venison chops to the pan and top with chilies, jalapeño peppers, and onions. Pour tomatoes and their juice over all. Cover and slowly simmer for about 1 hour, or until chops are tender. During cooking, add water if the sauce gets too thick. This dish can also be simmered in a slow cooker—4 to 5 hours on high, or 8 hours on low. To save time, you can brown the chops in advance, layer the ingredients in your cooker, and go to work knowing that by the time you get home, dinner will be well on its way.

Potato Bake

6 to 8 medium potatoes (about 2½ pounds)
salt and pepper
¼ teaspoon nutmeg
2 cups Gruyère cheese, shredded
¾ cup chicken broth
½ stick butter, melted
paprika

Preheat oven to 400 degrees. Peel and slice potatoes in ¼-inch slices, and layer in the bottom of a buttered casserole dish or a 9- by 13-inch pan. Sprinkle with a bit of salt and pepper and a pinch of nutmeg, followed by a sprinkling of cheese; repeat the layers, ending with cheese on top. If you salt each layer of potatoes, be careful not to overdo it. Pour chicken broth over all, drizzle with melted butter, and add a sprinkle of paprika. Bake covered for 45 minutes, and check for doneness. When nearly tender, remove cover and bake an additional 10 to 15 minutes, until top is crispy and browned.

Green Beans in Tomato Sauce

2 pounds green beans
4 slices bacon, cut into thin strips
1 onion, chopped
1 cup tomato sauce
¼ teaspoon ground allspice
salt and pepper

Snip ends from beans. Cook, covered, in boiling salted water until just tender, about 15 to 20 minutes. Drain, place in a serving bowl, and tent with foil to keep warm. Meanwhile, fry bacon until crisp, remove from pan, and sauté onion until just golden but not browned. Add tomato sauce, allspice, and salt and pepper. Simmer for 4 to 5 minutes to blend flavors. Pour over green beans, garnish with bacon, and serve.

Mexican Chocolate Cheesecake

1 sleeve cinnamon graham crackers
3 tablespoons butter, melted
½ cup finely chopped almonds (plus extra for
    garnish)
3 8-ounce packages cream cheese, softened
1 ½ cups granulated sugar
6 eggs
1 cup evaporated milk or heavy cream
6 ounces semisweet chocolate
2 tablespoons prepared coffee
1 teaspoon vanilla extract
1 teaspoon almond extract
2 teaspoons cinnamon
2 to 4 ounces semisweet chocolate, melted
    (for glaze, if desired)

Preheat oven to 350 degrees. Crush graham crackers into fine crumbs. In a small saucepan, melt the butter, stir in cracker crumbs and almonds, and mix thoroughly. Butter the bottom and sides of a 9-inch springform pan. Pat the crumb mixture in an even layer over the bottom of the pan.

With a mixer, combine cream cheese, sugar, eggs, and evaporated milk or heavy cream. Blend until smooth.

Melt 6 ounces chocolate in coffee over low heat, stirring until smooth and well blended. Cool slightly. Stir chocolate, vanilla and almond extracts, and cinnamon into the cheese mixture. Mix thoroughly. Pour the mixture over the crumb crust. Bake for 1 hour, or until the cake is set and the center is firm. Cool; then chill thoroughly before removing the sides of the pan. Glaze, if desired, with 2 to 4 ounces melted semisweet chocolate, and garnish with finely chopped almonds.

Man-of-the-House Venison Steaks with Portobello Mushrooms

Here's another recipe that's perfect for the grill or broiler. Using an outdoor grill makes cleanup easier, and the mushrooms and corn can be cooked at the same time as the meat.

menu

Appetizer:	*Smoked Salmon on Lavash or Pita Bread*
Salad:	*BLT Salad*
Entrée:	*Broiled Venison Steaks*
Sides:	*Grilled or Broiled Portobello Mushrooms; Grilled Corn Wheels*
Dessert:	*Chocolate and Peanut Butter Marbled Brownies*

Smoked Salmon on Lavash or Pita Bread

4 ounces cream cheese
1 tablespoon lemon juice
1 teaspoon prepared horseradish
4 small lavash or 2 small pita breads split in half to
    form 4 thin circles
4 ounces smoked salmon
½ small red onion, sliced very thinly
2 tablespoons capers

Blend cream cheese, lemon juice, and horseradish until smooth. Spread on lavash or pita bread. Top with sliced smoked salmon, then onion slices. Sprinkle with capers. Roll and secure with toothpicks. Cut diagonally into slices.

BLT Salad

romaine lettuce
½ head iceberg lettuce
3 medium tomatoes
1 cup croutons
8 slices bacon, cooked, drained, and crumbled
½ cup mayonnaise thinned with 2 tablespoons cider
    vinegar, or creamy dressing of your choice
salt and pepper

Line salad bowl with romaine leaves. Tear iceberg lettuce into bite-size pieces and add to the bowl. Cut each tomato into 6 or 8 wedges; add to the bowl. Add croutons, bacon, and mayonnaise or dressing. Toss lightly and season with salt and pepper to taste.

Broiled Venison Steaks

2 to 3 pounds venison steaks
1 12-ounce can evaporated milk
¼ cup olive oil
2 tablespoons vinegar
1 tablespoon Worcestershire sauce
1 clove garlic, crushed
salt and pepper

Soak steaks in evaporated milk for several hours or overnight. Remove from milk, rinse, and pat dry. Mix the remaining ingredients to make the marinade, and place in a nonmetallic bowl or a resealable plastic bag. Add steaks and coat; let them marinate 1 hour. Preheat broiler or grill. Arrange steaks on broiler pan or grill and cook until desired doneness—for steaks about 1 inch thick, 5 minutes per side for medium to medium rare.

Grilled or Broiled Portobello Mushrooms

4 large portobello mushrooms
½ cup olive oil
¼ cup cider vinegar
¼ cup balsamic vinegar
1 shallot, finely minced
1 clove garlic, finely minced
2 tablespoons Parmesan cheese

Preheat grill or broiler. Brush mushrooms clean with a damp paper towel. Remove stems. Combine marinade ingredients in a small bowl or plastic bag (for a shortcut, use bottled oil and vinegar dressing with ¼ cup balsamic vinegar added). Brush both sides of mushrooms with marinade mixture or toss together in a plastic bag; let mushrooms soak up marinade for about 5 minutes. Place mushrooms on grill or broiler pan, top side up. Cook 3 to 4 minutes, brush with remaining marinade, and turn over. Continue cooking for 2 to 3 minutes. Turn again and baste, one more time on each side. When both sides are tender, sprinkle undersides with Parmesan and broil or grill for 1 to 2 minutes until cheese bubbles. Slice into ½-inch strips. Serve with steak.

Grilled Corn Wheels

4 ears of corn
melted butter or oil
salt

Boil corn in salted water for 1 minute. Cut into 1 ½-inch slices or wheels. Brush with melted butter or oil, and grill or broil until corn is cooked and a little golden, 2 to 3 minutes per side. Serve with additional butter and a sprinkling of salt.

Chocolate and Peanut Butter Marbled Brownies

Chocolate Batter
    2 cups sugar
    2 sticks butter, softened
    2 teaspoons vanilla extract
    4 eggs
    1 ½ cups flour
    ¾ cup unsweetened cocoa powder
    1 teaspoon baking powder
    ½ teaspoon salt
    ½ cup peanut butter chips
    ½ cup semisweet chocolate chips

Peanut Butter Batter
> ¾ **cup peanut butter**
> ½ **stick butter, softened**
> ¼ **cup sugar**
> 2 **tablespoons flour**
> 2 **eggs**
> 1 **teaspoon vanilla extract**

Icing
> 3 **squares unsweetened chocolate**
> 3 **tablespoons butter**
> 3 **cups confectioners' sugar**
> ¼ **teaspoon salt**
> 1 **teaspoon vanilla extract**
> 3–4 **tablespoons water (to reach desired spreading consistency)**

Preheat oven to 350 degrees. Grease and flour a 13- by 9-inch baking pan. For the chocolate mixture: Cream sugar and butter until light and fluffy. Add vanilla and eggs, one at a time, beating well after each addition. Gradually add flour, cocoa, baking powder, and salt to the creamed mixture. Mix well. Stir in peanut butter chips and chocolate chips.

For the peanut butter mixture: In a small bowl, mix peanut butter and butter. Add sugar and flour; blend well. Add eggs and vanilla; beat until smooth.

To assemble the brownies: Spread half of the chocolate batter in the prepared pan. Top with the peanut butter batter and smooth. Spread the remaining chocolate batter over the top. Gently swirl a knife through the layers to marble. Bake for 40 to 45 minutes, or until the top feels firm when lightly touched in the center. Brownies should begin to pull away from the sides of the pan. Cool completely in pan.

For the icing: In a small saucepan over low heat, melt the chocolate in the butter, stirring occasionally. Remove from heat and cool. In a mixing bowl, combine confectioners' sugar and salt. Mix in cooled chocolate and add vanilla. Add enough water to make a smooth icing of spreading consistency. Spread over the cooled brownies; let it set. Cut into squares. Serve alone or with a scoop of ice cream.

MORE GAME MEAT RECIPES

Many of the following recipes feature ground game meat prepared with seasonal fruits and vegetables, providing some wonderful ways to enjoy these treasures. When nature explodes with the brilliant colors of the harvest—bright orange pumpkins, rich green squash, ruby red apples—what could be better than to pair the bounty of the field with the bounty of the hunt? You can use whatever game meat you have on hand for these recipes.

Game Meat and Apple Pie

The perfect pairing of fruit and game makes a splendid meat pie. You can double this recipe, serve one pie, and pop the other in the freezer. Use a prepared crust if you're in a hurry, or make your own from scratch. If you prefer, you can top the pie with mashed potatoes rather than pie pastry. Just brush the mashed potatoes with butter and bake until done, covering with foil if they brown too quickly.

> 3 slices bacon, diced
> ¾ to 1 pound game meat, cut into ½-inch cubes
> 1 onion, chopped
> 1 stalk celery, sliced
> 3 carrots, peeled and cut into slices
> ½ cup white turnip, peeled and cut into ½-inch cubes
> 1 large apple, peeled, cored, and cut into ½-inch cubes
> 2 tablespoons raisins
> 1 tablespoon flour
> ¾ teaspoon dried sage
> ¼ teaspoon thyme
> salt and pepper to taste
> 1 cup apple cider
> 9-inch deep-dish pie crust

Preheat oven to 350 degrees. Crisp bacon in a skillet. Remove bacon from pan and pour off all but 2 tablespoons of drippings. Brown meat chunks in bacon drippings. Remove from pan and set aside. Add the vegetables and fruit to the skillet and toss to coat. Stir in the flour and spices. Pour in cider and bring to a boil over high heat, stirring constantly. Return meat to skillet and mix. Return to a boil and cook for 1 minute. Spoon mixture into a 9-inch deep-dish pie pan and top it with the pastry crust. Flute the edge and cut several vents in the top to allow steam to escape. Bake uncovered for 1 hour and 20 minutes. Test a piece of meat through a vent hole for tenderness. If it's not done, bake 15 minutes more. Cover crust with foil if it browns too quickly.

Stuffed Acorn Squash

This version of stuffed squash features ground game meat. It can be served as a side dish or as a meal in itself. If your butcher doesn't add pork fat to your ground meat, you can mix ½ pound ground pork with the game burger.

2 acorn squash, halved lengthwise and seeded
1 pound ground game meat
½ cup sliced celery
½ cup chopped onion
1 egg, beaten
½ cup grated Parmesan cheese
¼ cup firmly packed brown sugar
1 apple, peeled, cored, and chopped
½ teaspoon ground sage or 3 or 4 fresh leaves,
minced
¼ teaspoon fennel seeds
¼ teaspoon anise seeds

Place squash cut side down on a large baking pan. Bake in a 350-degree oven for 30 to 40 minutes until just tender. Alternatively, pierce the skin in several places and microwave on high until soft. Meanwhile, in a skillet, brown the game meat; add celery and onion and cook until tender. Drain. Add egg, cheese, brown sugar, apple, and seasonings and mix well. Mound the meat mixture into the squash shells. Cover and bake for 20 to 25 minutes until hot throughout and cheese is melted.

Zucchini Boats

Are you looking for yet another way to use up those abundant zucchini? Trying to clear out your freezer in preparation for this year's game meat? Want to stretch those last few pounds of ground meat? Here's a way to do all three. This dish can be prepared in advance. You can also double or triple the recipe and freeze the leftovers for a quick reheat in the microwave.

4 medium zucchini
1 pound ground game burger
½ pound ground pork
1 small onion, finely minced
2 cloves garlic, minced
2 tablespoons grated Parmesan cheese
2 eggs, beaten
salt and pepper to taste
bread crumbs
olive oil

Preheat oven to 350 degrees. Slice the squash lengthwise and scoop out the seeds, making a canoe. Finely chop the removed pulp and reserve. Mix the remaining ingredients, except for the bread crumbs and oil. Stir in the squash pulp. Make sure the mixture isn't too stiff; add a bit of milk if it is. Fill the zucchini with the meat mixture. Sprinkle tops with bread crumbs and a few drops of olive oil. Place in a shallow baking dish; add enough water to bring the level halfway up the sides of the squash boats. Cover with foil and bake for 45 minutes. Tomato sauce can be substituted for the water. Remove the foil for last 10 to 15 minutes of baking to allow the bread crumbs to brown.

Venison Porcupines

These little meatballs are sure to please the kids. The rice swells as it cooks and pokes through the meat, creating the quills on the porcupines.

1 ½ pounds ground venison burger
½ pound ground pork
1 tablespoon finely minced parsley
2 cloves garlic, finely minced
1 tablespoon finely minced onion
½ cup uncooked rice (not instant)
¼ cup milk
1 egg
salt and pepper to taste
2 10¾-ounce cans tomato soup plus 2 cans water, or
    3 15-ounce cans tomato sauce

Preheat oven to 400 degrees. Combine all ingredients except soup. Form venison mixture into 10 or 12 balls for entrée size or 30 to 40 balls for appetizer size. Put in a Dutch oven, and cover with soup and water; if you're using tomato sauce, don't dilute. Bake covered for 30 minutes. Remove cover, reduce heat to 350 degrees, and continue baking for approximately 30 minutes more. Add more water if meatballs seem to be drying out.

Game Lettuce Wraps

1 large head leaf lettuce
1 pound ground game meat
1 tablespoon oil
½ cup chopped onion
2 shallots, minced
1 teaspoon minced garlic
1 can sliced water chestnuts, chopped
½ cup sweet red pepper, finely chopped
2 tablespoons hoisin sauce
2 tablespoons soy sauce
1 tablespoon fresh cilantro, chopped

Separate leaves of lettuce, discarding the tough outer leaves. Wash thoroughly and drain well or spin dry. Brown ground meat in oil over medium-high heat. Add onion, shallots, and garlic and cook until soft. Stir in water chestnuts, red pepper, hoisin sauce, and soy sauce. Cook until pepper is crisp-tender and most of the liquid has evaporated. Remove from heat. Mix in cilantro. Mound meat mixture in the center of a platter and arrange lettuce leaves around it in a wreath. To assemble, fill a lettuce leaf with the meat mixture and fold the lettuce around the filling. You can also prefill the lettuce leaves and tie the bundles with strips of green onion or secure them with fancy toothpicks. Stack in a pyramid for serving.

part 2

WILD FOWL

UPLAND GAME BIRDS

Upland game birds include wild turkey, grouse, pheasant, partridge, quail, and dove. These birds are found in numerous species across the country. A major difference between wild game birds and those that are domestically produced is the fat content. Therefore, your cooking techniques must be adjusted to take advantage of the natural flavor of low-fat game birds while preserving their moistness. A good rule of thumb is that the age of the bird should be the determining factor in choosing a cooking method. Older birds should never be fried, roasted, or broiled. They require braising or some other moist cooking method to tenderize the meat, as well as larding or repeated basting to avoid drying out the meat. When cooking an older bird, a marinade made with lemon juice or vinegar can help tenderize and freshen the meat, as well as imbuing flavor. And don't forget to add a spritz inside the body cavity.

Wild turkey tastes like a more intense version of domestic turkey. Although the breasts of wild turkeys are less meaty, the breast meat is white and the leg quarters yield dark meat, just like their domestic counterparts. This monarch of the upland birds is a wily prey, and the reward for outwitting a turkey in the field is a dining experience par excellence. The age and size of the turkey should determine how you cook it. Remember, a turkey doesn't always have to be stuffed and roasted and served with giblet gravy. In the fall, young males weigh about 10 pounds; the females weigh less—mature hens weigh approximately 8 pounds, and young hens about 6. Spring toms are larger and weigh more: 17 pounds for a mature adult and about 12 pounds for a young one. To determine the age of a tom turkey, check his beard and the length of his spur. Young, lightly bearded birds have just a bump or a nubbin. Older, mature birds have a full, long beard and a long, very obvious spur—sometimes it's so long that it curls. A mature bird should be braised or smoked. A younger, smaller bird can be fried, roasted, or cut into pieces and used in various ways. If you decide to take the classic route and roast your turkey, remember to baste it often to keep the meat moist. An oven cooking bag is also a good option to lock in the juices.

Pheasants usually range from 2 to 2 ½ pounds dressed. Males are heavier and may weigh as much as 3 or 4 pounds. In general, one pheasant can serve two people. Pheasant is a delectable bird. It is very similar in taste to chicken, so it is sure to please. You will find that the breast meat is light and the legs and thighs dark. Although preserve birds are usually tender, mature birds shot in the field can be tough.

Quail and grouse are much smaller birds, weighing between ¼ and ½ pound, depending on the species. Generally, cooks should count on two birds to serve each person. These birds can be split and grilled or cut up and broiled. They can also be braised or roasted whole. Most grouse, including the ruffed grouse, have white breast meat and darker haunches.

The average chukar, or partridge, weighs less than 1 pound dressed. One partridge can serve one or two people, depending on their appetites. Partridge can be cooked in the same ways as domestic birds of a similar size. Partridge is also delicious smoked.

Doves boast a tender, flavorful dark meat. Because they are very small (weighing only about ¼ pound feathered and undrawn), a hearty appetite won't be satisfied with one or two of these tasty morsels. Plan on three doves per person, if you're lucky enough to bag that many.

Mustard-Scented Chukar Partridge

Chukar partridges, which have both white and dark meat, will be a big hit at your next grill party. Remember to baste and turn the birds often to prevent burning, and use a meat thermometer to ensure that they're thoroughly cooked. If the weather isn't cooperating, bring them indoors and broil or roast in a hot oven.

menu

Appetizer: Fried Mushroom and Prosciutto
Ravioli with Spicy Marinara Sauce

Entrée: Mustard-Scented Chukar Partridge

Sides: Warm German Potato Salad;
Italian Asparagus Spears

Dessert: Melba Peach Shortcake

Fried Mushroom and Prosciutto
Ravioli with Spicy Marinara Sauce

This recipe is easily doubled or tripled. You can freeze the extra ravioli before boiling. Place them on a cookie sheet lined with plastic wrap, cover with more wrap, and freeze. Place the frozen ravioli in zipper-style plastic bags.

Ravioli
> 1 package wonton wrappers (or homemade pasta
>   dough)
> 1 egg beaten with 2 tablespoons water for egg wash

Filling
> 2 tablespoons olive oil
> 1 shallot, minced
> 3 cloves garlic, minced
> ¼ pound prosciutto, finely chopped
> 1 cup fresh mushrooms, thinly sliced
> 1 cup ricotta cheese
> 1 egg, beaten
> 1 tablespoon chopped parsley
> ½ cup grated pecorino Romano cheese
>   (or Parmesan)
> salt and pepper

Sauce
>   4 tablespoons olive oil
>   4 cloves garlic, minced
>   1 onion, finely chopped
>   3 hot Italian cherry peppers, chopped
>   2 28-ounce cans crushed tomatoes in puree
>   crushed red pepper flakes to taste
>   1 cup red wine
>   2 tablespoons chopped parsley
>   2 tablespoons chopped basil
>   2 tablespoons chopped oregano
>   1 tablespoon sugar
>   salt and pepper

For the filling: Heat olive oil in a skillet over medium heat. Add shallot and garlic and sauté until softened. Add prosciutto and sauté 5 minutes more. Add mushrooms and cook until they turn golden brown, about 10 to 15 minutes. Transfer to a bowl and let cool. When cooled, add ricotta, egg, parsley and Romano cheese. Mix well and season with salt and pepper.

To assemble: On a floured work surface, spread several wonton wrappers and brush with egg wash. Drop filling by teaspoon onto the pasta. Fold in half to form a triangle, pressing out any trapped air as you go and gently pressing to seal.

For the sauce: In a large saucepan, heat olive oil over medium heat. Add garlic and onion and sauté until soft. Add cherry peppers, tomatoes and puree, red pepper flakes, and wine. Stir to combine. Bring to a simmer. Reduce heat to medium-low. Simmer for 30 minutes. Add parsley, basil, oregano, and sugar. Simmer 30 minutes more. Season with salt and pepper to taste. Keep hot.

Meanwhile, bring a large pot of salted water to boil. Add the ravioli and boil until they are al dente. Drain, and rest on waxed paper. Let the ravioli air-dry, or pat with a paper towel; then cover with additional waxed paper or plastic wrap.

Heat about ½ inch olive oil in a large skillet until very hot. Carefully add ravioli and cook about 5 minutes on each side, until deep golden brown. Drain on paper towels and serve immediately with sauce.

Mustard-Scented Chukar Partridge

4 chukars, cleaned (1 per person)
4 tablespoons Dijon mustard
4 tablespoons white wine
2 shallots, minced
2 scallions, minced,
2 cloves garlic, minced
½ teaspoon dried thyme
½ teaspoon tarragon
salt and pepper

Soak chukars in salted water for several hours. Combine mustard, wine, shallots, scallions, garlic, thyme, and tarragon in a large glass baking dish. Cover birds with mustard mixture. Carefully separate skin from breast with fingers, and rub some mixture under the skin. Cover and refrigerate overnight. Season chukar with salt and pepper. Grill on high heat until cooked through, brushing with additional mustard marinade, until juices run clear—about 10 to 15 minutes per side, depending on size. An instant meat thermometer should read 165 degrees when done.

Warm German Potato Salad

8 cooked potatoes, peeled and sliced
½ cup chopped onion
1 teaspoon chopped parsley
¼ cup red wine vinegar
¼ cup vegetable oil
½ cup warm chicken stock
¼ teaspoon dry mustard
¼ teaspoon celery seed (optional)
salt and pepper

Start potatoes in cold salted water and boil until tender. Peel and slice. Combine remaining ingredients, and gently mix with potatoes until well blended. Serve warm or at room temperature.

Italian Asparagus Spears

2 tablespoons butter
1 pound asparagus spears, tough ends removed
1 celery stalk, sliced
1 clove garlic, minced
1 small onion, thinly sliced
¼ teaspoon oregano
2 plum tomatoes, sliced crosswise
2 tablespoons grated Parmesan cheese

Preheat oven to 350 degrees. Melt butter in a skillet. Cut asparagus spears into 1-to 1 ½-inch pieces on the diagonal, and sauté in butter with the celery until just tender and bright green, 3 to 4 minutes. Add garlic, onion, and oregano, and cook for 1 to 2 minutes more. Place in a buttered gratin dish, add tomato slices, and mix. Top with grated cheese and bake in the oven for 20 minutes, until heated through and vegetables are tender. This dish can also be wrapped in foil and finished on a covered grill if you're cooking outdoors.

Melba Peach Shortcake

With a store-bought jelly roll as a base, this dessert is both quick and delicious. Strawberries or any summer fruit can be substituted for the peaches.

6 to 8 fresh ripe peaches
½ cup sugar
1 tablespoon orange juice concentrate
2 cups whipping cream
½ cup confectioners' sugar
1 raspberry jelly roll (store bought)

Blanch peaches in boiling water to remove skins. Pit and slice peaches and toss with sugar and orange juice concentrate. Set aside. Whip cream and sugar until stiff peaks form. Slice cake into generous pieces at least 1 inch thick, top with peach slices and juice, and finish with a mound of whipped cream.

Lovey-Dovey Marsala

It may be hard to find enough of these tender little morsels to feed a crew, but if you hunt with a group, you may be able to fill a game bag. If not, add some other game birds to the doves and make it a mixed bag.

menu

Appetizer:	Tomato and Spinach Soup with Tortellini
Salad:	Chopped Salad with Ranch Dressing
Entrée:	Wild Dove Marsala
Sides:	Confetti Rice Mold; Stir-Fried Broccoli
Dessert:	Raspberry Cheese Bars

Tomato and Spinach Soup with Tortellini

1 package fresh tortellini
2 tablespoons olive oil
1 small onion, minced
2 cloves garlic, minced
8 cups chicken stock
14-ounce can whole tomatoes in juice, coarsely
 chopped
10 ounces fresh spinach, chopped; or frozen
 chopped spinach, thawed
salt and pepper to taste
$\frac{1}{4}$ cup grated Parmesan cheese

Cook tortellini in salted water until al dente. Rinse in a colander and set aside. In a medium soup pot, heat olive oil over medium heat and sauté the onion until soft, about 5 minutes; add the garlic and cook for 1 or 2 minutes, stirring often. Add chicken stock and tomatoes, turn heat up to high, and bring to a boil. Simmer for 15 minutes. Add the tortellini and spinach and season with salt and pepper. Serve immediately, garnished with Parmesan cheese. Serve with garlic toast.

To make garlic toast, slice a French baguette into ½-inch slices, brush with olive oil, and rub each slice with a clove of garlic. Bake in a 350-degree oven until golden, turning once. Sprinkle Parmesan cheese on top and bake or broil until melted.

Chopped Salad with Ranch Dressing

6 cups head lettuce (iceberg, romaine, or Boston),
chopped into bite-size pieces
1 large tomato, diced
1 cucumber, peeled and diced
½ cup black olives, sliced
½ cup crumbled Gorgonzola cheese
4 canned pear halves, diced

Dressing
1 cup mayonnaise
½ cup sour cream
1 teaspoon garlic powder
1 teaspoon dill weed
¼ cup buttermilk or powdered buttermilk mixed
according to package directions
1 tablespoon parsley
salt and pepper

For the dressing: Mix all ingredients until smooth. Chill until serving time. For the salad: Prepare all ingredients and toss together in a large salad bowl. Top with dressing and serve.

Wild Dove Marsala

10 to 12 doves, cleaned (2 to 3 per person)
1 cup butter
2 cups flour seasoned with 1 teaspoon seasoned salt
and ½ teaspoon pepper
½ cup finely chopped onion
¼ cup finely chopped shallot
2 tablespoons fresh, minced garlic
4 cups sliced mushrooms
2 tablespoons flour
3 cups Marsala wine
4 cups chicken stock
salt and pepper
parsley, chopped

Wash birds well inside and out. Remove any visible shot. In a large Dutch oven, melt butter over medium-high heat. Dust doves in seasoned flour and brown well on all sides in butter. Remove and set aside. Add onion, shallot, garlic, and mushrooms. Sauté approximately 3 to 5 minutes, until vegetables begin to soften. Sprinkle in 2 tablespoons flour and blend well into vegetable mixture; stir until a thick paste is formed. Boil for 2 minutes, stirring constantly. Stir in Marsala wine and chicken stock and blend well. Bring to a rolling boil, reduce to simmer, and return birds to sauce. Check seasoning and adjust with salt and pepper. Cover and cook in a 325-degree oven for 45 minutes to 1 hour, depending on the size of the doves. Alternatively, you can finish cooking the doves on the stove top, adding a small amount of chicken stock if the mixture becomes too thick. Arrange doves around rice mold (recipe follows), and garnish with chopped parsley; serve sauce on the side.

Confetti Rice Mold

2 chicken bouillon cubes or 2 teaspoons granules
2 cups water
½ teaspoon salt
2 tablespoons butter
1 cup white rice
10-ounce package frozen mixed vegetables

Dissolve bouillon in water. Add salt and 1 tablespoon butter and bring to a boil. Stir in rice, cover, and reduce heat to low. Let rice cook for 18 to 20 minutes, or until tender. While rice is cooking, cook and drain vegetables, add remaining butter, and keep warm. Fluff cooked rice with a fork, stir in vegetables, and press mixture into a small, lightly buttered bowl. Unmold in the center of a serving platter, and arrange the doves and mushrooms around the outside.

Stir-Fried Broccoli

2 tablespoons oil
1 pound broccoli florets
1 red pepper, cut into strips
½ cup walnuts, coarsely chopped
2 green onions with tops, sliced
1 clove garlic, minced
1 tablespoon Worcestershire sauce
salt and pepper

In a large, heavy skillet, heat oil until hot. Add broccoli and red pepper and stir-fry for 3 or 4 minutes. Add walnuts, green onions, garlic, and Worcestershire sauce, and continue to cook 1 or 2 minutes longer. Season with salt and pepper. Serve immediately.

Raspberry Cheese Bars

Make these bars the day before and let the flavors blend.

4 tablespoons butter, melted
1 cup firmly packed brown sugar
3 large eggs
2 teaspoons vanilla extract, divided
½ teaspoon salt
1½ cups flour
8-ounce package cream cheese
1 cup sour cream
½ cup sugar
1 teaspoon grated lemon peel
1 tablespoon fresh lemon juice
1 can raspberry pie filling

Preheat oven to 350 degrees. Cream butter and brown sugar in a mixing bowl until creamy. Add eggs, 1 teaspoon vanilla, and salt; beat until smooth. Add flour and stir until flour is just moistened. In another bowl, beat cream cheese, sour cream, 1 teaspoon vanilla, sugar, lemon peel, and lemon juice until light and fluffy. Line a 9- by 13-inch baking pan with foil, extending 1 inch beyond the sides. Coat the foil with butter or cooking spray. Spread half the flour mixture in the bottom of the pan. Layer with the cream cheese mixture, and top with raspberry pie filling. Drop the remaining batter on top of the raspberries with a tablespoon. Swirl the top batter, raspberries, and cream cheese layer together with a knife. Bake for 35 minutes, or until a toothpick inserted in the center comes out clean. Cool completely on a rack. Chill. To remove, lift foil. Cut into bars and serve.

Golden Greek Memories and Grilled Grouse

When I was a child, a Greek family lived in my grandparents' neighborhood, and I spent many Sunday afternoons sampling the wonderful flavors of Greek cuisine: stuffed grape leaves, spinach triangles, lemony chicken soup, sweet baklava. Greek fried cheese was one of my favorites long before mozzarella sticks were on the menu in every pub and bar. Kefalotyri is a hard yellow cheese made from sheep's or goat's milk. Fried in olive oil, it makes an interesting appetizer when served with olives and warm pita triangles. If you can't find it, substitute pecorino Romano.

menu

Appetizer:	*Fried Cheese*
Salad:	*Greek Mixed Salad*
Entrée:	*Greek-Flavored Grilled Grouse*
Sides:	*Roasted Potato Wedges;*
	Peppers and Peas with Dill
Dessert:	*Creamy Stirred Lemon Rice*
	Pudding with Broiled Figs

Fried Cheese

1 pound kefalotyri cheese
⅔ cup flour for dredging
2 eggs, beaten
½ cup olive oil
2 lemons, quartered

Cut the cheese into slices or wedges that are ½ inch thick by 3 inches wide. Dip in cold water, dredge in flour, and dip in the beaten egg. In a small, heavy-bottomed skillet (cast iron is best), heat the oil over medium-high heat and fry the cheese until golden brown on both sides. Serve with lemon wedges (for a tableside squeeze of fresh lemon juice), ouzo or wine, olives, and crusty bread.

Greek Mixed Salad

4 very ripe tomatoes, cut into bite-size chunks
1 large red onion, thinly sliced
1 cucumber, peeled, cut in half lengthwise, and
   sliced
1 green bell pepper, cut into strips
1 roasted red pepper (fresh or jarred), cut into strips
1 teaspoon dried oregano
2 cloves garlic, finely minced
½ cup extra virgin olive oil
⅓ cup red wine vinegar
2 tablespoons water
2 ounces feta cheese, sliced or crumbled
¼ pound olives, kalamata or green Greek style
pepperoncini (pickled hot peppers) for garnish

Combine the tomatoes, onion, cucumber, green pepper, and roasted red pepper in a large salad bowl. Sprinkle with garlic and oregano, pour olive oil and vinegar over the salad, and toss. Taste; if too tart, add water. Just before serving, add the feta, pepperoncini, and olives to the top of the salad.

Greek-Flavored Grilled Grouse

Grouse are rich in flavor and very lean, so you have to add fat. This can be accomplished by wrapping the birds in bacon, using larding pork, or marinating to keep the birds moist. In this recipe, mayonnaise adds moisture and serves as a clinging base for the seasoning. I usually soak the grouse overnight in buttermilk before adding the marinade.

> **3 young grouse split in half**
> **salt and pepper**

Marinade
> **½ cup mayonnaise**
> **1 teaspoon oregano**
> **½ teaspoon garlic powder**
> **1 teaspoon grated lemon peel**
> **1 tablespoon lemon juice**
> **1 teaspoon sage**

Mix all marinade ingredients. Wash and dry grouse breasts. Season both sides with salt and pepper. Brush both sides of birds with marinade. You can also wrap a slice or two of bacon around the grouse. Grill over a hot grill about 8 minutes per side, basting each side several times and turning frequently. Don't overcook. If you're using bacon and it makes the grill flames flare, reduce the heat and extend the cooking time, or raise the grill rack.

Roasted Potato Wedges

> **6 large potatoes, cut into large wedges**
> **2 cloves garlic, minced**
> **2 shallots, minced**
> **½ cup olive oil**
> **1 cup water**
> **1 tablespoon oregano**
> **juice of 1 lemon**
> **salt and pepper to taste**

Preheat oven to 400 degrees. Put all the ingredients into a baking pan large enough to hold them. Toss potato wedges to coat evenly. Bake for 40 minutes. Potatoes should form a golden brown crust on top. Stir gently to turn undersides up. Add ½ cup more water and a drizzle of olive oil if the pan appears to be getting dry. Continue cooking until the potatoes are browned and tender when pierced with a knife tip.

These potatoes can also be cooked on the grill in large, heavy skillet, but watch them carefully to prevent burning.

Peppers and Peas with Dill

1 green bell pepper, seeded and diced
1 red bell pepper, seeded and diced
4 scallions, thinly sliced (keep white and green parts
    separate)
⅓ cup olive oil
1 pound frozen peas
salt and pepper
½ cup water
1 bunch fresh dill, tender stems and leaves, minced

In a saucepan or skillet with a cover, sauté peppers and white part of scallions in olive oil until peppers are just softened, 4 to 5 minutes. Add peas, salt and pepper, and water, and bring to a boil over medium-high heat. Reduce heat to low and cook for 5 minutes. Add dill and green onion tops and cook uncovered for 2 minutes more, letting the water evaporate. Serve hot or cold.

Creamy Stirred Lemon Rice Pudding

½ cup long-grain rice
3 cups whole milk
½ cup sugar
lemon peel from 1 lemon (in 1 long piece, if
    possible) or 1 teaspoon lemon extract
2 egg yolks
1 ½ teaspoons cornstarch (with milk for mixing)
½ teaspoon vanilla extract
cinnamon

Rinse rice under cold running water in a fine strainer, until water runs clear. Parboil rice for 8 minutes in water. Place milk, sugar, and lemon peel in a heavy saucepan. Bring mixture to a boil over medium heat, stirring constantly until sugar melts. Reduce heat to low, and stir in the rice. Cover and simmer until most of the milk has been absorbed (about 20 minutes). Remove from heat. Discard lemon peel. In a small bowl, beat egg yolks. Quickly stir eggs into the rice, making sure they are well incorporated. Mix cornstarch with a few tablespoons of milk until a smooth paste is formed. Add the cornstarch mixture, vanilla, and lemon extract (if you're using it) to the rice. Keep stirring to ensure that the egg yolks are incorporated and don't curdle. Spoon pudding into four individual serving dishes, sprinkle with a dusting of cinnamon, and let cool. Serve with a broiled fig (recipe follows) on the side.

Broiled Figs

8 ripe figs
2 tablespoons butter
4 tablespoons honey
cinnamon

Heat broiler, and place oven rack near the top position. Cut a deep cross in the top of each fig and press down to flatten, like a four-petal flower. Place figs in a flat pan, and drop an even amount of butter in the center of each fig. Drizzle honey over figs, and sprinkle with cinnamon. Broil 4 or 5 minutes until figs are softened and honey and butter have melted and formed a sticky sauce. Serve warm with rice pudding.

Pheasant in Cream Sauce

This creamy sauce, which is flavored with mushrooms and capers, works well with many upland game birds. It's a great way to tenderize a wild pheasant that may have a bit of age on it.

menu

Appetizer:	*White Bean and Escarole Soup with Blue Cheese Crostini*
Entrée:	*Creamy Capered Pheasant*
Side:	*Green Beans with Dill*
Dessert:	*Lemon Pie*

White Bean and Escarole Soup with Blue Cheese Crostini

2 strips bacon
6 cups chicken stock or chicken broth
2 16-ounce cans white cannelini beans
1 small onion
salt and pepper
1 small head escarole, torn into bite-size pieces

Crostini
1 loaf French bread
1 clove garlic
olive oil
4 ounces blue cheese

Cut bacon strips into thin slices and cook in a medium-sized pot until browned. Add chicken stock, beans, and onion, simmering slowly until onion is translucent. Check for seasoning and add salt and pepper to taste. Just before serving, add escarole, stir, and remove from heat. Serve immediately.

For the crostini: Thinly slice the French bread on a diagonal. Bake in a 350-degree oven until lightly toasted. Rub each slice with a clove of garlic, and drizzle with a few drops of olive oil. Place on a baking sheet and top each slice of bread with a sprinkle of crumbled blue cheese. Broil or bake until cheese melts. Serve with the soup.

Creamy Capered Pheasant

2 pheasants, quartered
½ cup flour
¼ cup cornstarch
salt and pepper to taste
¼ teaspoon paprika
¼ teaspoon ground sage
2 tablespoons butter
¼ cup oil
2 shallots, minced
¼ cup dry sherry
1 pound white mushrooms, sliced
1 small onion, finely sliced
2 stalks celery, finely sliced
2 tablespoons capers, drained and rinsed
    (reserve 1 teaspoon)
2 cups sour cream

Mix flour and cornstarch and season with salt, pepper, paprika, and sage. Dredge pheasant pieces in the flour mixture. Heat butter and oil in a large skillet. Brown birds, and remove to a shallow baking dish. Add the remaining ingredients, except for the sour cream and the reserved capers, to the skillet and stir. Pour sauce over pheasant pieces and bake for approximately 1 ½ to 2 hours in a 300-degree oven. When done, remove pheasant pieces and stir sour cream into the sauce. Pour over pheasant pieces; garnish with reserved capers. Serve over buttered white rice.

Green Beans with Dill

**1 pound fresh green beans
2 tablespoons butter
1 tablespoon olive oil
1 teaspoon snipped fresh dill
splash lemon juice
salt and pepper**

Remove stem ends from beans. Boil beans in salted water until tender. Drain and refresh in ice water to preserve the bright green color. In a skillet, melt butter and oil. Toss beans with dill and lemon juice, add to skillet, and cook over medium heat until hot. Season with salt and pepper. Serve while hot.

Lemon Pie

**9-inch pie shell, baked (or 1 graham cracker
    crumb shell)
1 cup sugar
½ cup cornstarch
½ teaspoon salt
2 cups cold milk
3 egg yolks
½ stick butter
1 ½ teaspoons grated lemon zest
¼ cup lemon juice (fresh is best)
½ cup sour cream
whipped cream for topping**

Mix sugar, cornstarch, and salt in a heavy saucepan. Gradually stir in milk. Cook, stirring constantly, over medium heat until thick and boiling. Reduce heat; cook and stir 2 more minutes. Remove from heat.

Beat egg yolks slightly. Gradually stir 1 cup of milk mixture into yolks. Return yolk mixture to saucepan, and bring to a gentle boil. Continue to cook and stir for 2 minutes. Remove from heat. Stir in butter, lemon zest, and lemon juice; mix well. Fold in sour cream and stir until well incorporated. Pour filling into pie shell and cool. Refrigerate until set and cold. Top with whipped cream.

Cider-Braised Pheasant Breasts

When the season's apples are ripe for the picking, take advantages of the fresh flavors of late summer or early fall and enjoy your pheasant with the taste of apple cider.

menu

Appetizer:	*Linguine with Clam Sauce*
Entrée:	*Pheasant Breasts in Cider*
Sides:	*Colcannon (Mashed Potatoes with Cabbage); Braised Leeks*
Dessert:	*Apple Walnut Cake*

Linguine with Clam Sauce★

8 ounces linguine pasta
¼ cup olive oil
2 cloves garlic, minced
1 shallot, minced
¼ cup water or white wine
1 pound cleaned clams in the shell, or 1 cup canned
    whole clams and their juice
½ teaspoon salt
¼ teaspoon pepper
1 tablespoon fresh flat-leaf parsley, chopped

Cook linguine according to package directions until al dente. Drain and rinse with very hot water. Drain well, return to pasta pot, and cover to keep warm. Heat oil in a large pot with a cover if you are cooking fresh clams; otherwise, a saucepan will do. Sauté garlic and shallot until soft. Add wine and clams. Sprinkle with salt and pepper. Cover and cook for 4 or 5 minutes, until clams have opened up and are cooked. Discard any unopened clams. Sprinkle with parsley and serve over a bed of linguine.

   *For red clam sauce: Puree 3 ½ cups peeled Italian tomatoes packed in juice in a blender, add to the basic white clam sauce, and simmer for 15 minutes before adding the clams.

Pheasant Breasts in Cider

4 pheasant breasts
½ stick butter, softened
salt and pepper
4 slices bacon
2 cups cider
4 shallots
2 tablespoons sugar
½ cup flour
½ cup sour cream

Preheat oven to 400 degrees. Butter breasts, sprinkle with salt and pepper, and wrap each with 1 slice of bacon. Place in a baking pan and bake for 20 minutes. Reduce oven temperature to 325 degrees. Pour half the cider over the breasts, cover with foil, and continue braising for another 45 to 60 minutes. Check the pan during cooking, and add more cider if necessary. Meanwhile, reduce the remaining 1 cup of cider by half by boiling it in a small saucepan. Set aside. In a small skillet, sauté the shallots in 1 tablespoon butter until soft. Add the sugar and continue to cook until lightly browned and caramelized. Remove from heat and set aside. When pheasant is done, finish the sauce: reheat the shallots, add flour, and cook until thickened. Stir in the cider reduction. Let boil for 1–2 minutes. Then reduce the heat to low and gently stir in the sour cream; do not boil. Slice each breast and serve on individual plates with the sauce.

   When cooking a whole bird, cover the breasts with bacon, add cider halfway through roasting, and cook covered. Make sauce with the cooking juices.

Colcannon (Mashed Potatoes with Cabbage)

As far as I'm concerned, potatoes are good with everything. This classic combination of cabbage and mashed potatoes, which comes by way of my grandmother, goes well with any game recipe as well as with corned beef on St. Patrick's Day. Amounts aren't important; add more or less cabbage to suit yourself. You can use leftover potatoes or start with fresh; just be sure to add plenty of butter.

> **8 cooked potatoes**
> **½ cup milk**
> **1 stick butter (reserve 3 tablespoons)**
> **salt and pepper**
> **4 cups finely shredded green cabbage**
> **1 onion, finely chopped**
> **¼ cup water**

Mash potatoes with milk and butter, and season with salt and pepper. Place shredded cabbage, onion, and water in a skillet with 2 tablespoons melted butter, and sauté for a few minutes until cabbage softens and is tender. Do not overcook. Add cabbage mixture to mashed potatoes and stir well to combine. Mound in a serving bowl, make a well in the center, and fill with 1 tablespoon butter. Serve hot.

Braised Leeks

> **3 large leeks**
> **1 tablespoon olive oil**
> **1 tablespoon butter**
> **½ to 1 cup chicken stock**
> **salt and pepper**
> **1 cup grated Parmesan cheese**
> **½ cup bread crumbs**
> **fresh chopped parsley for garnish**

Wash the leeks well; trim bottoms and dark green tops. Slice in half lengthwise and run under cold water, separating layers of leaves. Cut into 3-inch-long pieces; do not separate individual leaves; keep in halves. Heat a large sauté pan over medium heat, and add the olive oil and butter. When the butter has stopped sizzling, add the leeks, cut side down. Brown well and turn. Add enough chicken stock so that it comes halfway up the sides of the leeks.

Bring the stock to a simmer; then reduce heat to very low. Cover with a tight-fitting lid and simmer for 10 minutes, or until the leeks are tender to a knife point. Add salt and pepper to taste.

When the leeks are tender, preheat the broiler. Increase the heat under the leeks and reduce the chicken stock until it just covers the bottom of the pan. Transfer the leeks to an ovenproof serving dish, and top them with cheese and bread crumbs. Broil until the cheese melts and starts to turn brown. Garnish with additional shaved slices of Parmesan and fresh chopped parsley.

Apple Walnut Cake

2 eggs
2 cups sugar
1 cup vegetable oil
1 teaspoon vanilla extract
2 cups flour
2 teaspoons cinnamon
½ teaspoon salt
1 teaspoon baking soda
1 ½ teaspoons water
4 cups peeled, cored, and coarsely chopped apples
1 cup chopped walnuts
confectioners' sugar for dusting on top

Preheat oven to 350 degrees. Grease and flour a 9- by 13-inch pan. Beat eggs, sugar, oil, and vanilla until smooth. In a separate bowl (or a plastic bag for easy cleanup) blend flour, cinnamon, and salt. Add the flour mixture to the batter and mix well. Dissolve baking soda in water and add it to the batter. Stir in apples and nuts and mix well by hand. Spoon batter into pan and bake for 55 minutes. Cool and dust with confectioners' sugar. This cake tastes better the next day, and it keeps for 2 days at room temperature or 1 week if refrigerated.

Hunter's-Style Pheasant Cacciatore

Pheasant has the taste of wild chicken. It is a bit more flavorful but delectable. Young, tender birds can be prepared in any number of ways, but older birds require braising, as in this wonderful Italian-style stew. *Cacciatore* means "hunter" in Italian, and the pheasant is simmered in a hunter's-style tomato sauce with mushrooms, peppers, and onions and flavored with red wine. Serve it over your favorite pasta, and don't forget the rest of the wine.

menu

Appetizer: *Eggplant Relish (Caponata) with Radicchio Lettuce*

Salad: *Caesar Salad*

Entrée: *Pheasant Cacciatore*

Dessert: *Chocolate Silk Pie*

Eggplant Relish (Caponata) with Radicchio Lettuce

1 large eggplant
1 large onion, chopped
1 green pepper, chopped
2 cloves garlic, minced
½ cup olive oil
2 large tomatoes, diced small; or 1 cup crushed or diced canned tomatoes
1 tablespoon capers
salt and cayenne pepper
4 tablespoons dry white wine
1 head radicchio lettuce or other leaf lettuce

Preheat oven to 400 degrees. Place the whole eggplant in a lightly oiled baking dish, prick with a fork in several places, and cook for 1 hour. Let cool. When the eggplant can be handled, scoop out the pulp and cut it into a fine dice. Set aside. Place the onion, green pepper, garlic, and olive oil in a skillet and sauté over medium-low heat until softened. Do not brown. Add the eggplant, tomatoes, capers, salt, cayenne pepper, and wine. Stir gently and let simmer over low heat about 20 minutes, stirring occasionally, until the mixture is thick. Transfer to a bowl, cover, and refrigerate overnight.

To make lettuce cups: Carefully unpeel whole lettuce leaves to form a cup. Use 2 overlapping leaves if the radicchio is small. Alternatively, use any leaf lettuce of your choice. Serve the caponata in radicchio cups or over lettuce leaves, along with bread or an assortment of crackers.

Caesar Salad

The use of a raw egg in Caesar dressing is controversial, owing to health and safety issues. You can coddle the egg in boiling water for 1 minute, if you like.

2 heads romaine lettuce, torn into bite-size pieces
1 cup flavored croutons (or homemade)
shaved slices Parmesan cheese for garnish

Dressing
1 teaspoon anchovy paste, or 2 flat anchovies
1 medium clove garlic, crushed
1 large egg (coddled 1 minute)
1 teaspoon Worcestershire sauce
3 tablespoons fresh lemon juice
pinch salt
¼ teaspoon freshly ground pepper
1 teaspoon capers
1 teaspoon Dijon mustard
½ cup olive oil

For the dressing: In a blender, puree anchovies and garlic; you can add a tablespoon of oil to help the process. Add all the remaining ingredients, except for the olive oil, and process until well blended. Pour the oil in a slow, steady stream through the cap, and blend until completely incorporated. Toss with romaine lettuce and croutons, and garnish with shaved slices of Parmesan.

Pheasant Cacciatore

2 pheasants
buttermilk
2 tablespoons olive oil
2 cloves garlic, minced
2 onions, quartered
1 6-ounce can tomato paste
2 28-ounce cans crushed or diced tomatoes
3 tablespoons fresh oregano or 1 tablespoon dried
1 tablespoon fresh chopped basil or 1 teaspoon
    dried, crushed
2 green peppers, chopped into 1-inch pieces
1 pound fresh mushrooms, sliced (if large) or cut in
    half (if buttons)
salt and pepper
1 cup dry red or white wine
pasta (hot and cooked)

Soak pheasants in buttermilk overnight (or at least for several hours). When the birds are ready, cut into quarters. Preheat oven to 325 degrees. In a large skillet, cook garlic and onions in oil over medium heat until onions are tender. Remove onions and set aside. Add more cooking oil to skillet, if needed. In the same skillet, season pheasant pieces with salt and pepper and brown over medium heat about 15 minutes, turning once. Place pheasant pieces in a large Dutch oven or covered pan. Fry tomato paste in the oil remaining in the skillet for 1 or 2 minutes. Stir in 1 can of tomatoes. Mix in oregano and basil, and add cooked onions. Layer green peppers and mushrooms over pheasant pieces. Season with salt and pepper. Pour wine, 1 can tomatoes, and tomato paste mixture over the pheasant and vegetables. Mix gently. Cover the Dutch oven and bake in the oven for about 1 ½ hours, checking for doneness at that time. Cook an additional 30 minutes or so, until the pheasant is tender. Remove the cover for the last 15 minutes. If the cacciatore is too dry, add more liquid (wine, water, or tomato sauce); if it's too thin, remove the cover and let some liquid evaporate.

Alternatively, you can cook this dish on the stove top, but it requires more watching to avoid sticking or burning. On the stove top, cover the Dutch oven and simmer for about 1 hour over low heat. Check for doneness, and cook about 15 to 30 minutes longer, or until the meat is tender, turning occasionally. Add more liquid if needed. Remove the cover for the last 15 minutes, pulling several pieces from the bottom up to the top.

With either cooking method, transfer pheasant pieces and sauce to a serving dish. Serve with hot cooked pasta.

Chocolate Silk Pie

This pie is scrumptious and very easy to make, but you'll need a stand mixer, because it has to be beaten for a long time. The mixture should be light and fluffy and silky smooth on the tongue—hence the name. If you take short-cuts, the final result will be disappointing. I often use cookies for the crust, rather than graham crackers. You might also consider a nut crust or even toasted coconut.

Crust
> **2 cups graham cracker crumbs**
> **½ stick butter, melted**
> **1 tablespoon sugar**

Filling
> **4 squares unsweetened chocolate**
> **2 sticks unsalted butter, softened**
> **1 ½ cups sugar**
> **2 teaspoons vanilla extract**
> **4 eggs**

For the crust: Mix all ingredients and form a crust on the bottom and about 1 inch up the sides of a 9-inch springform pan. Bake for 5 minutes, until set. Let cool completely.

For the filling: Melt chocolate over low heat and let cool slightly. Cream butter and sugar until well blended, light, and fluffy. Add the vanilla and melted chocolate, beating well. Add 2 eggs and beat for 5 minutes. Add the remaining 2 eggs and beat 5 minutes more. Taste to make sure the sugar has dissolved. Beat a few minutes longer if the sugar is still grainy. Spoon onto the graham cracker crust, smooth the top, and chill several hours or overnight, until cold. Serve with a dollop of whipped cream.

Oven-Fried Quail

Quail are tender, succulent little morsels—with *little* being the operative word. Averaging from about 5 to 8 ounces dressed, they cook quickly and taste delicious. Plan on serving at least two quail per person, and make sure you have substantial side dishes to round out the meal.

menu

>>>—><——<<<

Appetizer: Butternut Squash Soup

Salad: Pineapple Coleslaw

Entrée: Oven-Fried Quail

Side: Linguine with Green Pea and
Basil Sauce

Dessert: Chocolate Pie with Macadamia
Nut Crust

Butternut Squash Soup

Removing the outer peel from a large, firm winter squash can be daunting. To soften the outer shell and make the job easier, pierce the squash in several places with a sharp knife. (Make sure the knife actually goes into the squash, or you may have an explosion!) Microwave on high for 3 minutes, let the squash cool, and remove the outer peel.

> **2 butternut or acorn squash (or more, depending
>   on size)**
> **2 tablespoons butter**
> **1 small onion, chopped**
> **2 apples, peeled, cored, and chopped**
> **3 cups chicken or vegetable stock**
> **½ teaspoon cinnamon or ground ginger**
> **¼ teaspoon dried thyme**
> **salt and pepper**
> **chopped pecans for garnish (optional)**

Peel and chop 3 cups of squash. Melt the butter in a medium saucepan over medium heat. Add onion and cook until softened, about 5 minutes, stirring often. Add chopped squash, apples, stock, cinnamon, and thyme. Bring to a boil, reduce heat, cover, and simmer until squash is tender, about 20 minutes.

Remove from heat and puree in batches in a food processor or blender until smooth. Season with salt and pepper. Serve hot or cold. Garnish each serving with chopped pecans if desired.

Pineapple Coleslaw

This coleslaw has just a hint of sweetness, which complements the quail.

> **2 tablespoons sugar**
> **2 tablespoons cider vinegar**
> **1 head green cabbage, finely shredded, or 1-pound**
> **bag precut slaw mix**
> **1 8-ounce can crushed pineapple, drained**
> **½ cup mayonnaise**
> **salt and pepper**

Mix sugar in vinegar and let dissolve. In a large bowl, mix together cabbage, pineapple, mayonnaise, and the sugar-vinegar mixture. Check seasoning, and add salt and pepper to taste. The slaw should have just a hint of sweetness.

Oven-Fried Quail

> **1 stick butter, melted**
> **8 whole quail, with skin on (2 quail per person)**
> **1 cup garlic cheese croutons or seasoned stuffing**
> **mix, crushed finely into crumbs**
> **¼ cup grated Parmesan cheese**
> **¼ teaspoon thyme**
> **½ teaspoon celery flakes**

Preheat oven to 350 degrees. Brush some of the melted butter in a roasting pan large enough to accommodate the quail. Split each quail through the backbone and flatten. Mix crumbs, cheese, and herbs, and pour out on a large plate. Dip quail in melted butter and coat with stuffing mix, pressing crumbs in with your hand. Place in the prepared pan. Bake 30 to 45 minutes, depending on the size of the quail, until the meat can be removed easily from the bone. Cover with foil if the birds brown too quickly.

Linguine with Green Pea and Basil Sauce

1 pound linguine pasta
4 tablespoons butter, divided
½ cup chopped leek
1 cup chicken stock
1-pound package frozen green peas
1 cup fresh basil leaves
1 tablespoon olive oil
1 pound fresh mushrooms, sliced
2 cloves garlic, minced
2 shallots, minced
salt and pepper
several basil leaves cut into chiffonade for garnish

Cook pasta in boiling salted water until al dente. Set aside and keep warm. Melt 1 tablespoon butter in a large skillet over medium heat. Add leek and cook for 3 to 4 minutes, stirring often. Add 1 cup chicken stock and peas, bring to a boil, reduce heat, and simmer for 5 minutes. Place 1 ½ cups of pea mixture in a blender, add basil leaves and 1 tablespoon olive oil, and puree until smooth. Add pureed mixture to remaining pea mixture. Thin with additional chicken stock if too thick. In a skillet, melt the remaining 3 tablespoons butter over medium-high heat. Sauté the mushrooms, garlic, and shallots until mushrooms are tender. Toss pasta with pea mixture and mushroom mixture, add salt and pepper to taste. Place in a large bowl and garnish with basil leaves.

Chocolate Pie with Macadamia Nut Crust

Crust
2 cups chopped macadamia (or other) nuts
¼ cup sugar
½ cup mini semisweet chocolate chips
½ stick butter, melted

Filling
1 ½ cups semisweet chocolate chips
1 stick butter
1 teaspoon vanilla extract
4 egg yolks
¼ cup sugar

Topping
½ cup chocolate chips
¼ cup heavy cream
1 tablespoon butter

Preheat oven to 375 degrees. For the crust: In a medium bowl, combine the nuts, sugar, mini chips, and melted butter. Press into a 9-inch pie pan to create the crust. Bake for 7 to 8 minutes, until set. Cool completely.

For the filling: Melt chocolate chips and butter in a saucepan set in simmering water, or in the microwave. Stir until melted and smooth. Remove from heat, stir in vanilla. Set aside. In the mixing bowl of your electric mixer, beat egg yolks with sugar until pale yellow, at least 5 minutes. Stir egg mixture into the melted chocolate and return to the pan of simmering water. Whisk constantly until thick, about 5 minutes. Pour into the cooled crust.

For the topping: Melt the chocolate chips with the heavy cream and butter. Stir over low heat until smooth. Let cool slightly before pouring over the filling. Or, top with bottled hot fudge sauce.

Citrus Sharptail

The citrus marinade is piquant and fragrant, and it's easy to prepare. So get that grill going!

menu

Appetizer: *Sweet and Sour Slaw*

Entrée: *Barbecued Citrus Sharptail*

Sides: *Rice Pilaf; Summer Squash Medley*

Dessert: *Cream Cheese Pound Cake*

Sweet and Sour Slaw

½ cup white wine vinegar
½ cup sugar
¼ cup orange juice concentrate
8 cups very thinly sliced green or red cabbage, or a
    combination of the two
½ cup finely chopped red onion
¼ teaspoon celery seed
¼ teaspoon poppy seeds
½ teaspoon salt
1 serrano chili, seeded and finely minced
orange zest and chopped parsley for garnish

In a small saucepan, mix vinegar, sugar, and orange juice concentrate over low heat until sugar is dissolved. Chill. In a large bowl, combine cabbage, onion, spices, and chili. Add dressing, and toss to coat well. Chill and toss again before serving. Garnish with some orange zest strips and fresh chopped parsley.

Barbecued Citrus Sharptail

This glaze is delicious, and the caramelization from grilling makes it even tastier. Start the recipe the day before to allow time for marinating.

1 large bird cut into 8 pieces, or 2 smaller birds
    quartered
½ cup fresh lemon juice
½ cup orange juice concentrate
½ cup white wine
3 tablespoons soy sauce
2 cloves garlic, minced
½ teaspoon ground allspice
salt and pepper
¼ cup orange marmalade

Combine juices, wine, soy sauce, garlic, and allspice in a large baking dish or large zipper-style plastic bag. Salt and pepper poultry, add pieces to marinade, and turn to coat. Refrigerate overnight, turning pieces occasionally.

Prepare barbecue or grill (set gas grill to medium-high heat). Remove sharptail from the marinade, and place the leftover marinade in a small saucepan. Grill sharptail pieces until cooked through, about 20 minutes, turning often.

Meanwhile, add marmalade to the marinade. Boil until reduced to a thick, syrupy glaze. Brush bird pieces with the glaze and continue grilling until the glaze is set, about 2 minutes per side.

Rice Pilaf

2 tablespoons butter
½ cup minced onion
1 cup long-grain rice
1 ½ cups chicken stock
1 teaspoon dried parsley
1 teaspoon salt
black pepper to taste

Melt butter in a saucepan with a tight-fitting lid. Sauté onion over medium heat until just softened. Add rice and stir to coat. Add stock, parsley, and salt, and bring to a boil. Reduce heat and simmer for 20 minutes, until just tender. Check for seasoning; add black pepper and more salt if needed.

Summer Squash Medley

½ pound yellow wax beans or green string beans,
    cut in 2-inch lengths
2 tablespoons butter
1 onion, sliced in vertical pieces
1 medium yellow summer squash, cut in ¼-inch
    slices
1 medium zucchini, cut in ¼-inch slices
salt and pepper
2 tablespoons lemon juice
½ teaspoon dill

Precook beans in boiling salted water for 6 to 7 minutes or until tender-crisp. Drain and set aside. In a large skillet, melt butter and sauté onion for 2 minutes, until just beginning to soften. Add squash and salt and pepper, cover, and cook over medium heat until squash is tender. Return beans to the pan; continue to cook until desired degree of doneness is attained. Remove from heat, add lemon juice and dill, and stir gently. Place in a serving dish.

Cream Cheese Pound Cake

8 ounces cream cheese
1 ½ sticks butter
1 ½ cups sugar
1 teaspoon vanilla extract
1 teaspoon lemon extract
4 eggs
2 cups sifted flour
1 ½ teaspoons baking powder

Preheat oven to 350 degrees. Combine softened cream cheese, butter, sugar, and extracts. Add eggs, beating until well blended. Mix flour with baking powder, and add gradually to the wet mixture. Blend well. Pour into a greased and floured tube pan. Bake for 1 hour or until done. Check with a toothpick. Do not overbake. Serve with fresh berries topped with whipped cream. This cake tastes better the next day and should be refrigerated to allow the flavors to mellow.

Wild Turkey with Pear Glaze and Roasted Turnips

Forget the bread stuffing and gravy; this wild turkey is served with a pear glaze. The accompanying roasted turnips are a far cry from the mashed version and will convince even die-hard turnip haters to give them a try.

menu

Appetizer:	*Savory Sausage Puff Pastry*
Salad:	*Mixed Green Salad with Tomatoes and Thousand Island Dressing*
Entrée:	*Wild Turkey with Pear Glaze*
Sides:	*Roasted Turnips; Au Gratin–Style Potatoes*
Dessert:	*Baked Apples*

Savory Sausage Puff Pastry

2 sheets frozen puff pastry dough, thawed according
   to package directions
2 eggs
1 tablespoon water
½ pound bulk sausage meat
½ pound ground venison or other game meat
1 cup packaged herb stuffing cubes
1 small onion, chopped
1 shallot, finely minced
2 cups chopped fresh mushrooms
½ teaspoon sage or Bell's seasoning
¼ teaspoon celery salt
¼ teaspoon marjoram
¼ teaspoon thyme
salt and pepper

Preheat oven to 375 degrees. Mix 1 egg with 1 tablespoon water for egg
wash, and set aside. Mix sausage, ground game meat, stuffing, 1 egg, onion,
shallot, and mushrooms; add herbs and spices.

Open sheets of pastry on a cookie sheet (this way, you won't have to
move the assembled pastry). Cut 1-inch strips along the long edges of the
pastry up to the fold line on both sides; repeat with the second sheet. Spoon
the filling mixture into the center of the pastry. Beginning at the top, fold
over one strip at a time, alternating right and left, nearly covering the filling
(some sausage filling will show). Repeat with the second sheet. At this point,
you can wrap the pastry tightly in plastic wrap and then foil, and freeze it for
later use; just add 10 minutes to the baking time. When ready to use, brush
pastries with egg wash and bake in a 375-degree oven until puffed and
golden and filling is cooked, approximately 20–30 minutes. Slice and serve.
This delicious pastry can be served as an appetizer or as a main dish.

Mixed Green Salad with
Tomatoes and Thousand Island Dressing

4 cups lettuce leaves, washed and dried
2 tomatoes, cored and sliced into wedges
1 cucumber, peeled and sliced
1 small red onion, thinly sliced
1 hard-cooked egg, chopped
roasted, salted sunflower seeds for garnish

Dressing

>1 cup mayonnaise
>½ cup chili sauce
>½ cup ketchup
>1 tablespoon cider vinegar
>1 tablespoon sweet green pickle relish
>¼ teaspoon paprika
>¼ teaspoon dry mustard

For the dressing: Mix all ingredients until well combined. Chill until ready to serve. For the salad: In a large salad bowl, place lettuce and prepared vegetables; top with chopped egg. Serve dressing and sunflower seeds on the side.

Wild Turkey with Pear Glaze

>1 wild turkey
>salt and pepper
>1 teaspoon sage
>1 tablespoon minced garlic
>1 stick butter
>4 to 6 strips bacon
>precooked turnips (see recipe below)

Glaze

>2 cups pears, peeled, cored, and diced in 1-inch
>   pieces
>2 cups dry white wine
>½ cup honey
>½ cinnamon stick
>4 tablespoons butter, cut into 4 pieces

Preheat oven to 350 degrees. Place turkey in a roasting pan. Carefully separate skin from breast meat with fingertips. Mix salt, pepper, sage, and garlic with butter, and use your fingers to spread the mixture under the skin of the breast. Add a strip of bacon under the skin to cover the butter mixture. Place the skin back in its original position. Season the outside of the bird with additional salt and pepper. Place any unused bacon strips across the breast of the turkey. Roast in the oven for 1 hour. After 15 minutes, or when some bacon fat has rendered, arrange turnips around the turkey and continue to roast, basting with pan juices, until the turnips are soft.

To make the glaze: Combine pears, wine, honey, and cinnamon stick in a saucepan and simmer over medium heat until the pears are very tender.

Remove cinnamon stick and blend glaze ingredients with an immersion blender or in a food processor. Swirl butter into warm glaze 1 tablespoon at a time.

Reduce oven to 300 degrees, and baste the turkey with the pear glaze. Continue baking, glazing every 15 minutes, until the turkey is done (180 degrees on a meat thermometer). You can leave the turnips in the roasting pan when glazing or remove them to an ovenproof baking dish.

Roasted Turnips

2 pounds small to medium white turnips, peeled

Cook turnips in salted boiling water; leave whole if on the smallish side, or cut into halves or quarters if larger. Let simmer for 10 minutes or until barely tender. Drain, butter, and set aside. See directions above for adding to the turkey as it roasts.

Au Gratin–Style Potatoes

3 tablespoons unsalted butter, softened
8 to 10 small Yukon Gold potatoes (about 3 pounds)
1 ½ cups milk
1 cup heavy cream
1 clove garlic, minced
salt to taste
¼ teaspoon freshly grated nutmeg
1 dried bay leaf
pepper to taste
1 cup finely grated Gruyère cheese

Preheat oven to 400 degrees. Generously butter a 9- by 12-inch glass baking dish with 1 tablespoon softened butter. Peel potatoes, and cut into ⅛-inch-thick slices. Place potato slices in a bowl of cold salted water to prevent discoloration. Mix milk, heavy cream, garlic, salt, nutmeg, and bay leaf in a saucepan. Bring to a simmer over medium heat. Drain potatoes and transfer to the prepared baking dish. Discard bay leaf and pour milk mixture over sliced potatoes. Carefully toss potatoes with milk mixture, pressing down gently to distribute the potato slices evenly. Season with pepper. Dot top with remaining butter; sprinkle with cheese. Place uncovered in the oven and bake until potatoes are tender (easily pierced with a fork) and the top is brown, 45 to 50 minutes. Cover with foil if the top browns too quickly. Serve immediately.

Baked Apples

This recipe is both simple and simply delicious. Use any firm apple such as Cortland or Granny Smith. Your only other decision is to stuff or not to stuff. These apples can also be baked or reheated in the microwave.

8 tart apples
½ cup sugar
1 cup water
½ teaspoon cinnamon
granola or oatmeal cookies, crushed (optional,
for stuffing)

Preheat oven to 350 degrees. Prepare syrup by combining the sugar, water, and cinnamon in a small saucepan. Bring to a simmer and let cook for 4 or 5 minutes. Meanwhile, peel the top third from each apple and remove the core with a melon baller or apple corer. If you're going to refill the apples with granola or crushed cookies, leave a bit of the bottom after the seeds have been removed to hold the filling in place. For the unfilled version, remove the entire core. Arrange the apples in a buttered baking dish and pour the syrup over them. Add filling to the core, if desired. Sprinkle each apple with a pinch of extra sugar and a shake of cinnamon. Cover with foil and bake for about 30 minutes, until apples are tender. Remove the foil for the last few minutes, or place them under the broiler for a minute if you want them browned. Serve warm or cold with cream, whipped cream, or vanilla ice cream.

Grilled Turkey Rolls

If you're looking for a change from roast turkey, try grilling wild turkey breasts on an outdoor grill. Butterfly the meat, spread with the flavors of the Mediterranean, roll, and grill to perfection. You may never want bread stuffing again.

menu

Salad: *Mixed Greek Salad with Feta Cheese Dressing*

Entrée: *Grilled Wild Turkey Breasts*

Sides: *Baked Wild Rice with Cranberries and Walnuts; Glazed Baby Carrots*

Dessert: *Blueberry Buckle*

Mixed Greek Salad with Feta Cheese Dressing

My husband and I honeymooned in Greece, and it was there in the Plaka marketplace that we had our first taste of this delicious salad. Strips of green cabbage combined with lettuce greens, thick slices of feta, black olives, and extra virgin olive oil make a hearty salad. Serve it with warm pita wedges.

> **4 cups torn lettuce (iceberg or romaine)**
> **2 cups fresh green cabbage, cut in 1-inch strips**
> **2 ripe tomatoes, cut into eighths**
> **4 slices feta cheese**
> **2 ounces brine-cured black olives, such as kalamata**

Dressing
> **4 ounces feta cheese**
> **2 tablespoons wine or cider vinegar**
> **1 tablespoon lemon juice**
> **1 tablespoon water**
> **1 teaspoon oregano**
> **1 clove garlic, minced**
> **4 tablespoons extra virgin olive oil**
> **salt and pepper**

Blend all the dressing ingredients in a blender or food processor until well mixed. Combine salad ingredients, and add dressing.

Grilled Wild Turkey Breasts

2 turkey breasts
salt and pepper
4 tablespoons fresh lemon juice
4 tablespoons olive oil
2 tablespoons oregano
½ cup chopped, pitted, ripe olives
1 cup shredded Monterey Jack cheese
½ cup roasted red pepper, cut into thin strips

Butterfly each turkey breast, creating a flat piece of meat that resembles a book. Pound to about ½ inch thick with a meat mallet or a rolling pin on plastic wrap. Season both sides with salt and pepper. Mix together lemon juice, olive oil, and oregano, and spread 2 to 3 tablespoons on top of each breast. Spread half the olives and cheese on each breast; arrange half the pepper strips on top. Roll up lengthwise, jelly-roll style. Tie with butcher's string in several places. Coat the outside with the remaining oregano mixture. Refrigerate covered for at least 4 hours, or overnight.

Preheat gas grill or barbecue to high heat. Grill the turkey rolls, turning them occasionally so that all sides are browned. Cook about 8 to 10 minutes per side. Check the temperature with a meat thermometer, and continue cooking and rotating the rolls until the internal temperature reaches 170 degrees. The total time depends on the size of the rolls and how tightly they're wrapped.

Baked Wild Rice with Cranberries and Walnuts

1 cup raw wild rice
4 cups water
2 tablespoons butter
1 medium yellow onion, chopped
1 stalk celery, thinly chopped
1 cup sliced mushrooms
2 to 3 cups heated chicken stock
1 clove garlic, finely minced
½ teaspoon sage
salt and pepper
1 cup dried cranberries
½ cup chopped walnuts or pecans

Preheat oven to 350 degrees. Butter an 8- by 8-inch baking dish. Rinse wild rice thoroughly by running cold water through a pot with the rice in the bottom. Bring rice and water to a boil, reduce heat, and simmer gently for 20 minutes. Change water once if it gets very dark. Drain and set aside.

Melt butter in a skillet over medium heat. Cook onion, celery, and mushrooms until celery is tender. Mix rice and onion mixture in the baking dish. Stir in chicken stock, garlic, sage, salt, and pepper. Cover and bake 1 hour. Check liquid and add more stock if needed. Stir in cranberries and nuts. Cover and cook for 15 minutes more, or until rice is cooked.

Glazed Baby Carrots

This recipe is made even easier with the wide availability of peeled baby carrots in the supermarket. If you can't find them (or if you prefer), peel a pound of carrots, slice or julienne, and adjust the boiling time.

1 pound peeled baby carrots
2 tablespoons butter
2 tablespoon brown sugar

Cook carrots in boiling salted water until tender. In a skillet, melt butter and sugar until sugar is dissolved. Add carrots and cook 3 to 4 minutes, stirring frequently, until carrots begin to caramelize.

Blueberry Buckle

For years we lived in the small town of Granville, Massachusetts, which is famous for its forests, whitetails, cheddar cheese, apples, and blueberries. This recipe remains one of my favorites because of its generous use of blueberries—no skimping here.

Topping
½ cup sugar or brown sugar
⅓ cup flour
½ teaspoon cinnamon
4 tablespoons butter, softened

Cake Batter
>   4 tablespoons butter, softened
>   ½ cup sugar
>   1 egg
>   1 teaspoon vanilla extract
>   1 cup flour
>   1 teaspoon baking powder
>   ¼ teaspoon salt
>   ⅓ cup milk
>   2 cups fresh blueberries

Preheat oven to 375 degrees. Grease and flour a 9-inch-square pan.

For the topping: Mix sugar, flour, and cinnamon in a medium bowl. Cut in butter with a fork or pastry blender until crumbly. Set aside.

For the cake batter: Beat butter and sugar in a large bowl until creamy; add the egg and vanilla, and beat until fluffy. Mix together the flour, baking powder, and salt; add alternately with the milk to the creamed mixture, beating well after each addition. Spread the batter in the prepared pan. Top with blueberries. Sprinkle with topping. Bake for 40 minutes, or until a toothpick comes out clean.

A Trio of Wild Turkeys

Don't be shy about serving wild turkey for your holiday dinner. However, because there's less breast meat than on a domestic bird, one turkey probably won't feed a crowd. So unless your hunter has bagged two birds, you can stretch the meal by offering plenty of appetizers and filling side dishes. This menu offers three methods of preparing wild turkey, just in case you're feeling adventurous and want a new slant on an old favorite.

menu

Appetizer:	*Cranberry Cheese Spread*
Salad:	*Shrimp and Avocado Salad*
Entrée:	*Turkey—Fried, Smoked, or Oven Roasted*
Side:	*Potato Filling*
Dessert:	*Pumpkin Mousse*

Cranberry Cheese Spread

Besides being easy and delicious, this spread is also very colorful. It would be great to serve on Valentine's Day as well.

1 pound small-curd cottage cheese
½ 16-ounce can whole cranberry sauce
1 to 2 tablespoons prepared horseradish, plain or
with beets (or more to taste)

Mix cottage cheese and cranberry sauce together until well blended. Add horseradish to taste. This spread should be tangy—a bit sweet and a bit zippy. Serve with savory crackers or sesame seed crackers.

Shrimp and Avocado Salad

½ pound cooked cocktail shrimp
2 tablespoons chopped fresh chives
¼ cup mayonnaise
1 tablespoon Worcestershire sauce
2 tablespoons chili sauce
salt
2 avocados, halved lengthwise and pitted
2 tablespoons lemon juice
Bibb lettuce leaves
½ teaspoon paprika
4 lemon wedges

Mix the shrimp, chives, mayonnaise, Worcestershire sauce, and chili sauce in a small bowl. Season with salt. Mound the shrimp mixture into avocado halves, and sprinkle with lemon juice. Place avocado halves on Bibb lettuce leaves. Garnish with a sprinkle of paprika and a lemon wedge.

Fried Turkey

Deep-fried turkey is moist and delicious and not at all greasy. As far as the turkey itself goes, smaller birds—15 pounds or less—work better for frying, so a wild turkey is perfect. For a more flavorful bird, you can inject the turkey with your favorite marinade (see below), or use a dry spice rub before cooking.

You'll need a 40- or 50-quart pot with a basket or turkey frying hardware, plus a propane gas tank and burner, a candy or deep-fry thermometer, a meat thermometer, and about 5 gallons of corn, peanut, or canola oil. Or you can purchase a turkey fryer with everything you need except for the thermometers and the propane tank. Because oil is flammable, you should never fry a turkey indoors. Place the fryer outdoors on a level dirt or grassy area. Avoid frying on wood decks, which could catch fire, as well as concrete surfaces, unless you don't mind oil stains. Always keep a fire extinguisher nearby.

Before beginning (and before you even season or marinate your turkey), determine the amount of oil you'll need by placing the turkey in the pot. Add water until it reaches about 2 inches above the turkey. Remove the turkey and note the water level by using a ruler to measure the distance from the top of the pot to the surface of the water. Remove the water and thoroughly dry the pot. This is the amount of oil you'll need to completely submerge the bird.

1 wild turkey
sufficient oil for frying

Lemon Marinade
3 tablespoons melted butter
1 tablespoon Worcestershire sauce
⅔ cup chicken stock
3 tablespoons lemon juice
1 tablespoon garlic power
1 teaspoon onion powder
1 tablespoon sugar
½ teaspoon salt
½ teaspoon finely ground black pepper
1 teaspoon Tabasco sauce (optional; or more to taste)

Mix all marinade ingredients, and use an injector to flavor the bird. Follow injector directions.

Heat the appropriate amount of oil (see above) to approximately 325 degrees (but no higher than 350 degrees). This should take about 20 to 30 minutes, but use a candy thermometer to check the temperature. Once the oil is hot enough, place the turkey in the basket or on the turkey hanger and slowly lower it into the pot.

To estimate cooking time, figure about 3 minutes per pound. After the appropriate amount of time, remove the turkey and check the temperature with a meat thermometer. It should read 170 degrees in the breast and 180 degrees in the thigh.

Smoked Turkey

Commercial smokers are readily available at grill shops, from catalogs, and online. A water smoker not only imbues flavor but also keeps the turkey moist. Charcoal smokers have two pans—one for the wood chips or charcoal, and one for the water or cooking liquid that creates the moist, hot smoke needed for cooking.

1 wild turkey
salt and pepper or poultry seasoning (optional)
onion, orange, or apple (optional)

You can add a little salt, pepper, or poultry seasoning or place an onion, orange, or apple in the cavity if you like, but the smoke provides the real flavor. You can flavor the bird by using different kinds of hardwood, such as hickory or apple, and wine or juice for the liquid.

Once the fire is going nicely, set the water pan in place, along with the smoker's cylindrical body. Strain presoaked wood chips out of the soaking liquid, add the liquid to the water pan, and then fill the pan with additional liquids or water. Place the lid on the smoker, and wait for the internal temperature to reach 250 to 300 degrees. Some smokers have built-in thermometers; if not, use an oven thermometer. When the smoker is preheated, place the turkey on the top grill rack and quickly replace the cover to avoid heat loss. Add charcoal every hour, as necessary, to maintain the temperature. Add more liquid and wood chips as necessary. Heat and liquid are critical to maintaining the hot smoke that cooks the turkey. The turkey is done when a meat thermometer placed in the inner thigh reaches 180 degrees.

Oven-Roasted Turkey

You can roast the turkey in a pan or use a roasting bag to help keep the bird moist.

> **1 wild turkey**
> **salt and pepper**
> **1 onion, peeled**
> **1 carrot, quartered**
> **1 celery stalk, quartered**
> **1 apple, quartered**
> **1 orange, quartered**
> **1 lemon, quartered**
> **1 stick butter**

Wash the turkey, pat it dry, season the inside with salt and pepper, and fill cavity with the vegetable-fruit mixture. Truss the legs to close the cavity. Loosen the breast skin carefully with your fingers, and smear softened butter under the skin. Butter the outside of the bird, and season with salt and pepper. Place in a roasting pan or oven bag, following directions. Roast at 325 degrees until the internal temperature reaches 180 degrees in the thickest part of the thigh. To estimate cooking time, figure 20 minutes per pound.

Potato Filling

With this recipe from the Pennsylvania Dutch, you get a twofer: the creamy taste of mashed potatoes and the savory taste of crunchy stuffing. Potato filling also works with many other meats.

> **5 pounds potatoes, cooked and mashed**
> **1 stick butter, divided**
> **1 cup milk**
> **2 eggs, lightly beaten**
> **1 teaspoon salt**
> **½ teaspoon pepper**
> **1 cup finely chopped celery**
> **1 onion, finely chopped**
> **2 tablespoons fresh chopped parsley**
> **   or 1 tablespoon dried**
> **1 package seasoned stuffing cubes**

Preheat oven to 375 degrees. Add ½ stick butter, milk, lightly beaten eggs, salt, and pepper to the mashed potatoes; they should be a bit loose, because the stuffing will absorb some of their moisture. Set aside. Melt 2 tablespoons butter in a very large skillet. Add the celery and onion and sauté until tender. Add the parsley and continue cooking for a few minutes longer. Place the vegetable mixture in a bowl and set aside. Melt the remaining 2 tablespoons butter in the skillet. Add the stuffing cubes to the skillet, toss to coat, and sauté until the cubes are very lightly browned. Combine the stuffing cubes with the vegetable mixture. In a very large bowl, combine the mashed potato mixture with the vegetable and stuffing mixture. Stir until thoroughly mixed. Add more milk, if needed. Spoon the mixture into a large buttered casserole or oven-safe bowls. Dot with additional butter. Bake for 30 minutes.

Potato filling can be prepared a day ahead of time, refrigerated, and baked just before serving. Allow about 15 minutes additional baking time if the filling has been chilled. Stir once or twice during baking.

Pumpkin Mousse

Experience the taste of pumpkin pie in a scrumptious light dessert. Make the toffee nut crunch in advance, or if you're short on time, use crushed gingersnaps.

> ¼ cup cold water
> 1 envelope unflavored gelatin
> 15-ounce can pumpkin
> ¾ cup firmly packed light brown sugar
> 3 eggs, separated
> 2 teaspoons grated orange zest
> 1 teaspoon pumpkin pie spice
> ¼ teaspoon salt
> 3 cups heavy cream, divided
> 2 teaspoons vanilla extract, divided
> ¼ cup confectioners' sugar
> toffee nut crunch (recipe follows), or 10 gingersnap
>   cookies, chopped

> *Toffee Nut Crunch*
> vegetable oil
> 1 cup pecan pieces
> ⅔ cup toffee bits or broken Heath bars
> 4 teaspoons packed dark brown sugar
> ⅛ teaspoon salt
> 1 tablespoon butter, melted

For the toffee nut crunch: Preheat oven to 350 degrees. Cover a cookie sheet with aluminum foil and brush with vegetable oil. Add all the ingredients together in a small bowl and mix well. Spread mixture evenly on the cookie sheet. Bake for about 10 to 15 minutes. Cool completely. Remove to a work surface and break into crumbly pieces. Set aside.

For the mousse: Place the water in a heat-proof bowl and sprinkle the gelatin over it. Set aside for 10 minutes to allow the gelatin to soften.

In a large bowl, whisk together the pumpkin, brown sugar, egg yolks, orange zest, pumpkin pie spice, and salt until well blended. Set the bowl of gelatin over a pan of simmering water and cook until the gelatin is clear. Add the hot gelatin to the pumpkin mixture, whisking to incorporate. Using an electric mixer, whip 2 cups of heavy cream and 1 teaspoon vanilla until soft peaks form. Fold this whipped cream into the pumpkin mixture. Whip the second batch of cream: 1 cup of heavy cream, 1 teaspoon vanilla, and ¼ cup confectioners' sugar until stiff peaks form (or substitute ready-made whipped cream).

To assemble: Spoon some of the pumpkin mixture into parfait glasses, add a layer of whipped cream, then some toffee nut crunch or crushed cookies. Repeat layers, ending with a third layer of pumpkin. Cover with plastic wrap and refrigerate for 4 hours or overnight. To serve, decorate with additional whipped cream and toffee nut crunch or a gingersnap.

WATERFOWL

Geese and ducks make fine eating. There are many varieties of each, and the size of the bird varies with its sex and species. Most wild geese weigh 6 to 10 pounds undrawn and with feathers, or about 4 to 6 pounds dressed; one goose will feed four to six people, depending on their appetites. Mallards are considered large ducks, and one can feed two people. Smaller species, such as the teal, can feed one guest per bird in a pinch, but cook a couple of extra if you have some big eaters. I will always prepare an extra bird because my husband can eat a whole duck all by himself. Remember, a substantial appetizer or soup can take the edge off a hearty appetite, and an extra side dish can ensure that all your diners are satisfied. I always prepare too much because of my fear that someone will leave the table hungry, but at least I end up with some great leftovers.

Chinese-Spiced Teal Breasts

Cooking a Chinese duck dinner at home is relatively easy. Most supermarkets carry all the ingredients you need. The preparation time, with all that chopping, is actually longer than the cooking time, but most of that work can be done beforehand.

menu

Appetizer: Wonton Soup

Entrée: Spiced Teal Duck Breasts

Sides: Chinese Green Beans; Fried Rice

Dessert: Coconut Macaroons with Pineapple Chunks

Wonton Soup

The wontons can be prepared well in advance and frozen. The soup itself can be heated and left simmering, and the vegetables and wontons can be added a few minutes before serving to avoid overcooking.

wonton wrappers (available in most supermarkets or Asian grocery stores)
¾ pound ground pork
1 egg
¼ cup water chestnuts, finely minced
1 glove garlic, minced
3 green onions
2 tablespoons soy sauce
6 cups clear chicken stock with splash soy sauce
1 cup assorted vegetables, thinly sliced: mushrooms, carrots, pea pods, water chestnuts, bok choy, Chinese cabbage, spinach

Mix ground pork, egg, water chestnuts, garlic, and the white and light green parts of two green onions finely minced; slice the remaining green onion into thin slices crosswise, and reserve for garnish. Stir in soy sauce. Place a wonton skin on your work surface, and place a teaspoon of filling in the center of the wrapper. Moisten edges with water. Bring one point of the wrapper up and over the filling to form a triangle. Continue to seal the edge, pressing out air. Moisten one point on the right, and pull the left and right points back behind the lump of filling. Pinch to seal. Repeat, until all the filling is used. Plan on 4 to 6 wontons per serving. If you have extra wontons, let them air-dry, and then dust them with cornstarch. Freeze them on a cookie sheet, and then transfer to an airtight container or freezer bag. Freeze any leftover skins as well, making sure they are wrapped tightly.

Drop several wontons in boiling salted water and cook for 3 to 4 minutes, until skin becomes white and filling is cooked. Remove with a slotted spoon. Cook in batches. Meanwhile, bring chicken stock to a boil, and add the vegetables of your choice. Simmer 1 or 2 minutes, add wontons, and simmer until wontons are heated through. Serve immediately with a sprinkling of green onions.

Spiced Teal Duck Breasts

2 large duck breasts or 4 smaller breasts (about 1 ½ to 2 pounds), with skin still attached
salt and pepper

Sauce
3 tablespoons rice wine
1 teaspoon fresh ginger root, peeled and grated or very finely minced
1 clove garlic, finely minced
2 star anises or ½ teaspoon anise seed
crushed red pepper flakes
¼ teaspoon Chinese five-spice powder
3 tablespoons honey
3 tablespoons mushroom soy sauce
1 tablespoon tomato chili sauce or ketchup
½ cup chicken stock
hot Szechuan chili oil
scallions, sliced into rings for garnish

Preheat oven to 425 degrees. Lightly score the skin on the duck breasts with a crisscross pattern, then salt and pepper both sides. Heat an ovenproof skillet over medium heat and brush with oil. Place the duck breasts skin-side down in the skillet and let brown and crisp for about 5 minutes. Pour off any accumulated fat, turn breasts over, and sear the other side (about 1 minute). With the breasts in the skin-side-up position, place the skillet in the preheated oven, and continue cooking until desired degree of doneness is achieved: for large breasts, about 4 minutes for rare, 6 minutes for medium, and 8 to 10 minutes for well-done; smaller breasts cook faster. Or you can use an instant-read meat thermometer: 130 degrees for medium rare, 170 degrees for well-done. Remove the breasts from the hot pan and let them rest in a warm place while you make the sauce.

For the sauce: Pour off any fat left in the skillet. Deglaze the pan with the rice wine, scraping any browned bits into the sauce. Add the remaining ingredients, except for the Szechuan oil, to the pan; bring to a boil; and let simmer for 2 to 3 minutes to reduce, stirring constantly. When the sauce has thickened, remove the star anises. Taste the sauce and add more soy sauce, rice wine, or honey if needed. Add hot Szechuan oil if desired. Pour sauce over duck breasts served on a bed of shredded lettuce. Garnish with scallion rings.

Chinese Green Beans

   3 tablespoons peanut or other vegetable oil
   1 clove garlic, minced
   1 dime-sized slice fresh ginger root, peeled
   1 pound green beans
   1 teaspoon cornstarch
   2 tablespoons light soy sauce (light in color or
       flavor, not necessarily in calories)
   ½ cup chicken stock
   2 green onions, sliced in circles

Heat oil in a wok or skillet. Sauté garlic and ginger root for about 1 minute; do not burn. Remove the ginger slice from the pan. Add green beans and sauté until crisp-tender. Mix cornstarch and soy sauce into cold chicken stock and stir well. Add chicken stock mixture to wok and continue to cook until sauce thickens and becomes clear, stirring constantly, about 2 minutes. Remove from heat, add green onions, toss, and remove to a serving platter.

Fried Rice

The secret to good fried rice is starting with firm, cold rice and adding it to the other ingredients near the end of cooking to prevent it from becoming mushy or starchy. Prewashing the rice helps remove excess starch and keeps the grains from sticking together.

> **4 cups cold white rice**
> **¼ pound pork, chicken, steak, or shrimp, diced in small pieces**
> **4 tablespoons vegetable oil**
> **1 egg, beaten**
> **1 medium onion, diced**
> **2 ounces fresh pea pods, chopped into pieces; or ½ cup frozen peas, thawed**
> **1 cup fresh bean sprouts**
> **2 tablespoons dark soy sauce**
> **1 scallion, sliced in circles for garnish**

Marinade
> **2 tablespoons dark soy sauce**
> **2 tablespoons water**
> **2 tablespoons rice wine**

The rice must be cooked in advance so that it's cold when you're making the fried rice. Begin by prewashing the rice under cold running water until the water runs clear. In a saucepan with a tight-fitting lid, bring 1 ½ cups water and 1 teaspoon salt to a boil. Add rice, bring to a full boil, reduce heat, and cover. Cook very slowly; if the rice is simmering too fast, move the pan partway off the burner if possible. Listen for the sound of crackling after about 12 to 15 minutes. This means that all the water has been absorbed. Test for doneness. The rice should be very firm, because it will continue to cook when added to the main recipe. Add a bit more water if needed, but don't add too much or cook too long; if you do, the rice will be mushy. Rinse the cooked rice under cold water, drain well, and put in the refrigerator until cold. Rice can be cooked the day before, or you can use leftover rice from home or from your local Chinese restaurant.

Combine the marinade ingredients, and marinate the meat or shrimp while you cook the egg and onion. Heat oil in a wok or large skillet. Pour beaten egg into the oil and stir, breaking it up into small, thin strips. When done, remove and set aside. In the same oil, sauté the onion until tender but not browned. Add meat and marinade and cook until done. Remove onion and meat from the wok. Sauté pea pods or peas for 1 to 2 minutes. Add rice, breaking up clumps, and heat until grains separate. Add bean sprouts and toss to mix. Pour in soy sauce and stir to mix evenly. When rice is hot, return egg, meat, and onions to the mixture. Remove to a serving dish and garnish with sliced scallions.

Coconut Macaroons with Pineapple Chunks

2 egg whites
14 ounces sweetened condensed milk
14 ounces sweetened flaked coconut
1 teaspoon vanilla extract
1 pineapple, peeled, cored, and cut into chunks; or 1
    20-ounce can pineapple chunks in juice, drained

Preheat oven to 325 degrees. Spray a baking sheet with cooking spray. Beat egg whites until frothy and soft peaks form. Mix in condensed milk, coconut, and vanilla. Stir until well blended. Drop by heaping teaspoonful on the baking sheet. Bake for 25 to 30 minutes until set and very lightly browned. Remove from sheet and cool on a wire rack. Serve with chilled pineapple chunks.

Roast Mallard Duck with Fruit Sauce

It doesn't get any better than roasted duck. Fruit is the perfect accompaniment for this bird, and the flavors of the roasted fruit sauce add something special to the dinner.

menu

Appetizer:	*Spicy Red Bean Soup*
Entrée:	*Mallard Duck with Roasted Fruit Sauce*
Sides:	*New Potatoes with Balsamic and Shallot Butter; Creamed Cauliflower*
Dessert:	*Ginger Biscotti*

Spicy Red Bean Soup

2 tablespoons oil
1 small onion, minced
3 cloves garlic, minced
1 quart chicken stock or broth
4 16-ounce cans red beans or red kidney beans
¼ cup red hot pepper sauce (more or less to taste)
¼ cup minced fresh cilantro
2 teaspoons ground cumin or 1 tablespoon dried
1 teaspoon dried oregano
sour cream and shredded Monterey Jack cheese for
    garnish

Heat oil in a 6-quart pot. Cook onion and garlic over medium heat until soft; do not brown. Add the chicken stock, the beans with their liquid, and all other soup ingredients. Bring to a boil. Reduce heat and simmer for 30 minutes. Remove about 2 cups of beans and soup base, puree them in a blender, and return them to the pot. Alternatively, you can use an immersion blender, being careful not to overblend, and leaving some beans whole. Adjust spiciness with more or less pepper sauce. Serve garnished with sour cream, shredded cheese, or both.

Mallard Duck with Roasted Fruit Sauce

2 large or 4 small ducks
dry red wine for basting (reserve for fruit compote)
kosher salt
pepper
1 cup coarsely chopped celery
1 cup coarsely chopped carrot
1 medium onion, quartered
4 shallots, sliced
2 cloves garlic, crushed and coarsely chopped
1 orange, quartered
1 apple, quartered

Preheat oven to 400 degrees. To prepare the ducks, rinse well under cold water and pat dry; remove any excess fat. Sprinkle inside cavities with salt and pepper. Divide celery, carrot, onion, shallots, garlic, orange, and apple evenly among ducks, and stuff the cavities with the vegetables and fruits. Tie the legs together with kitchen twine. Lift the wing tips up and over the back, and tuck under the duck. Prick the ducks all over with a fork, piercing the skin to allow fat to escape. Rub the outside of the ducks with half an orange. Place the ducks on a rack in a roasting pan. Roast for 20 minutes; reduce heat to 350 degrees and roast for at least 1 ½ hours, depending on size. Baste with wine every 30 minutes. Remove from oven when done (internal temperature 170 to 180 degrees); cover with foil and keep warm while you make the fruit sauce (recipe follows).

Roasted Fruit Sauce
  2 cups pitted cherries
  2 peaches, peeled
  2 pears, peeled
  2 Granny Smith apples, peeled
  2 plums
  ½ teaspoon each: cinnamon, allspice, and ginger
  ½ cup red wine (from basting)

Increase oven temperature to 450 degrees. Cut all fruit into 1-inch pieces. Combine cherries, peaches, pears, apples, plums, and spices. Drain all but 1 tablespoon of drippings from the duck roasting pan. Add fruit to the pan and toss gently to coat. Bake for 20 to 30 minutes until very soft, stirring occasionally. Stir in the wine and cook 5 minutes more. The fruit should be soft, and sauce syrupy. Serve with duck.

New Potatoes with Balsamic and Shallot Butter

  ⅔ cup balsamic vinegar
  ½ stick butter, softened
  1 tablespoon fresh minced parsley
  1 shallot, finely minced
  salt and pepper to taste
  3 to 4 pounds small red potatoes, cleaned but not
      peeled

In a small saucepan, reduce vinegar to 2 tablespoons. Cool completely. Add butter, parsley, shallot, salt, and pepper, and mix well to combine. Remove to a small bowl and set aside. Meanwhile, place potatoes in a pot, cover with cold salted water, and bring to a boil. Reduce heat and simmer for about 20 minutes, or until potatoes are tender. Drain. Cut potatoes in half and place in a serving bowl. Add butter mixture, and toss gently to coat. Add more salt and pepper if needed. Serve hot.

Creamed Cauliflower

**1 medium head cauliflower, broken into florets, or 2
    10-ounce packages frozen cauliflower florets
2 cups cauliflower cooking liquid, reserved
4 tablespoons butter
4 tablespoons flour
1 cup milk
salt and pepper to taste
dash cayenne pepper or nutmeg (optional)**

In a large saucepan of boiling salted water, cook cauliflower until tender. Drain and reserve 2 cups cooking water. Set cauliflower aside and keep liquid simmering. In a small skillet, melt butter. Add flour and stir over medium-low heat until well blended and a thick paste forms; cook for 2 minutes. Add flour mixture to the hot cauliflower water and whisk until a thick sauce if formed. Gradually add milk, stirring constantly, and cook until thick and smooth. Adjust seasoning if necessary. Return florets to the sauce and gently stir to coat. Keep on very low heat until serving time. Add more milk if the sauce gets too thick. Dust with a dash of cayenne pepper or nutmeg if desired.

Ginger Biscotti

**1 cup sugar
1 stick butter
2 eggs
1 teaspoon vanilla extract
1 teaspoon ground ginger
1 teaspoon ground cinnamon
1 teaspoon ground cloves
1 teaspoon ground allspice
2 cups flour
1 cup quick-cooking rolled oats
½ teaspoon baking powder
1 cup chopped almonds**

Preheat oven to 350 degrees. In a large mixing bowl, cream together sugar and butter until light and fluffy. Add eggs and vanilla and blend well. In a separate bowl or paper bag, mix together all dry ingredients, including almonds. Gradually add dry ingredients to the creamed mixture, and blend until a dough is formed. Do not overmix. Divide dough in half and roll each half into a 12-inch log about 1 inch in diameter. Place the logs on an ungreased cookie sheet, and bake for 25 minutes or until lightly browned.

Cool at least 30 minutes. Using a sharp, serrated knife, cut each log diagonally into ½-inch-thick slices. Arrange the slices on the cookie sheet and bake at 350 degrees for about 15 minutes, turning once, until dry, crisp, and lightly browned. Cool and store in an airtight container. Makes about 3 dozen. Serve with ice cream, pudding, or coffee.

Cajun Cookin' Duck Gumbo

Serve up some Louisiana-style duck with a rib-sticking, crowd-pleasing gumbo. You can use duck, goose, or other wild fowl pieces for this hearty dish.

menu

Appetizer:	*Crawfish, Crab, or Shrimp Salad*
Entrée:	*Duck and Oyster Gumbo*
Sides:	*Dirty Rice;*
	Baked Sweet Potato Soufflé
Dessert:	*French Puffs*

Crawfish, Crab, or Shrimp Salad

2 cups cooked crawfish or other seafood
½ cup chopped celery
½ cup chopped green pepper
1 small onion, chopped
2 hard-boiled eggs, chopped
2 teaspoons green pickle relish (sweet or dill)
½ to 1 cup mayonnaise
3 tablespoons chili sauce or ketchup
1 teaspoon Worcestershire sauce
salt and pepper
Tabasco sauce (optional)
lettuce leaves
lemon slices for garnish

In a large salad bowl, mix all ingredients except lettuce and lemon slices. Check seasoning and adjust as desired. Arrange lettuce leaves on individual salad plates or on a serving platter, and mound with seafood salad, and garnish with a lemon slice.

Duck and Oyster Gumbo

Cook the duck and make the stock the day before to help streamline the final recipe.

> **1 large or 2 small diving ducks (or any species)**
> **½ cup vegetable oil**
> **1 cup flour**
> **2 stalks celery, chopped**
> **2 green bell peppers, chopped**
> **2 medium onions, chopped**
> **3 cloves garlic, finely minced**
> **2 tablespoons tomato paste**
> **2 quarts duck stock**
> **2 teaspoons filé seasoning**
> **2 teaspoons Creole seasoning (Tony Chachere's)**
> **1 bay leaf**
> **salt, black pepper, and cayenne pepper to taste**
> **bottled hot sauce to taste**
> **4 to 5 cups duck meat**
> **½ pound smoked andouille sausage, cut into ½-inch slices**
> **½ pound fresh or frozen okra**
> **12 ounces fresh shucked oysters**
> **green onions, sliced, for garnish**

If you use a diving duck for this gumbo, the simmering will tenderize the meat and give a richness to the stock. The day before, cook the duck in a large stockpot covered with salted water. You need at least 8 to 10 cups of stock when finished. Skin the duck and remove the meat, and shred or chop it into bite-size pieces; you need at least 4 cups.

Heat oil over medium heat in a large, heavy pot or Dutch oven. Add the flour and cook, stirring constantly, until dark brown (a dark roux is essential to a good gumbo). Don't rush this step—it should take about 30 minutes. Be careful not to burn it. Add the celery, green peppers, garlic, and onions, and cook until just crisp-tender; stir in tomato paste. Add the warmed stock 1 cup at a time until the base is as thick as a very thick soup. Add filé powder, Creole seasoning, and bay leaf, and finish with salt, black pepper, red pepper, and hot sauce to taste. Add duck meat and simmer for 1 hour, uncovered, on low heat. Add sausage and okra and cook 15 minutes longer, until okra is cooked. Add the oysters just before serving. Cook 3 minutes longer, until oysters have frilled around the edges. Serve over hot white rice or with dirty rice (recipe follows). Garnish with sliced green onions.

Dirty Rice

A must with any Cajun food, dirty rice has as many recipes as it does cooks, so experiment until you get it the way you like it. I've added some ground game meat to this recipe just to jazz it up.

> 3 ½ cups chicken stock
> 1 teaspoon salt
> 1 ½ cups white rice
> ½ pound chicken livers
> 2 chicken giblets
> 2 tablespoons bacon drippings
> 1 medium onion, finely chopped
> 1 green pepper, finely chopped
> 1 red bell pepper, finely chopped
> 3 celery stalks and leaves, finely chopped
> 1 clove garlic, finely minced
> ½ pound ground game meat (your choice)
> 2 tablespoons Worcestershire sauce
> salt and pepper to taste
> Tabasco sauce to taste

Bring chicken stock and salt to a boil in a medium saucepan. Add the rice, cover, and reduce heat to low. Simmer until liquid is absorbed and rice is cooked, about 20 minutes. Meanwhile, in a food processor or meat grinder, finely chop the chicken livers and giblets. Heat the bacon drippings in a skillet. Add onion, peppers, celery, and garlic. Sauté, stirring often, until vegetables are softened. Add ground game meat and cook until no longer pink. Add giblets and chicken livers and sauté until they are browned. Add Worcestershire, salt and pepper, and Tabasco. Stir in the hot rice. Combine well. Garnish with parsley or sliced green onions.

Baked Sweet Potato Soufflé

Take a break from the spice and enjoy this sweet potato casserole—no marsh-mallows, honest!

> **8 medium sweet potatoes or yams**
> **1 cup milk**
> **½ cup packed brown sugar**
> **½ stick butter**
> **1 egg**
> **1 teaspoon vanilla extract**
> **1 teaspoon cinnamon**
> **pinch nutmeg**
> **2 tablespoons orange juice concentrate**
> **8 canned pear halves, pureed**
> **1 cup chopped pecans**

Preheat oven to 350 degrees. Bake, peel, and mash the sweet potatoes. Mix the milk, sugar, and butter, and heat until the butter is melted. Add to the potatoes and mix. Add the remaining ingredients and beat with an electric mixer until well blended and light. Transfer to a buttered baking dish and bake for 20 to 30 minutes, until hot throughout.

French Puffs

An easy version of the classic French beignet, these little puffs are great for dessert served with chicory coffee.

> **2 cups flour**
> **⅓ cup sugar**
> **½ teaspoon salt**
> **½ teaspoon nutmeg**
> **1 tablespoon baking powder**
> **¼ cup vegetable oil**
> **¾ cup milk**
> **1 egg**
> **confectioners' sugar or cinnamon-sugar mixture for**
> **dusting**

Mix the dry ingredients together in the bowl of an electric mixer. Add oil, milk, and egg. Mix thoroughly until a smooth batter is formed. Drop by tea-spoonful into hot fat (375 degrees). (Anything larger and the batter will cook on the outside before it's done on the inside.) Fry about 2 to 3 minutes; puffs will rise to the top of the oil. Turn to brown on all sides. Remove from fryer and drain on paper towels. Shake warm puffs in a paper bag with powdered sugar or cinnamon-sugar mixture. Makes about 36. The batter can be made beforehand and held in the refrigerator for several days.

Duck, Duck, Duck

The entrée calls for duck breast, so to be thrifty, you can use the rest of the duck in the appetizers.

menu

Appetizer: *Duck and Mushroom Crepes*

Salad: *Mixed Salad*

Entrée: *Duck Breast with Cranberry and Dried Cherry Chutney*

Sides: *Cheesy Potato and Onion Bake; Herbed Green Beans*

Dessert: *Ricotta Cheesecake*

Duck and Mushroom Crepes

Crepes
> 1 cup all-purpose flour
> 2 eggs
> 1¼ cups milk
> ¼ teaspoon salt
> 3 tablespoons butter, melted

Filling and Sauce
  1 ½ cups cooked duck meat, chopped
  1 stick butter, divided
  1 small onion, finely chopped
  4 ounces mushrooms, minced
  ½ cup chopped cooked spinach, squeezed dry
  1 teaspoon fresh minced parsley
  1 tablespoon fresh minced tarragon or chives,
    or 1 teaspoon dried
  6 tablespoons flour, divided
  ¾ cup milk
  2 tablespoons sour cream
  2 tablespoons Parmesan cheese
  salt and pepper to taste
  1 ½ cups duck or chicken stock
  1 ½ cups cheddar cheese, shredded (or half Swiss and
    half Parmesan)
  ½ cup milk
  ⅛ teaspoon cayenne pepper
  2 tablespoons Parmesan cheese (for topping)

For the crepes: In a blender, mix together the flour and eggs. Add the milk and water, stirring to combine. Add the salt and butter; blend until smooth. Let rest for at least 30 minutes. Whirl the blender just before making the crepes.

Heat a small nonstick skillet over medium–high heat. Brush with butter and remove the excess with a paper towel (the pan should just be filmed with butter). Pour or scoop ¼ cup batter into the pan. Tilt the pan with a circular motion so that the batter coats the surface evenly. Cook for about 2 minutes, until the bottom is slightly browned and the top is drying. Lower the heat if the crepe browns too quickly. Run a spatula around the edges, turn, and cook the other side for 1 minute. Stack between layers of waxed paper while you continue making crepes, using all the batter. Crepes can be sealed in plastic wrap and frozen for later use, or they will keep for several days in the refrigerator.

For the duck meat: After separating the breasts for the main course, remove any visible fat and simmer the saddles and bones in salted water until the meat is cooked. Reserve stock; let cool. Remove the meat from the bones and discard the skin and bones. Chop the duck meat and measure 1 ½ cups. Reserve any extra meat for another use. If you don't have enough stock, add chicken broth to make 1 ½ cups.

For the filling: Melt 2 tablespoons butter in a skillet. Add onion and cook until soft. Add mushrooms and sauté until the mushrooms give off their liquid. Add the spinach and sauté until the mixture is dry. Transfer to a large bowl; stir in duck meat, parsley, and tarragon or chives. Set aside.

Melt 2 tablespoons of the remaining butter in a small, heavy saucepan. Make a roux by adding 2 tablespoons flour and cooking, stirring constantly, for 2 to 3 minutes until thick and bubbly. Whisk in milk and return to a boil, stirring constantly. Reduce heat and simmer until thick and smooth. Stir white sauce into the duck-spinach mixture; blend in sour cream, 2 tablespoons Parmesan cheese, salt, and pepper.

For the cheese sauce: Melt the remaining butter in a heavy, medium-sized saucepan. Add the remaining 4 tablespoons of flour and cook until thick and bubbly. Whisk in the duck stock or broth, bring to a boil, and cook, stirring constantly, until thickened and smooth. Remove from heat and stir in the cheddar cheese. Stir in the milk and cayenne pepper. Set aside.

To assemble: Preheat oven to 350 degrees. Fill each crepe with 3 to 4 tablespoons filling, and roll. (At this point, the crepes can be refrigerated for 24 hours or frozen.) Place the crepes in a baking dish, pour the cheese sauce over all, and sprinkle with Parmesan. Bake, uncovered, for 30 to 40 minutes, until the sauce is bubbling. Run under the broiler to brown lightly if desired.

Mixed Salad

1 head red or green leaf lettuce
1 head curly endive
1 small head radicchio lettuce
2 ripe tomatoes, cut into wedges
½ cup pitted or stuffed green olives
½ cup Italian- or Greek-style black olives
1 small red onion, sliced
8–10 pepperoncini (small pickled peppers)
shaved Parmesan cheese
½ cup croutons

Dressing
¼ cup white wine vinegar
1 tablespoon minced fresh basil leaves
   or ½ teaspoon dried
2 tablespoons water
1 clove garlic, finely minced
1 teaspoon dried oregano
⅓ cup extra virgin olive oil
salt and pepper to taste

For the dressing: Mix all ingredients together in a jar; shake well and set aside. For the salad: Wash, dry, and tear lettuces into bite-size pieces. Mix in salad bowl. Add tomatoes, olives, onion slices, and pepperoncini, and toss to distribute. Just before serving, shave slices of cheese on top. Pass croutons and dressing for drizzling.

Duck Breast with Cranberry and Dried Cherry Chutney

Chutney is a sweet and sour sauce, kind of like a cooked fruit salsa. It is usually spicy and pungent. The dried cherry in this version adds the taste of the East to the duck breasts. Remember that chutney is a condiment, not a cooking sauce, and a little goes a long way.

Chutney
> 1 tablespoon olive oil
> 1 large shallot, minced
> 4 dime-sized slices fresh ginger root, minced
> 1 large clove garlic, minced
> 1 cup fresh or frozen cranberries
> 1 cup dried sweet cherries
> ½ cup sweet vermouth or apple juice
> 3 tablespoons honey
> 2 tablespoons lemon juice
> 1 tablespoon orange juice
> 1 teaspoon lemon or orange zest, or a combination
>   of both
> ¼ teaspoon crushed red pepper flakes (optional for a
>   hot and spicy taste)
> salt and ground white pepper

Duck
> 3 full or 6 halved mallard duck breasts
> ½ teaspoon ground cinnamon
> ½ teaspoon powdered ginger
> dash cayenne pepper or finely crushed red pepper
>   flakes
> salt and ground black pepper
> 2 tablespoons oil

For the chutney: Heat oil in a heavy, medium-sized saucepan. Sauté shallot, ginger, and garlic over low heat until shallot is tender. Add cranberries, cherries, and vermouth, and cook over medium heat, stirring frequently, until cranberries pop and cherries soften—3 to 5 minutes. Stir in honey, lemon juice, orange juice, zest, and pepper flakes if desired. Heat thoroughly; add salt and pepper to taste. Set aside.

For the duck: Use a very sharp knife to score the skin down to the flesh. In a small bowl, mix together the spices. Rub the mixture into both sides of the duck breast. Heat oil in a heavy skillet (cast iron if you have one) over medium heat. Add the duck breast, skin-side down, and cook until skin is well browned, about 5 minutes. Turn and cook the second side until the flesh is firm to the touch, 3 to 5 minutes. Duck should be cooked to the medium-rare stage; add more time if you want it well-done, or put the duck in a 300-degree oven to keep it warm, where it will continue to cook a bit.

Using a sharp knife, slice the duck ⅛ inch thick, and arrange the slices on a platter. Reheat chutney, if necessary, and serve on the side.

Cheesy Potato and Onion Bake

8 cups thinly sliced, unpeeled russet potatoes
½ cup thinly sliced small yellow onions, separated
**   into rings**
2 cups shredded cheddar or Monterey Jack cheese
½ stick butter, melted
salt and pepper to taste

Preheat oven to 400 degrees. Arrange overlapping potatoes slices in the bottom of a 9- by 13-inch baking pan; sprinkle with salt and pepper. Layer with the onions and half the cheese. Cover with the remaining potatoes, drizzle with the melted butter, and season with salt and pepper. Cover with aluminum foil and bake for about 40 minutes. Remove the foil, check for doneness, and continue baking uncovered until the potatoes are tender. Replace the foil if the casserole browns too much. When the potatoes are tender, add the remaining cheese to the top of the casserole and return to the oven until the cheese is melted. Let stand for 5 minutes before serving. Top with a sprinkle of chives.

Herbed Green Beans

1 pound broad, flat, Italian green beans
1 teaspoon extra virgin olive oil
1 teaspoon fresh lemon juice
1 tablespoon chopped fresh basil leaves
salt and pepper

Steam or boil the green beans until just tender. Rinse under cold water to stop cooking, drain, and set aside. Just before serving, heat oil over medium heat in a large skillet; add green beans and toss to heat. When beans are hot, add lemon juice and basil, and stir for 1 minute to heat through. Season with salt and pepper and serve immediately.

Ricotta Cheesecake

2 pounds ricotta cheese
⅔ cup sugar
⅓ cup flour
6 eggs
2 teaspoons vanilla extract
½ teaspoon salt

Berry Sauce
1 cup strawberries
½ cup sugar
1 tablespoon balsamic vinegar
1 cup raspberries

For the berry sauce: Slice the strawberries and mix with sugar and balsamic vinegar. Gently stir in the raspberries. Cover and let macerate.

For the cheesecake: Preheat oven to 300 degrees. Butter and flour a 9-inch springform pan, and tap out the excess flour. Place the ricotta in a large mixing bowl and beat until smooth. Add sugar and flour and beat thoroughly. Beat in the eggs one at a time, on low speed. Blend in the vanilla and salt. Pour the batter into the prepared pan. Bake in the center of the oven for about 1 ¼ to 1 ½ hours, until a light golden color. Cake is done when a knife inserted in the center comes out clean and the middle is firm. Cool on a wire rack for 10 minutes; run a sharp knife around the inside edge of the pan and continue to cool. Cheesecake will sink slightly as it cools. Cover and chill until serving time. Remove the sides of the pan, move the cheesecake to a serving plate, and serve with berries.

Mahogany Mallard

Duck with orange sauce used to be my husband's favorite way to eat duck; in fact, it may have been his favorite meal. Having worked in a Chinese restaurant, I developed a love for the mahogany browned roasted duck found hanging in the windows of markets in Boston's Chinatown. I made a convert of my husband, and now this is his favorite duck dish too. Since I can't get to Boston as often as I'd like, I came up with this version, which is pretty close. One duck serves two people (although my husband will eat a whole one if he gets the chance). If you want to serve this dish in the authentic Chinese style, chop the duck into pieces with a cleaver, bones and all, and arrange on a platter.

---

menu

Appetizer:	*Sesame Pork Appetizers*
Entrée:	*Chinese Mahogany Mallard*
Sides:	*Steamed Rice; Chinese Broccoli (Rapini)*
Dessert:	*Chilled Cream of Coconut Soup*

Sesame Pork Appetizers

2 pounds pork tenderloin
½ cup rice wine or dry sherry
½ cup soy sauce
½ cup water
1 tablespoon hoisin sauce
½ teaspoon garlic powder
pinch crushed red pepper flakes
½ cup honey
½ cup white sesame seeds

Dipping Sauce
1 tablespoon sesame oil
⅓ cup soy sauce
1 tablespoon rice wine or dry sherry
1 clove garlic, crushed
½ teaspoon grated fresh ginger
1 green onion, finely chopped

Place pork in a large zipper-style plastic bag. Add rice wine, soy sauce, water, hoisin sauce, garlic powder, and crushed red pepper flakes, and turn pork to evenly coat. Let meat marinate in the refrigerator for 1 to 2 hours, turning it in the bag several times. Remove pork from marinade. Pour honey on one paper plate, sesame seeds on another. Roll meat in honey and then in sesame seeds. Place pork on a roasting rack in a roasting pan. Bake at 350 degrees for 30 to 45 minutes, or until a meat thermometer reads 155 degrees. Let stand 10 minutes. Slice pork thinly on the diagonal. Arrange in a spiral on a bed of shredded Chinese or green cabbage. Serve at room temperature with dipping sauce (made by mixing together the ingredients listed above).

Chinese Mahogany Mallard

2 4-pound oven-ready mallard ducks
3 teaspoons salt

Basting Sauce
1 cup dark soy sauce
2 teaspoons sesame oil
¼ cup dark corn syrup
¼ cup rice wine or dry sherry
2 tablespoons oil
1 teaspoon garlic powder
2 tablespoons hoisin sauce
2 teaspoons Chinese five-spice powder
2 star anises
1 teaspoon crushed red peppercorns

Clean the ducks well. Remove the wing tips and the lumps of fat from inside the vent. Blanch in a pot of boiling water for a few minutes, remove, and dry well. Rub the ducks with salt inside and out, and refrigerate overnight.

For the basting sauce: Heat all the ingredients, bring to a boil, and blend well. Set aside. When the ducks are ready, brush basting sauce all over them; give them several coatings. Then let them dry, uncovered, in a cool and airy place, such as the refrigerator, for at least 4 to 5 hours.

To cook: Preheat oven to 400 degrees. Arrange oven racks so the ducks will fit on the top rack of the oven. To catch drips and prevent smoking, place a large tray or shallow pan with 1 inch of water on the bottom rack of the oven under the ducks. Roast the ducks for 30 minutes. Baste again and reduce oven to 350 degrees. Roast for another 60 minutes or until done, basting with the remaining sauce every 20 minutes.

To serve: Let the ducks cool down a little, and chop them into bite-size pieces. Serve hot or cold with steamed white rice (recipe follows). Reboil the extra basting liquid and serve as a sauce or dip.

Steamed Rice

2 cups white rice, rinsed well
3 cups water
1 teaspoon salt

Rinse long-grain rice under running water until the water runs clear. Using a ratio of 1 cup rice to 1 ½ cups water, plan your serving amounts. Here, I'm using 2 cups of rice to 3 cups of water, which will make about 4 cups of cooked rice. If you add extra water, the rice will boil, absorb too much, and become mushy. Bring salted water to a boil, add rice, stir, and cover tightly. Reduce heat to the lowest setting; you may have to slide the pan partway off the burner if it's simmering too hard. Cook until you can just hear the pan crackle. This means that the water is gone and the rice is done. Listen carefully, or you may scorch the rice.

Chinese Broccoli (Rapini)

Chinese broccoli (also called broccoli rabe or rapini) is a pungent and, some say, bitter green. It is very popular in Chinese cuisine and is delicious if cooked tender-crisp. Add more garlic if you like.

1 pound Chinese broccoli
2 to 3 tablespoons olive oil
1 clove garlic, minced
1 tablespoon soy sauce

Cut the dry ends from the bottom of the stalks. Cut greens into 2-inch pieces. Blanch for 1 minute in boiling salted water and drain well. Plunge immediately into ice water to stop cooking, and drain well. Meanwhile, heat olive oil in the bottom of a skillet and slowly cook the garlic until soft. Add rapini and soy sauce and toss to coat evenly. Serve immediately.

Chilled Cream of Coconut Soup

The duck is the star of the menu, but watch out for this dessert. This delicious concoction is a sweet finish to any meal.

1 ½ cups crème fraîche or sour cream
2 tablespoons lemon juice
1 teaspoon vanilla extract
1 tablespoon honey
½ cup Coco Lopez
11-ounce can unsweetened coconut juice
    or coconut water
13.5-ounce can coconut milk
1 cup cream of coconut
1 ½ cups heavy cream
sweetened flaked coconut, toasted; and mandarin
    orange segments for garnish

In a large bowl, mix crème fraîche or sour cream with lemon juice, vanilla, and honey (add more to taste). Whisk until smooth. Next add Coco Lopez, coconut juice, coconut milk, and cream of coconut. Stir well. Slowly add heavy cream, and stir gently (stirring too much will make the soup too thick). Add more cream of coconut or cream to taste. Chill thoroughly. Serve garnished with coconut flakes and orange segments.

Christmas Goose

Bring back an old English tradition—the Christmas goose. This is a great way to celebrate the holiday, especially if you've bagged a Canada goose.

menu

Appetizer:	*Shrimp Salad in Boston Lettuce Cups*
Entrée:	*Festive Roast Goose with Cranberry Apricot Stuffing and Giblet Gravy*
Sides:	*Mashed Potatoes; Brussels Sprouts with Balsamic Vinegar; Sweet Potato Bake*
Dessert:	*Berry Trifle*

Shrimp Salad in Boston Lettuce Cups

This dish is an appetizer and a salad course all in one.

> **1 head Boston lettuce per person**
> **4 to 6 cocktail shrimp per person, cooked, peeled, and deveined**
> **lemon wedges**

Cocktail Sauce
> **1 cup chili sauce or ketchup**
> **2 tablespoons prepared horseradish (or more to taste)**
> **5 or 6 drops Tabasco sauce**
> **juice of ½ lemon**

Vinaigrette Dressing
> **½ cup olive oil**
> **¼ cup white wine vinegar**
> **1 teaspoon Dijon mustard**
> **2 tablespoons water**
> **1 clove garlic, finely minced**
> **1 shallot, finely minced**

For the cocktail sauce: Mix all ingredients, and adjust heat to taste. For the dressing: Mix or shake all the ingredients together. For the salad: Scoop out the center of each head of lettuce, chop coarsely, and toss with half the dressing. Fill each lettuce bowl with dressed lettuce strips; top with shrimp. Ladle cocktail sauce on top. Serve on a salad plate with lemon wedges. Pass additional dressing and cocktail sauce on the side.

Festive Roast Goose with Cranberry Apricot Stuffing and Giblet Gravy

1 Canada goose
1 lemon, cut in half
salt and pepper

Stuffing
1 cup dried cranberries
1 cup dried apricots, cut into small pieces
1 cup port wine, heated
1 stick butter, melted
1 pound bulk pork sausage (or links with the casing
    removed)
1 large onion, diced
2 ribs celery, sliced
1-pound bag seasoned stuffing cubes
½ cup coarsely chopped walnuts
1 to 2 cups chicken stock
½ to 1 teaspoon Bell's seasoning or ground sage
    to taste
salt and pepper

For the stuffing: Soak the dried fruits in hot port wine while preparing the remaining stuffing ingredients. Melt butter in a large skillet. Crumble sausage meat, and sauté until no pink shows. Add onion and celery and cook until they begin to soften. In a large bowl, mix stuffing cubes, sausage mixture, drained soaked cranberries and apricots, and walnuts. Pour chicken stock over the stuffing, using enough liquid to make moist but not mushy cubes. Add more stock or water if needed. Mix thoroughly and add seasonings to taste.

For the goose: Preheat oven to 400 degrees, and position the rack in the center of the oven. Carefully wash and dry the outside and inside of the goose. Rub the cavity with lemon and salt and pepper. Fill the cavity and neck area with stuffing, but don't pack it too tightly. (Leftover stuffing can be baked in a covered dish during the last hour of roasting. Baste it once or twice with chicken stock to keep it moist.) Tie the goose's legs together, and close the opening with string and skewers to keep the stuffing inside. Place the goose, breast side up, on a rack set in a large roasting pan. Rub the skin with salt. Pierce the skin (not meat) with a fork to allow fat to escape and self-baste while roasting. Roast for 20 minutes. Then cover the breast with greased foil, reduce heat to 350 degrees, and cook for about 2 ½ hours, or until the juices run clear when a skewer is inserted into the thickest part of the thigh (185 degrees, if you're using a meat thermometer). To make the skin really crispy, remove the foil for the last 20 minutes. It isn't necessary to baste the goose, but if the fat drippings cause smoking, add some water to the bottom of the roasting pan.

For the giblet gravy: Simmer the giblets and neck bone in 4 cups water for 1 ½ hours; then strain and season the stock with salt and pepper. (You can also cook the heart or liver, grind it up, and add it to your gravy.) Set aside. Once the goose is fully cooked, remove it from the roasting pan and let it rest for 15 minutes before carving, while you finish the gravy. Pour off most of the fat from the roasting pan and add 2 to 3 tablespoons flour, making a roux. Cook over medium heat, stirring and scraping all the dark bits from the pan into the sauce. Gradually add giblet stock, stirring as it thickens. Let it boil for a minute or two, then season to taste. Serve roast goose with stuffing and gravy.

Mashed Potatoes

There are a lot of decisions to make regarding mashed potatoes. Which type of potato—waxy or mealy? Which method of mashing—hand masher or electric mixer? What additions? It all depends on the personal preferences of the cook. In general, however, waxy potatoes hold up better when cooked, absorb less water, and, some say, have more flavor. Yukon Gold is one type of waxy potato, whereas russets are drier and mealier. For mashing, you can get out the old hand masher and pound away until you achieve the perfect texture, but if you like a light, fluffy potato, an electric mixer is your best bet. If you demand lump-free spuds, use a ricer for an extremely smooth consistency. As for additions, you can choose cream, butter, onions, other vegetables, or cheese—the sky's the limit. The one thing that's always the same is the cooking: peel, quarter, and cook your potatoes in cold salted water until tender. Drain and return to the pan on low heat for several minutes to dry any excess water; then mash as you like.

4 to 5 pounds Yukon Gold potatoes
1 ½ cups milk or cream
½ stick butter
1 teaspoon salt
½ teaspoon pepper

Peel, quarter, and rinse the potatoes. Place in a large pot of cold, salted water and boil until tender. The time depends on how many potatoes, but figure on 20 to 30 minutes. Drain and return to the pan over low heat for several minutes to remove excess moisture. Add milk or cream, butter, and seasoning. Mash to desired consistency. Remove to a serving dish, make a well in the center of the mound, and add a dollop of butter. Sprinkle with chives or paprika if desired.

Brussels Sprouts with Balsamic Vinegar

I had a sprout hater in my family, but I reformed him with this recipe. Fresh sprouts and careful cooking, along with the right seasoning, may make a few converts in your family too.

1 ½ pounds fresh brussels sprouts
1 shallot, minced
2 cloves garlic, minced
2 tablespoons olive oil
¼ cup balsamic vinegar
2 tablespoons butter
salt and pepper
orange zest for garnish

Clean spouts, removing any discolored outer leaves, and trim ends. Parboil for 3 minutes in salted water; drain and stop the cooking process by plunging them in an ice-water bath. Meanwhile, in a large skillet, sauté the shallot and garlic in olive oil until soft but not brown. Add the balsamic vinegar and butter, and return the brussels sprouts to the pan. Continue cooking until they are just cooked through—firm, not mushy. Don't overcook. Add salt and pepper to taste. Remove to a serving dish and garnish with orange zest if desired.

Sweet Potato Bake

6 to 8 sweet potatoes (depending on size),
    precooked
1 cup cranberry sauce, jellied or whole berry
¾ cup orange juice
⅓ cup brown sugar
½ teaspoon grated orange rind
1 cup chopped fresh cranberries
½ teaspoon cinnamon
¼ teaspoon nutmeg
2 tablespoons butter
ground walnuts or almonds (optional)

Preheat oven to 350 degrees. Precook sweet potatoes in boiling water or in the oven. Peel and cut into thick slices, and arrange in a casserole dish. Melt cranberry sauce with orange juice, brown sugar, orange rind, fresh cranberries, spices, and butter. Pour over the top of the sweet potatoes, and sprinkle with ground walnuts or almonds. Bake until hot, bubbly, and golden on top. Cover if they brown too quickly.

Berry Trifle

Trifle is a decadent Victorian dessert. Besides being a delicious end to a meal, it also makes a great presentation when layered in a deep bowl with clear sides. The good news is that if you use a store-bought sponge cake, yellow cake mix, or store-bought ladyfingers, you can simplify the process and assemble this luscious treat in advance, allowing time for the flavors to blend. You can also substitute prepared whipped topping instead of whipping the cream yourself. I've included the from-scratch recipes, but by all means, feel free to take advantage of the shortcuts—I often do.

Cake Layer
    1 stick butter
    ½ cup sugar
    2 eggs
    1¾ cups flour
    ½ teaspoon baking powder
    ½ teaspoon salt
    1 small jar seedless raspberry or strawberry jam
    ½ cup sherry (optional)

Cream Layer
> 2 cups heavy cream
> ¼ cup sugar
> 1 teaspoon vanilla extract
> 4.6-ounce package vanilla pudding (not instant)

Fruit Layer
> 1 small can sliced peaches
> 1 pint fresh strawberries, sliced
> 1 pint fresh blueberries

For the cake: Preheat oven to 350 degrees. Grease and flour an 8- by 8-inch cake pan. In a mixing bowl, cream together butter and sugar. Beat in eggs one at a time until mixture is light and fluffy. Combine dry ingredients in a separate bowl. Fold dry ingredients into butter mixture. Pour into pan. Bake 20 to 25 minutes until cake springs back when touched lightly in center, or toothpick comes out clean. Cool for 5 minutes; then remove from pan and continue cooling on a wire rack. When cool, spread cake with jam and cut into 1-inch cubes. Set aside.

For the cream: In a large mixing bowl, beat cream until soft peaks form. Add sugar and vanilla and continue to beat until stiff peaks form. Set aside. Prepare vanilla pudding according to the package directions. Set aside.

To assemble: Line the bottom of a trifle bowl or glass bowl with cake squares. If using sherry, sprinkle half of it on top of the cake. Layer half of the fruit over the cake. Cover with half of the pudding and the whipped cream. Repeat layers, ending with whipped cream. Chill in the refrigerator at least 30 minutes. Trifle can be prepared the day before, which allows the flavors to blend.

Golden Goose

This goose dinner is enhanced by a fruited stuffing of wild rice. Nothing quite compares with a roasted golden goose; it is quite a treasure and a festive way to celebrate an important occasion.

menu

Appetizer:	*Mushroom Ring*
Salad:	*Tossed Green Salad with Creamy French Dressing*
Entrée:	*Roast Canada Goose with Wild Rice Stuffing*
Side:	*Vegetables Julienne*
Dessert:	*Pear Tart*

Mushroom Ring

This scrumptious, savory pastry makes a great starter. It can be made ahead and baked just before serving. It says, "You're special!" to family and friends alike.

Pastry
¾ cup water
6 tablespoons butter
½ cup flour
½ teaspoon salt
3 eggs, beaten
¾ cup shredded or diced Gruyère or Gouda cheese
(or Swiss if others are not available)

Filling

> 1 small onion, sliced vertically
>
> 8 ounces sliced white mushrooms or baby portobellos
>
> 3 tablespoons butter
>
> 2 tablespoons flour
>
> 1 ¼ cups milk
>
> 2 tablespoons Marsala wine
>
> salt and pepper
>
> 2 tablespoons chopped fresh parsley

Preheat oven to 400 degrees. Butter a 9- or 10-inch glass pie plate.

For the pastry: Heat the water and butter in a saucepan until the butter is just melted. Do not boil. Mix the flour and salt together; add all at once to the saucepan. With a heavy wooden spoon, beat the mixture quickly until the lumps become smooth and the mixture pulls away from the sides of the pan. Cool for 15 minutes. Add the eggs a little at a time, beating well after each addition. You want a dough with a stiff but droppable consistency. Stir in the cheese. Drop spoonfuls of the mixture along the outside edge of the pie plate only, forming a ring around the center. Use a spoon to fill in the gaps and smooth it out. Set aside.

For the filling: Sauté the onion and mushrooms in butter for about 4 or 5 minutes. Stir in the flour and mix well. Cook until thickened. Gradually stir in the milk and Marsala, and continue to heat until thick and bubbling. Season with salt and pepper, mix in the parsley, and pour the filling into the center of the pastry. Bake for 35 to 40 minutes until the pastry puffs and is a golden brown. Serve hot.

Tossed Green Salad with Creamy French Dressing

> 8 cup fresh washed salad greens, torn into bite-size pieces
>
> 1 small red onion, thinly sliced crosswise
>
> 2 tomatoes, cut into eighths
>
> ½ cucumber, sliced

Dressing
> ¼ cup cider vinegar
> 2 tablespoons sugar
> ¼ teaspoon onion powder or 1 teaspoon dried onion
>   flakes
> ¼ teaspoon garlic powder
> ½ teaspoon brown mustard
> ½ teaspoon paprika
> dash cayenne pepper
> ½ to ¾ cup ketchup
> ½ cup vegetable oil
> salt and pepper

For the dressing: Blend all ingredients in a tightly covered jar, or whirl them in a blender. Refrigerate for 15 minutes to let flavors develop. For the salad: Toss vegetables in a large salad bowl, drizzle with dressing, and toss again to coat.

Roast Canada Goose with Wild Rice Stuffing

> 1 dressed goose
> salt and pepper
> 2 cups chicken stock (sufficient to cook giblets
>   and neck)

Stuffing
> 1 cup wild rice
> 3 cups hot water
> 1 teaspoon salt
> 1 stick plus 1 tablespoon butter
> 2 large onions, chopped
> 1 cup chopped celery
> ¼ cup chopped pitted prunes
> 2 Granny Smith apples, peeled, cored, and chopped
> 1 teaspoon ground sage or Bell's seasoning
> salt and pepper

Remove the neck and wing tips from the goose, as well as any extra skin covering the neck opening (keep just enough neck skin to fold over the stuffing). Add the giblets (if available), skin, wing tips, and neck to a saucepan with chicken stock, and simmer gently until the meat falls from the bones.

Strain, refrigerate, and reserve this stock to add to pan drippings to make gravy. Wash the goose inside and out, dry with paper towels, and salt and pepper the cavity. Set aside.

For the stuffing: Put the wild rice, water, and salt in a saucepan, and bring to a boil. Lower the heat, cover, and let simmer for 10 minutes. Drain the rice, rinse, and continue to boil in fresh salted water for another 20 minutes. When the rice is soft and plumped, drain, rinse (if needed), add 1 tablespoon butter, mix, and set aside. Melt the remaining butter in a skillet, and cook the onions and celery until soft. Add the fruit and rice to the pan and mix together. Adjust sage, salt, and pepper to taste. Stuff the front of the goose, fold skin over, and secure with poultry pins or toothpicks. Stuff the body cavity, and sew up the opening or skewer it closed.

To cook: Place the bird on a rack in a large roasting pan. Rub salt and pepper into the skin. Bake in a 425-degree oven for 30 minutes. Lower heat to 350 degrees and continue cooking until a leg pulls away from the body easily, about 20 to 25 minutes per pound. Check the internal temperature with a meat thermometer to avoid under- or overcooking. The temperature should be at least 165 degrees in the innermost part of the thigh or the thickest part of the breast (personal preferences may demand cooking to a higher degree of doneness). Baste occasionally during roasting. When fully cooked, remove to a platter and cover with foil. Let stand 20 minutes before carving.

To make gravy: Skim fat from the reserved stock and pan juices. Combine both in a saucepan and heat. Melt 3 tablespoons butter in a small pan and stir in 3 tablespoons flour. Make a roux by cooking until a thick paste has formed, stirring constantly. Whisk the roux into the warmed stock, and cook stirring constantly until boiling and thickened. Serve the gravy with the stuffing and sliced goose.

Vegetables Julienne

This dish is a fresh vegetable medley that looks as good as it tastes.

> ¼ **pound asparagus spears, green beans, snow pea pods, or cauliflower or broccoli crowns**
> 1 **small yellow squash or zucchini**
> 1 **carrot**
> 1 **sweet red pepper**
> **juice of 1 lemon**
> **butter**
> **dill leaves for garnish**

Choose a selection of vegetables from the preceding list, using some or all, and adjusting amounts based on the number selected. Julienne the vegetables, keeping them as close to the size of the asparagus spears as possible. Steam over salted boiling water to which lemon juice has been added. When crisp-tender, remove to a serving bowl, add a dollop of butter and a sprinkle of fresh lemon juice, and garnish with fresh dill leaves. Leftovers can be tossed with olive oil, vinegar, and a dash of garlic powder; refrigerated; and served cold the next day.

Pear Tart

Shell
> **2 cups flour**
> **1 stick butter**
> **3 tablespoons water**

Filling
> **½ cup flour**
> **1 teaspoon baking powder**
> **1 cup ground almonds**
> **1 teaspoon vanilla extract**
> **¼ cup sugar**
> **½ stick butter, softened**
> **2 eggs, beaten**
> **3 tablespoons raspberry jam**
> **1 large can pear halves in natural juice**

For the shell: Blend flour and butter with a pastry cutter or your fingers until it resembles fine crumbs. Add enough water to form a firm dough. Roll out the pastry and line a 10-inch tart pan with it. Press dough firmly to the bottom, and trim the top edge. Press dough on the sides so that it sits above the rim of the pan all around. Prick the base, line with waxed paper, and fill with dried beans or pie weights. Chill for 30 to 40 minutes. Bake in a preheated 400-degree oven for 15 minutes. Remove beans and waxed paper and bake for an additional 5 minutes. Reduce oven temperature to 350 degrees.

For the filling: Mix the flour, baking powder, ground almonds, vanilla, sugar, butter, and eggs together. If the mixture appears too thick, thin with a little pear juice. Spread the pastry bottom with jam. Spoon the filling into the crust. Drain pears well, and arrange cut side down in the filling. Bake for 30 minutes, until the filling has risen and is firm to the touch and golden brown. Serve warm with cream or ice cream or at room temperature.

Braised Sandhill Crane Breasts with Mushrooms in White Wine

Sandhill cranes are very large birds. They can be as tall as a man and have a wingspan around 7 feet. That's quite a bird. Their meat is dark, like a turkey's dark meat, and they are called the "rib eye of the sky."

menu

Appetizer: Cock-a-Leekie Soup

Salad: Cabbage-Apple Slaw with Raisins

Entrée: Braised Sandhill Crane Breasts with Mushrooms in White Wine

Sides: Stuffed Baked Potatoes with Caramelized Onions; Deep-Fried Cauliflower Nuggets with Mustard Sauce

Dessert: Lemon Berry Coffee Cake

Cock-a-Leekie Soup

This delicious soup flavored with barley is a great way to use the haunches and other tougher sections of wild fowl.

> **1 goose, duck, or other wild fowl, or 4 to 6 leg**
> **quarters from the fowl of your choice**
> **2 tablespoons oil**
> **10 cups water**
> **½ cup pearl barley**
> **2 cups chicken broth**
> **6 leeks, sliced**
> **2 stalks celery with leaves, thickly sliced**
> **2 carrots, thinly sliced**
> **1 sprig fresh thyme, chopped**
> **1 tablespoon chopped fresh parsley**
> **1 teaspoon salt**
> **1 teaspoon ground black pepper**

In a large stockpot over high heat, brown the skin of the birds in oil. Add the water and barley. Bring to a boil, reduce heat to low, and simmer for 1 hour. Remove the bird, discard the bones and skin, chop the meat into bite-size pieces, and return to the soup pot. Add the chicken broth, leeks, celery, carrots, thyme, parsley, salt, and pepper. Simmer for 30 more minutes, or until all vegetables are tender.

Cabbage-Apple Slaw with Raisins

> **⅓ cup cider vinegar**
> **¼ cup packed brown sugar**
> **1 tablespoon peanut oil**
> **¼ cup mayonnaise**
> **½ teaspoon salt**
> **¼ teaspoon pepper**
> **½ teaspoon poppy seeds**
> **2 cups coarsely chopped Granny Smith apples**
> **½ cup golden raisins**
> **¼ cup unsalted peanuts**
> **1-pound package cabbage and carrot coleslaw mix;**
> **or 1 small head cabbage, finely shredded**

Mix the first seven ingredients to make the dressing. Whisk until the sugar is dissolved. Taste and add a bit more mayonnaise if it's too sour. In a large mixing bowl, toss apples, raisins, peanuts, and coleslaw mix together. Pour dressing over all. Mix well. Chill for at least 1 hour.

Braised Sandhill Crane Breasts with Mushrooms in White Wine

breast meat from 1 sandhill crane
½ stick butter
salt and pepper
3 cloves garlic, minced
salt and pepper
1 750 ml. bottle white wine
3–4 whole cloves
pinch red pepper
1 onion, sliced
8 ounces fresh mushrooms, sliced
1 cup heavy cream
1 tablespoon minced parsley

Rub the crane with butter. Place it in a casserole or oven roasting bag. Sprinkle with garlic and a pinch of salt and pepper. Add the white wine, cloves, red pepper, onion, and mushrooms. Bake securely covered in the casserole or in the roasting bag at 325 degrees for 1 to 1 ½ hours, depending on thickness, until the breasts are cooked to the desired degree of doneness. Some prefer it rare like the "rib eye." Do not overcook. Remove the crane breasts to a serving platter; tent with foil to keep warm. Pour pan drippings and juices into a small saucepan, and skim off the fat. Add the cream and parsley to the saucepan. Cook at medium heat until slightly thickened. Serve over slices of the breast meat.

Stuffed Baked Potatoes with Caramelized Onions

4 medium baking potatoes
2 tablespoons butter, divided
½ cup shredded Gruyère cheese, divided
4 tablespoons sour cream
salt and pepper
2 cups vertically sliced red or sweet white onions
(e.g., Vidalia)
1 tablespoon sugar
2 tablespoons sherry
1 tablespoon Worcestershire sauce
¼ teaspoon thyme

Pierce potatoes with a fork and bake in a microwave or conventional oven until tender. Remove the top third from each potato and scoop out the white pulp; discard the skin or reserve for another use. Scoop the pulp from the remaining potato, leaving a shell about ¼ inch thick. Mash the potato pulp with a fork or masher, and mix with 1 tablespoon butter, ¼ cup cheese, sour cream, salt, and pepper. Spoon filling mixture back into potato shells, mounding slightly.

Meanwhile, melt the remaining tablespoon of butter in a skillet over medium-high heat. Add onions and sauté until softened, 4 to 5 minutes. Stir in sugar and continue to cook until browned. Stir in sherry, Worcestershire sauce, and thyme and cook for several minutes more, until liquid has evaporated. Top each potato with one-fourth of the onion mixture, and top with the remaining cheese. Place the potatoes in the oven at 350 degrees until heated through and cheese is melted.

Deep-Fried Cauliflower Nuggets with Mustard Sauce

Although I love cauliflower any way you can think of—from raw to pickled to steamed—deep-fried is my favorite. Other vegetables such as onion rings, batons of eggplant, or mushrooms can be prepared the same way for a fantastic appetizer.

1 head cauliflower
2 eggs beaten with ¼ cup milk
2 cups (or more) flavored bread crumbs
oil for deep-frying

Creamy Mustard Dipping Sauce
>   ½ **cup mayonnaise or sour cream**
>   **3 tablespoons Dijon-style or spicy brown mustard**
>   **1 tablespoon lemon juice**
>   ¼ **teaspoon seasoned salt**
>   **black pepper (for more zip, use cayenne pepper)**

Break cauliflower into similar-sized florets. Blanch for 2 minutes in boiling salted water. Plunge in cold water to stop cooking, and drain well. Dip cauliflower pieces in egg mixture, then shake with bread crumbs in a paper or plastic bag. Set on a cookie sheet and let dry. When you're finished with all the florets, repeat the process, giving each piece a double coating of crumbs. This can be done in advance and the nuggets refrigerated until cooking time.

Heat oil to 350 degrees in a deep-fryer or a deep, heavy saucepan. Fry cauliflower in batches until golden brown, about 3 to 4 minutes. Cauliflower should remain firm, not mushy. Drain on paper towels and keep warm in a 250- to 300-degree oven until ready for service. Or you can fry the cauliflower in advance, drain, and reheat in a 375-degree oven.

For the sauce: Whisk mayonnaise and mustard together with the lemon juice. Add seasoned salt, and adjust seasonings to your liking.

Lemon Berry Coffee Cake

⅓ **cup vegetable oil**
1 cup sugar
4 large eggs
¼ **cup water**
2 teaspoons lemon extract
1 teaspoon grated lemon peel
2 ½ **cups flour**
2 teaspoons baking powder
1 cup lemon yogurt or sour cream
1 cup fresh blueberries or very well drained frozen
      berries

Preheat oven to 350 degrees. Grease and flour a 9-inch Bundt pan. In a mixing bowl, beat oil and sugar until creamy; add eggs, water, extract, and lemon peel and mix well. In another bowl, stir flour and baking powder together and add alternately to the sugar mixture with the yogurt or sour cream. Do not overmix. Gently fold in berries. Pour into prepared pan and bake 30 to 35 minutes until a toothpick inserted in the center comes out clean. Cool for 10 minutes; then invert the pan on a cake rack and continue to cool.

Slow-Simmered Snow Goose

A snow goose is a very lean bird, and since the feathers are such a trial to remove, it is usually easier to skin it than to pluck it. This means that a snow goose lends itself to braising or being cooked in a sauce to add moisture to the dry meat. Here, the breasts are used for a variation on the classic coq au vin.

menu

Appetizer: *Spinach Orange Salad*

Entrée: *Snow Goose with Wine*

Sides: *Popovers; Roasted Cauliflower with Parmesan Cheese*

Dessert: *Pecan Pie*

Spinach Orange Salad

4 to 6 cups torn fresh spinach
2 navel oranges, peeled and cut into sections
½ cup sliced fresh mushrooms
¼ cup sliced almonds

Dressing
4 tablespoons salad oil
2 tablespoons lemon juice
2 tablespoons honey
¼ teaspoon poppy seeds

Place spinach in a large salad bowl. Add orange sections and mushrooms; toss lightly. Sprinkle with almonds. Mix all dressing ingredients in a screw-top jar. Shake well and pour over salad. Serve.

Snow Goose with Wine

4 slices bacon, cut into eighths
2 whole snow goose breasts (about 2 pounds),
   boned, skinned, and cut into large chunks
1 tablespoon flour
2 cups red wine
2 tablespoons tomato paste
2 cloves garlic, crushed
1 bay leaf
1 teaspoon thyme
1 cup small pearl onions, peeled
1 pound small white button mushrooms
salt and pepper

Fry the bacon in a large Dutch oven on medium-high heat; remove and drain on paper towels. Lightly brown the goose chunks in the bacon drippings. Remove the goose and drain on paper towels. Stir in flour and cook over medium heat for 2 minutes. Stir in the wine, tomato paste, garlic, bay leaf, thyme, onions, and mushrooms. Bring the mixture to a boil, add goose meat, and simmer for 20 to 30 minutes or until goose meat is tender. Season with salt and pepper to taste. Just before serving, stir in reserved bacon pieces. Serve over split popovers (recipe follows) or buttered noodles.

Popovers

Popovers are light and crunchy with a hollow center. They add flair to any meal when served dripping with butter, but they really shine when split and filled with this hearty stew. Use jumbo-sized muffin pans to make them large enough for a dinner serving.

3 tablespoons butter, divided
4 eggs
1 cup flour
1 cup milk

Preheat oven to 400 degrees. Use 1 tablespoon butter to grease 6 large or 12 regular-sized muffin cups. Melt the remaining butter. In a blender, mix the melted butter, eggs, flour, and milk until smooth, about 30 seconds. Scrape down the sides of the blender if necessary. Pour the batter into the prepared muffin cups, filling half full. Bake 30 to 40 minutes, until risen, browned, and firm. Remove from the oven and prick each popover with a sharp knife or a fork to let steam escape. To hold the popovers for serving, prick them and then return to the oven for 5 minutes, until heated through. Popovers must be served hot!

Roasted Cauliflower with Parmesan Cheese

1 head cauliflower, broken into florets
2 to 3 cloves garlic, peeled and coarsely minced
1 lemon
olive oil
salt and pepper
Parmesan cheese

Preheat oven to 400 degrees. Place cauliflower in a single layer in an oven-proof baking dish or on a baking sheet. Sprinkle with garlic. Squeeze the juice of a lemon over the cauliflower, and drizzle each piece with olive oil. Season with salt and pepper. Place cauliflower in the hot oven, uncovered, for 15 to 25 minutes, until the top is lightly browned. Test with a fork for desired doneness. Remove and sprinkle with Parmesan cheese.

Pecan Pie

1 unbaked pie shell

Filling
3 eggs
¾ cup sugar
1 teaspoon vanilla extract
2 tablespoons butter, melted
1 cup corn syrup
1 ½ cups pecan halves

Preheat oven to 375 degrees. In a mixing bowl, beat the eggs, sugar, and vanilla together. Mix in the butter and corn syrup. Stir in pecans. Pour into the pie shell and bake for 40 to 45 minutes, until a knife inserted in the center comes out clean. Cover edges of the crust with foil if it browns too quickly. Chill. Serve with a spoonful of whipped cream.

Roasted Savory Specklebelly Goose

Because the specklebelly goose has more fat than other geese, it is a great candidate for roasting. Specklebellies have light breast meat and dark thigh and leg meat, similar to the meat on a chicken, but with a more robust flavor. It has a milder flavor than duck, however, so it can be a nice way to initiate newcomers to the pleasures of dining on wild waterfowl.

menu

Appetizer: *Lobster Bisque*

Entrée: *Roasted Savory Specklebelly Goose*

Sides: *Risotto with Butternut Squash and Pancetta;*
                  Red Cabbage and Cranberries

Dessert: *Irish Cream Pie*

Lobster Bisque

1- to 1½-pound lobster
4 stalks celery, chopped, divided
2 carrots, chopped, divided
1 large onion, chopped
1 stick butter, melted
½ cup flour
4 cups lobster stock
salt and pepper
Tabasco sauce, to taste
1 tablespoon Worcestershire sauce
2 tablespoons tomato paste
¼ cup sherry (optional)
1 bay leaf
1 pint whipping cream

Boil the lobster, half the celery, half the carrots, and all the onion until lobster is cooked through. Remove lobster and separate meat from shells; return shells and body cavity to stockpot. Simmer until vegetables are tender and stock has concentrated. Strain and reserve stock. Chop lobster meat into small pieces.

In a large, heavy pan, make a roux by stirring melted butter and flour over medium-high heat until light brown. Add lobster stock, the remaining carrot and celery, salt, pepper, Tabasco, Worcestershire sauce, tomato paste, sherry, and bay leaf. Simmer 30 minutes. Remove the bay leaf. Strain and puree the vegetables and return to the soup base Add lobster meat and heat thoroughly. Before serving, add cream. Heat but do not boil.

Roasted Savory Specklebelly Goose

1 specklebelly goose
salt and pepper
2 tablespoons butter, softened
1 cup apple juice
½ cup currant jelly, melted with ¼ cup apple juice

Stuffing
½ pound bulk sausage meat or ½ pound ground venison
1 stick butter
1 small onion, chopped finely
1 green pepper, diced
2 ribs celery, chopped
1 apple, peeled, cored, and chopped
¼ cup chopped walnuts
1 bag seasoned bread stuffing cubes
1 teaspoon ground sage or Bell's seasoning
½ teaspoon celery seed
1 to 2 cups warm chicken stock or hot water

For the stuffing: Brown sausage or venison in butter until no pink remains. Add onion, pepper, celery, and apple, and cook until pepper and celery have softened. In a large bowl, combine cooked mixture with stuffing cubes and nuts; add sage and celery seed. Mix well. Add enough warm chicken stock or water to moisten and soften the bread. Avoid making the stuffing too wet. Do not stuff the bird until you are ready to roast it. If you prepare the stuffing a day in advance, keep it refrigerated in a bowl, not in the bird.

For the specklebelly: Preheat oven to 350 degrees. Remove any visible signs of fat. Rinse the bird inside and out, and season with salt and pepper. Fill the cavity with stuffing mixture; pack lightly. Close the opening with a lacing kit or kitchen twine. Spread melted butter over the entire bird. Place the goose in a roasting pan; add apple juice. Roast for 1 ½ hours. Baste with the jelly mixture two or three times during the last 30 to 40 minutes of cooking. The bird is done when a leg moves freely from the joint, or check for doneness with a meat thermometer.

To make gravy: Remove the goose from the pan, pour off drippings, and separate fat. Return juices to the pan and add chicken stock, wine, or water to deglaze. Scrape off any browned bits and reduce liquid a bit. Thicken drippings with a roux made from 2 tablespoons flour cooked to a paste with 2 tablespoons butter. Mix into drippings, and cook until thick. Thin to desired consistency with chicken stock, boiling for 2 to 3 minutes. Serve gravy with goose and stuffing.

Risotto with Butternut Squash and Pancetta

1 tablespoon olive oil
2 ounces pancetta or bacon, coarsely chopped
1 cup peeled butternut squash, cut into ½-inch
    cubes
1 onion, chopped
2 cloves garlic, minced
2 shallots, minced
1 cup Arborio rice
½ cup dry white wine
2 cups (or more) simmering chicken stock
2 tablespoons butter
½ cup grated pecorino Romano cheese
    (or Parmesan)
2 tablespoons chopped flat-leaf parsley
1 tablespoon finely chopped fresh rosemary
    or 1 teaspoon dried
salt and pepper

In a large saucepan, heat olive oil over medium-high heat. Add pancetta and cook until golden brown. Remove pancetta and set aside. Add squash to the pan drippings and cook until soft. Reduce heat to medium and sauté onion, garlic, and shallots. Cook until softened. Return the pancetta to the pan and add rice, stirring constantly. Cook 5 minutes, making sure rice doesn't brown. Increase heat to medium-high and add wine, stirring constantly until absorbed. When the liquid has evaporated, begin adding stock ½ cup at a time (use a ladle), letting the stock absorb before adding more. After the fourth addition of stock, begin tasting the rice; it should be firm when done. You may or may not have to use all the stock, or you may need to add a bit more. When the risotto is done, remove from heat and stir in butter, cheese, parsley, and rosemary. Season with salt and pepper. Serve immediately.

Red Cabbage and Cranberries

2 cups cranberries
1 cup apple cider or juice
½ stick butter
1 cup firmly packed light brown sugar
8 cups red cabbage, shredded
2 apples, peeled, cored, and finely chopped
salt and pepper

In a large pot, cook cranberries in cider until they pop; add butter and sugar, and stir until sugar is dissolved. Add remaining ingredients and simmer gently until cabbage is cooked tender and apples are very soft—about 30 minutes. Add more apple cider or brown sugar if more liquid is needed. Serve warm or at room temperature.

Irish Cream Pie

24 chocolate sandwich cookies
½ stick butter, melted
1 quart chocolate ice cream
1 quart coffee ice cream
1 12-ounce jar hot fudge ice cream topping
2 cups heavy cream
2 tablespoons sugar
½ cup Irish cream liqueur, such as Baileys
    (omit for a nonalcohol version)

Preheat oven to 375 degrees. Crush cookies in the bowl of a food processor. Add melted butter and mix well. Press crumb mixture in the bottom and about 1 inch up the sides of a 9-inch springform pan. Bake for 5 minutes, until set. Let cool completely.

Remove the chocolate ice cream from the freezer and let it soften slightly. Spread over cooled crust and return to the freezer. Remove the coffee ice cream from the freezer and let it soften slightly. Spread the hot fudge sauce over the chocolate ice cream and return to the freezer until set. Spread the coffee ice cream over the fudge topping. Cover with plastic wrap and return pie to the freezer until hardened. Whip the cream, add sugar and Irish cream, and continue to whip until stiff. If you're celebrating St. Patrick's Day, you can add a drop or two of green food coloring. Spread the whipped cream mixture over the coffee layer. Freeze until ready to serve. Remove from freezer about 20 minutes before serving (if it's too warm in the kitchen, put the pie in the refrigerator to soften). Remove the sides of the pan and place the pie on a serving plate. Garnish with crushed cookie crumbs or chocolate shavings.

part 3

WILD FISH

Many anglers are able to fish close to home and do so as often as possible, as opposed to deer hunters, for example, who may enter the woods only one week each season. One might think that these fishing enthusiasts would have devised many ingenious and delicious ways to prepare and enjoy their catch, but unfortunately, that's not always the case. Their recipes are often no more creative than frying or baking the fish with a sprinkling of lemon juice and bread crumbs. So fish is one type of wild game that can definitely use a shot of the gourmet.

Fish flesh is delicately flavored, so when it comes to seasoning with herbs and spices, a lighter hand is required than when cooking red meat or fowl. Herbs such as tarragon and dill complement fish, as do citrus flavors. Cooking fish also requires a light hand. Fish can be cooked in a variety of ways, from the ever-popular batter-fried to steamed, poached, grilled, baked, or even microwaved. It can also be salted or smoked. Many recipes can be used for different kinds of fish. Fish should never be overcooked; it should flake easily when prodded with a fork. Sealing in a packet, oven bag, or lettuce leaves can help keep it moist. When grilling fish, the grill should be very clean, very hot, and oiled. Turn the fish just once, to avoid breaking.

Fish come in freshwater and saltwater varieties. They can also be divided by size (large or small) and by fat content (fat or lean). Large fish are generally considered those that weigh more than 2 pounds. "Fat" fish are moist and can usually be cooked without any additional oil or fat.

Brown trout, lake trout, carp, and salmon (depending on where they're taken) are large, fat freshwater fish; small, fat fish include brook and rainbow trout. Freshwater fish considered both large and lean are catfish, bass, northern pike, and walleye; yellow perch, bluegills, and bullheads are considered small, lean fish.

Large, fat saltwater varieties include shad, salmon, albacore, and kingfish; mackerel and pompano are small, fat species. Large, lean saltwater fish are bluefish, cod, grouper, halibut, haddock, sea bass, and striped bass. Fish in the small, lean category include flounder, mullet, ocean perch, porgy, smelt, and whiting.

Whether you plan on fly-fishing for a rainbow trout or surf-casting for a striped bass, bring your catch home and enjoy the fruits of your labor.

Batter-Fried Northern Pike Fillets with Chips

Northern pike are called the gangsters of freshwater. They are sought by anglers for their explosive hits and aerial acrobatics. They love to fight! Northern pike are some of the largest freshwater fish caught; although an average fish weighs approximately 3 to 4 pounds, they can tip the scales at 20. The fish is bony, but because of its large size, it can produce some fine white fillets. Dipping in batter and deep-frying seals in the moisture, as pike can dry out if grilled or overcooked.

menu

Appetizer:	*Cheddar Cheese Chowder*
Salad:	*Cucumber Salad*
Entrée:	*Batter-Fried Northern Pike Fillets with Chips*
Dessert:	*Fruit Salad with Creamy Poppy Seed Dressing*

Cheddar Cheese Chowder

Kids love this soup. You can turn it into cheeseburger chowder by replacing the ham with ½ pound browned ground beef or ground game meat of your choice.

> **2 cups cubed potatoes**
> **2 carrots, sliced**
> **2 ribs celery, sliced**
> **1 medium onion, chopped**
> **1 teaspoon salt**
> **¼ teaspoon ground white pepper**
> **½ stick butter**
> **¼ cup flour**
> **2 cups milk (or 1 cup milk and 1 cup light cream)**
> **2 cups sharp cheddar cheese, shredded or cut into**
> **small cubes**
> **1 cup ham cubes**

In a covered pan, simmer vegetables and seasonings in 2 cups cold water until tender. Do not drain. Set aside. In a medium-sized saucepan, melt butter, stir in flour, and cook and stir until a roux forms. Boil for 1 minute. Whisk in milk. Stir until thick and bubbly. Add cheese and stir until melted. Add ham and vegetables with their broth to the cream mixture. Heat gently until hot. Do not boil.

Cucumber Salad

> **2 English cucumbers, peeled and sliced**
> **1 bell pepper, cut into thin strips**
> **1 stalk celery, sliced**
> **1 small red onion, chopped**
> **½ to ¾ cup mayonnaise**
> **2 tablespoons vinegar**
> **¼ teaspoon paprika**
> **salt and pepper**

In a bowl, combine cucumber, pepper, celery, and onion. Mix remaining ingredients in a small bowl. Check for seasoning; the dressing should be tangy. Pour dressing over vegetables, and toss to coat.

Batter-Fried Northern Pike Fillets with Chips

**2 pounds northern pike fillets, cut into serving-size
   pieces
3 cups flour, divided
½ cup white cornmeal
1 egg
½ teaspoon baking powder
2 teaspoons salt
1 teaspoon pepper
12-ounce can beer or club soda
vegetable oil for frying**

Mix 2 cups flour, cornmeal, egg, baking powder, salt, and pepper. Stir in beer
or club soda until a medium batter is formed. Add water if the batter is too
thick. Place the remaining 1 cup flour on a plate; dredge fish fillets in flour,
dip in batter, and immediately fry in hot oil over medium heat. Cook for 2
or 3 minutes per side, or until golden brown and flaky. Keep fish warm in a
250-degree oven until all pieces are fried and the chips are done (recipe follows). Serve with tartar sauce and lemon wedges.

Chips

**6 medium potatoes
oil for deep-frying**

Peel potatoes, if desired, or wash well and dry. Cut potatoes into even strips or
batons. Rinse the starch from the potatoes; drain and dry on paper towels to
avoid splattering oil. Heat oil to 325 degrees in a deep-fryer or saucepan. Fry
potatoes until lightly golden, about 5 minutes. Turn heat up to 350 degrees
to finish cooking. Chips should be golden on the outside and soft on the
inside. Drain well on paper towels to absorb the excess oil, and season with
salt. Keep hot in the oven until ready to serve.

Fruit Salad with Creamy Poppy Seed Dressing

Nothing cleanses the palate like a fresh fruit salad. Add your own favorites
here, and top with this creamy light dressing.

6 peaches, peeled, pitted, and sliced
1 pound strawberries, rinsed, hulled, and sliced
½ pound seedless green grapes
½ pound seedless red grapes
3 bananas, peeled and sliced
½ cup sugar (or less, to taste)

Dressing
    juice of 1 lime
    ½ cup pineapple juice
    ¼ cup mayonnaise, sour cream, or yogurt
      (plain, lemon, or vanilla)
    ¼ teaspoon poppy seeds

Cut all fruits as directed and lightly toss in a large salad bowl with sugar. Mix together dressing ingredients. Drizzle fruit with dressing, and toss to coat. Serve well chilled.

Barbecued Northern Pike

The northern pike is a voracious predator and easy to catch, because it doesn't fear chomping down on a lure. If you've never tried barbecued fish, you're in for a taste sensation.

menu

Appetizer: *Strawberry Soup*

Salad: *Greek Salad with Pita Bread*

Entrée: *Barbecued Northern Pike*

Sides: *Packet Potatoes; Grilled Artichokes with Lemon Butter*

Dessert: *Fudge Brownies*

Strawberry Soup

This cold soup can be served in a frosty glass so that backyard picnickers can enjoy it while moving about rather than being seated for a more formal gathering. It's refreshing, easy to make, and a luscious way to enjoy these little red jewels.

1 quart fresh strawberries, cleaned and hulled
1 cup sour cream
1 cup half-and-half
¼ cup sugar
2 tablespoons white wine or orange juice
mint leaves

Slice several berries into fans and reserve for garnish. Puree the remaining strawberries in a blender or food processor. Add remaining ingredients and mix well. Chill several hours or overnight. Whirl in the blender or whisk just before serving. Garnish each serving with a strawberry fan and a mint leaf.

Greek Salad with Pita Bread

2 6-inch pita breads
olive oil
1 head romaine lettuce, cut into bite-size pieces
1 cucumber, peeled and sliced (remove seeds if
** they're woody)**
2 medium tomatoes, chopped
3 to 4 scallions, sliced crosswise
¼ cup Greek olives
4 ounces feta cheese

Dressing
⅓ cup extra virgin olive oil
¼ cup lemon juice
1 clove garlic, minced
1 teaspoon fresh oregano or ½ teaspoon dried

Preheat oven to 350 degrees. Split each pita bread in half to form 2 large circles, for a total of 4 pieces. Brush with a drizzle of olive oil and bake until crisp. Remove from the oven, let cool, and break into bite-size pieces. In a large bowl, place romaine, cucumber, tomatoes, scallions, and olives. Mix dressing ingredients together, pour over salad, and add pita pieces. Toss gently to mix. Garnish with crumbled feta cheese.

Barbecued Northern Pike

A dry, firm fish, northern pike isn't usually grilled, but the barbecue sauce in this recipe allows the fish to remain moist. It is butterflied and then cooked skin-side down, to protect the white flesh from drying out.

> **1 whole northern pike (about 4 pounds), cleaned,**
> **with head and tail removed**
> **salt and pepper**
> **oil**
> **fresh chives for garnish**
> **lemon slices for garnish**

Sauce
> **½ cup tomato sauce**
> **1 tablespoon fresh lemon juice**
> **1 tablespoon Worcestershire sauce**
> **1 tablespoon molasses**
> **½ teaspoon dry mustard**
> **2 tablespoons olive oil**
> **1 clove garlic, finely minced, or ¼ teaspoon garlic**
> **powder**
> **salt and pepper**

Spray grill rack with cooking spray or brush with oil. Prepare charcoal grill or preheat gas grill for medium direct heat. In a small mixing bowl, combine the sauce ingredients. Set aside.

To butterfly the fish, cut from the inside cavity along each side of the backbone to release the bone from the flesh; don't cut through the skin. Discard the backbone and press the fish to spread out both sides, so it lies flat. Trim and discard the belly meat. Remove the rib bones. Season fish with salt and pepper. Oil the skin side of the fish to prevent sticking. Place the pike skin-side down on the prepared grill rack. Grill covered for 5 minutes. Spread sauce evenly over fish. Grill, covered, for 6 to10 minutes, or until fish is firm and opaque and just begins to flake. Garnish with snipped fresh chives and lemon slices.

Packet Potatoes

You can cook these potato packets first, then lower the temperature and move them away from the hottest part of the grill to keep them warm while the fish is grilling.

> **4 medium potatoes (peeled if desired), cut into**
> **bite-size chunks**
> **1 small onion, sliced**
> **2 tablespoons olive or vegetable oil**
> **1 teaspoon seasoned salt**
> **¼ teaspoon pepper**

Preheat grill to medium-high heat or oven to 450 degrees. Cut 4 large sheets of heavy-duty aluminum foil. Center ¼ of the potato pieces and some onion slices in the center of each piece of foil. Drizzle with oil, and sprinkle with salt and pepper. Bring up sides of foil and double fold. Cook for 25 to 30 minutes in a covered grill or on cookie sheet in the oven until potatoes are tender.

Grilled Artichokes with Lemon Butter

As long as the grill is going, you might as well toss your vegetables on the fire too. These artichokes take a bit of work, but they are well worth the effort.

> **4 large artichokes**
> **¼ cup salt**
> **½ lemon**
> **1 cup olive oil**
> **⅓ cup balsamic vinegar**
> **1 tablespoon minced garlic**
> **1 tablespoon chopped flat-leaf parsley**
> **½ teaspoon salt**
> **¼ teaspoon freshly ground black pepper**

Lemon Butter
> **1 stick butter, melted**
> **1 teaspoon minced garlic**
> **juice of 2 lemons**

For the lemon butter: Sauté garlic in melted butter for 2 minutes over low heat, or until just beginning to soften. Add lemon juice and keep warm until serving time.

For the artichokes: Fill a large pot ¾ full with water. Add ¼ cup salt and bring to a boil. Trim the bottoms of the artichokes and remove the top third of each; trim the sharp thorn from each leaf tip. Rub the cut sides and bottoms of the artichokes with a lemon half, and carefully add them to the boiling water. Simmer, covered, until the bottoms are just tender and can be pierced with a sharp knife, and an outer leaf pulls away easily—about 15 minutes. Drain the artichokes upside down in a colander and cool. Cut each artichoke into quarters and remove the prickly purple leaves and hairy choke.

In a bowl, combine the olive oil, vinegar, garlic, parsley, salt, and pepper. Add the artichoke quarters and toss to coat. Let them marinate for 2 to 4 hours, turning occasionally.

Preheat the grill to medium-high. Remove the artichokes from the marinade and grill them, turning, until warmed through and lightly charred around the edges—about 5 minutes. Place on a platter and drizzle with lemon. Serve lemon butter on the side for dipping.

Fudge Brownies

Chewy fudge brownies make a great grab-and-go dessert, or they can be dressed up with frosting or ice cream and a topping. Any way you serve them, they're an all-time favorite.

½ **cup flour, sifted before measuring**
¼ **teaspoon baking powder**
¼ **teaspoon salt**
1 **stick butter, at room temperature**
1 **cup sugar**
2 **eggs**
2 **squares (2 ounces) unsweetened chocolate, melted**
1 **teaspoon vanilla extract**
1 **cup chopped walnuts or pecans**
½ **cup semisweet chocolate chips**

Preheat oven to 325 degrees. Grease and flour an 8-inch-square baking pan. Sift together flour, baking powder, and salt. Set aside. In a mixing bowl, beat butter, sugar, and eggs together until light and fluffy. Beat in melted chocolate and vanilla. Stir in flour mixture; fold in chopped nuts and chocolate chips. Spread batter in the prepared pan. Bake for 25 to 30 minutes, or until sides pull away from the pan and brownies are firm in the center. Let cool, and cut into squares with a plastic knife. Serve alone or with a scoop of ice cream.

Blackened Redfish

The Creole taste of Louisiana grabs you with this spicy and delicious black-ened redfish. It's quick and easy and great for the grill or campsite, but it's too smoky for indoor cooking unless you have a powerful exhaust fan.

menu

Appetizer:	*Cold Potato and Leek Soup*
Salad:	*Marinated Vegetables*
Entrée:	*Blackened Redfish*
Side:	*Potato Pancake*
Dessert:	*Strawberry Shortcake with Grandpa's Biscuits*

Cold Potato and Leek Soup

Leeks tend to hold sand between their leaves, so they need to be cleaned carefully. Cut off the root end and the heavy, tough green tops. Then cut through the green leaves down toward the root end, leaving about 1 inch uncut. Spread and fan the leaves under running water to remove any grit.

½ **stick butter**
6 **leeks, thinly sliced**
4 **ribs celery, thinly sliced**
4 **cups salted water**
6 **potatoes, peeled and diced**
3 **cups milk**
1 **cup heavy cream**
freshly ground pepper
fresh chives for garnish

In a large pot, sauté leeks and celery in butter until soft, stirring often. Cook potatoes in salted water until they are tender. Stir in milk and cook for another 5 to 10 minutes. Puree the soup in small batches in a blender or with an immersion blender. Stir in heavy cream. Chill. Add salt and pepper to taste, garnish with fresh chives, and serve.

Marinated Vegetables

This salad is lettuce free, so it doesn't wilt easily. But if you prefer, you can serve it on a bed of greens. The vegetables can be marinated overnight, except for the broccoli, which should be marinated for only about 30 minutes before serving to keep it bright green.

> 1 pint grape or small cherry tomatoes (leave whole)
> 1 head broccoli, cut into bite-size pieces
> 1 cucumber, peeled and sliced
> 1 red onion, sliced
> 8 ounces small button mushrooms
> 1 green pepper, cut into strips
> 1 small zucchini or yellow squash, thinly sliced

Dressing
> ½ cup olive oil
> ¼ cup red wine vinegar
> ¼ cup water
> ½ teaspoon garlic powder
> 1 teaspoon Italian seasoning
> 2 tablespoons grated Parmesan cheese (optional)

Slice all vegetables and layer in a clear bowl. Put tomatoes and mushrooms near the top. Mix together dressing ingredients, or use an 8-ounce bottle of your favorite oil and vinegar Italian dressing. Marinate the vegetables, except for the broccoli, in dressing for at least 2 hours or overnight. Add broccoli for the last 30 minutes. Toss well before serving.

Blackened Redfish

2 pounds redfish fillets
1 stick butter, melted
2 tablespoons lemon juice
1 tablespoon paprika
2 teaspoons kosher salt
1 teaspoon onion powder
1 teaspoon cayenne pepper
1 teaspoon garlic powder
½ teaspoon ground white pepper
½ teaspoon ground black pepper
½ teaspoon dried thyme
½ teaspoon dried oregano
½ teaspoon celery seed

Mix melted butter and lemon juice in a shallow dish. Mix dry ingredients together in a shallow dish or pie plate. Dip fillets in butter-lemon mixture first, then in spice mixture, pressing to help spices adhere to the fish. Preheat a heavy cast-iron skillet until very hot, several minutes on high heat or over direct heat on the grill. Cook redfish in a dry pan for 2 minutes on one side; then turn over and cook about 1 minute more. This dish is smoky, so cook the rish outdoors and then bring it inside on a platter. Keep the fish warm in the oven if necessary.

Potato Pancake

Keep that skillet on the grill and make a crispy and golden potato pancake.

4 potatoes
salt and pepper
enough oil or bacon drippings to cover the bottom
of a skillet to a depth of ¼ inch

Peel and shred potatoes. If you need to prepare the potatoes in advance, put them in cold, salted water to prevent discoloration. Before cooking, remove excess water by squeezing the potatoes inside a clean kitchen towel or pressing them between layers of paper towels. Heat oil in a heavy skillet, and add the potatoes in an even layer in the bottom. Sprinkle with salt and pepper. Press down firmly. Cook over medium to medium-high heat until the bottom is crisped and brown. To avoid breaking the potato pancake when turning it, slide it out of the skillet onto a plate, invert it on a second plate, and return it to the skillet with the uncooked side down. Continue to cook until browned and potatoes are done.

Strawberry Shortcake with Grandpa's Biscuits

In my family, strawberries rule. My mother just liked to pick them, but the rest of us loved eating them with shortcake biscuits made by my grandfather. He never used a recipe but just scooped, poured, mixed, and patted and created light, mouthwatering biscuits every time. I watched him and took notes, and I've come up with a close version. Gramps never put sugar in his shortcake biscuits—we'd just add extra to the berries—but by all means, add some if you like.

> **2 quarts ripe strawberries**
> **½ to 1 cup sugar**
> **2 cups flour**
> **4 teaspoons baking powder**
> **½ teaspoon salt**
> **1 tablespoon sugar (optional)**
> **½ cup shortening**
> **¾ cup milk**
> **whipped cream for topping**

Clean the strawberries, cut them in half, and sweeten with ½ cup sugar or more, depending on the tartness of the berries and your personal preference. Let them macerate until the sugar has dissolved and the berries have given up some of their juice.

For the biscuits: Preheat oven to 450 degrees. Sift together flour, baking powder, salt, and sugar if desired. Cut in shortening with two knives, a pastry blender, or your fingertips. Do not overmix, and do not let the shortening melt. Add enough milk to form a soft dough. Again, do not overmix. Flour a work surface and gently knead the dough to form a soft ball. Press or gently roll into a flat disk about ¼ to ½ inch thick. Flour a biscuit cutter or the rim of a glass and cut out dough circles. Place on a lightly greased baking sheet and bake for 12 to 15 minutes, until risen and golden brown. Cool.

To assemble: Slice a shortcake biscuit in half horizontally. Put the bottom half in a dish, top with berries, add the top of the shortcake, and finish with more berries and a generous dollop of whipped cream. To make your shortcake extra special, place a scoop of strawberry or vanilla ice cream on the bottom biscuit before you add the berries.

Orange-Glazed Salmon Fillets

Salmon are found in both the Atlantic and Pacific oceans. They also populate the Great Lakes and other freshwaters when spawning. Their distinctive orange-colored flesh is loaded with omega-3 fatty acids, making them good for you as well as good tasting. Wild is best, so if you get a chance, try your luck at salmon fishing.

---

menu

Appetizer:	*Tossed Salad with Green Goddess Dressing*
Entrée:	*Orange-Glazed Salmon Fillets*
Sides:	*Country Fries; Rainbow Swiss Chard*
Dessert:	*Chocolate, Coconut, and Macadamia Pillows*

Tossed Salad with Green Goddess Dressing

Green goddess is one of my all-time favorite salad dressings. It used to be ubiquitous on restaurant menus and supermarket shelves, but sadly, it has lost favor—but not so with flavor. This creamy dressing is fantastic on salad greens and deserves a reincarnation. The anchovies add another level of flavor, but if you're not a fan, leave them out.

**4 to 6 cups torn, assorted salad greens or 1 head
iceberg lettuce, cut into 4 to 6 wedges**

Dressing

> 1 ½ cups mayonnaise
> 1 shallot, minced
> 1 large or 2 small cloves garlic, minced
> 1 tablespoon white wine vinegar
> 1 tablespoon fresh lemon juice
> 2 teaspoons fresh lime juice
> 2 tablespoons extra virgin olive oil
> 3 tablespoons chopped fresh parsley
> 1 tablespoon chopped fresh chives
> 1 tablespoon chopped fresh tarragon
> 1 tablespoon chopped fresh dill leaves
> 2 anchovy fillets, mashed, or 1 tablespoon
>   anchovy paste
> 1 tablespoon sugar
> salt and pepper

Blend all dressing ingredients in a food processor or blender until smooth. For best results, let sit overnight for flavors to develop. Serve over a bed of your favorite greens or iceberg lettuce wedges.

Orange-Glazed Salmon Fillets

> 2 pounds salmon fillets (skin removed)
> salt and pepper
> ¾ cup orange marmalade
> 1 shallot, finely minced
> 2 tablespoons orange juice concentrate
> 2 tablespoons dry white wine
> ½ teaspoon grated fresh ginger
> 1 tablespoon Dijon mustard
> ⅛ teaspoon Chinese five-spice powder
> ¼ to ½ teaspoon crushed red pepper flakes
>   (optional)
> sliced almonds for garnish

Preheat oven to 450 degrees. Rinse salmon and check for bones. Place in a shallow, buttered baking dish and sprinkle with salt and pepper. In a small bowl, mix marmalade, shallot, orange juice, wine, ginger, mustard, five-spice powder, and red pepper flakes. Spoon the mixture over the salmon fillets. Bake, uncovered, 5 minutes per ½-inch thickness, or until the salmon flakes easily when tested with a fork. Remove the fillets and glaze to a serving dish, and sprinkle with almonds.

If it's too hot to use the oven, or if you're in a hurry, these fillets can be prepared in the microwave. Cooking fish in the microwave is easy and fast, and the results are excellent. Place the fillets in a microwave-safe dish, cover, and cook on high for about 5 minutes. Rotate the dish at least once if your microwave isn't equipped with a turntable. Check for doneness with a fork, making sure the fish flakes easily.

Country Fries

4 cups potatoes, peeled and diced (raw or cooked)
6 tablespoons bacon fat, or 4 tablespoons butter and
    2 tablespoons olive oil
1 onion, chopped
1 green pepper, diced
¼ teaspoon paprika
salt and pepper

If potatoes are raw, place them in cold salted water and parboil for 5 minutes, until barely tender. Drain well. In a large skillet over medium heat, melt bacon fat and sauté onion and green pepper until just beginning to soften. Add potatoes and mix well. Continue cooking until potatoes are cooked through and browned and crispy on the outside. When done, season with paprika, salt, and pepper. Stir and serve.

Rainbow Swiss Chard

Rainbow chard is a perfect backdrop for the bright salmon.

1 bunch rainbow-colored Swiss chard (if unavailable,
    use red or green varieties)
1 tablespoon butter
1 teaspoon cider vinegar
1 tablespoon bread crumbs mixed with 1 tablespoon
    olive oil

Clean chard and slice crosswise into 1-inch strips. Cook in salted boiling water for 3 minutes. If you're not ready to serve it, plunge the chard into an ice bath to set the colors and stop cooking. Drain well. If the chard is hot, stir in butter, splash with vinegar (or pass vinegar on the side), and garnish with the bread crumb mixture. If the chard is cooled, place it in a serving dish, microwave until hot, and butter, season, and garnish. The chard can also be served at room temperature.

Chocolate, Coconut, and Macadamia Pillows

6 tablespoons mini chocolate chips
6 tablespoons flaked coconut
6 tablespoons chopped macadamia nuts
    (or other nuts)
wonton wrappers
oil for frying
confectioners' sugar

Mix chocolate chips, coconut, and nuts together. Place wonton wrappers on a flat surface. Place a teaspoon of filling in the center of each wrapper. Moisten the edges of the dough with water, using either a pastry brush or your fingers. Fold the wrapper in half to form a triangle. Press sides to seal, being careful to push out any air pockets. Drop several pillows in hot oil and fry to a golden brown, 1 to 2 minutes. Drain on paper towels. Dust with confectioners' sugar before serving. Alternatively, place the pillows on a baking sheet sprayed with butter-flavor cooking spray, then spray the top of the pillows with butter spray. Bake at 350 degrees for 10 to 12 minutes, until golden brown. Serve as above.

Poached Salmon with Beurre Blanc

Several years ago, my family vacationed in New Brunswick, Canada, where we went fly fishing in the Chapel Bar Pool, just below the Mactaquac Dam on the St. John River, for that renowned East Coast game fish: the Atlantic salmon. I actually managed to land a salmon, which was quite an experience. Here, I've re-created the recipe that the chef served us that evening, with my salmon crowning the meal, of course.

menu

Appetizer: Salmon Cakes

Salad: Mixed Greens with Lemon Vinaigrette

Entrée: Poached Salmon with Beurre Blanc

Sides: Duchess Potatoes; Sugar Snap Peas

Dessert: Blueberry Mousse Pie

Salmon Cakes

Use any leftover salmon in these salmon croquettes, which make a great starter.

> 1½ cups cooked salmon, flaked
> 1 cup cooked white rice
> 2 eggs
> 1 scallion, thinly sliced
> 1 tablespoon finely chopped parsley
> 1 tablespoon Dijon mustard
> 3 tablespoons mayonnaise
> salt and pepper
> 3 tablespoons water
> 1½ to 2 cups bread crumbs
> vegetable oil for frying

In a large bowl, stir together salmon, rice, 1 egg, scallion, parsley, mustard, and mayonnaise. Season with salt and pepper. Mixture should hold together; if it doesn't, add a bit of milk to moisten. Shape into 6 to 8 croquettes, and chill for 1 hour. Beat 1 egg with 3 tablespoons water. Dip cakes in egg; then cover with bread crumbs, lightly pressing them into each side. Heat oil in a non-stick skillet, and fry croquettes on each side until golden brown. For a first course, serve salmon cakes over mixed greens with lemon vinaigrette, and pass spicy mayonnaise on the side (recipes follow).

Spicy Mayonnaise
> **1 cup mayonnaise**
> **1 tablespoon lemon juice**
> **3 tablespoons chili sauce or ketchup**
> **1 teaspoon red pepper sauce**
> **¼ teaspoon cayenne pepper**

Stir all ingredients until well combined and chill. Adjust heat with more red pepper sauce and cayenne pepper.

Mixed Greens with Lemon Vinaigrette

mesclun salad greens, rinsed and spun dry

Dressing
> **4 tablespoons lemon juice**
> **1 clove garlic, crushed**
> **1 tablespoon Dijon mustard**
> **1 teaspoon grated lemon peel**
> **½ cup olive oil**
> **salt and pepper**

For the dressing: Combine all ingredients in a small jar, cover, and shake until well mixed. Add to salad greens and toss.

Poached Salmon with Beurre Blanc

Atlantic salmon is delicately flavored and is fantastic poached, baked, or grilled. This recipe calls for poaching the salmon in a court bouillon, which is a seasoned vegetable stock acidulated with vinegar, lemon juice, or wine.

> **1 whole salmon or 3 or 4 fillets**
> **olive oil**

If you don't have a whole fish poacher, or if you prefer to poach 3 or 4 fillets rather than a whole fish, you'll need a pan large enough to accommodate the fish in a single layer; the pan should have a cover, or you can use aluminum foil. If you're poaching a whole fish, you want to be sure that you can lift the fish without breaking it; if your fish cooker doesn't have a rack, you can wrap the fish in cheesecloth or foil to facilitate removal.

Gut and remove scales from the fish. Leave the head and tail on if you want a dramatic whole-fish presentation. Coat the entire fish with olive oil. Cover fish with cold court bouillon (recipe follows).

Court Bouillon
>   **6 quarts water**
>   **1 cup white wine vinegar**
>   **¼ cup lemon juice**
>   **1 teaspoon salt**
>   **1 teaspoon pepper**
>   **2 carrots**
>   **1 leek**
>   **2 celery stalks**
>   **2 shallots**
>   **2 sprigs parsley**
>   **1 small bay leaf**

Chop all vegetables and place them in a stockpot with the liquids. Bring to a boil; cover and simmer for 20 minutes. Strain. Add salt and pepper. Use to poach salmon or other fish.

To continue preparing the salmon: If you need more liquid to cover the fish, add wine, water, or fish stock. Cover the pan. Slowly bring fish to a gentle boil; reduce heat and slowly simmer for 3 or 4 minutes. Turn off heat and let salmon sit in hot poaching liquid. When the liquid has cooled to warm, remove fish carefully, unwrap, and remove skin. Serve on a tray with beurre blanc (recipe follows) and garnished with additional parsley, dill, or herbs of your choice. The salmon can also be served cold with a covering of tartar sauce, sliced cucumbers layered as scales, and an olive for the eye. A cold poached salmon (with head and tail intact) makes a great centerpiece for a buffet table.

Beurre Blanc
>   **3 shallots, minced**
>   **¼ cup dry white wine**
>   **¼ cup white wine vinegar**
>   **1 stick butter, cut into small pieces and chilled**
>   **splash fresh lemon juice**
>   **salt and white pepper**

Cook shallots in wine and vinegar until reduced to a syrup. Cool slightly. Over lowest heat, whisk butter into the liquid one piece at a time, until all is incorporated. If the butter melts, remove from heat. Add lemon juice. Season with salt and pepper. Serve immediately or keep warm over lowest heat setting, in a bowl over hot water, or in a warmed thermos bottle.

Duchess Potatoes

5 or 6 medium potatoes
½ stick butter, melted
1 teaspoon salt
½ teaspoon pepper
2 egg yolks, slightly beaten
⅓ cup cream
1 egg, beaten
2 teaspoons water

Preheat oven to 425 degrees. Peel and quarter potatoes. Place in cold salted water, bring to a boil, and simmer until tender. Mash hot cooked potatoes with butter, salt, pepper, egg yolks, and cream. Beat until light and fluffy. Spoon serving-size mounds onto a baking sheet, or place in an icing bag and squeeze out though a large star tip. Mix 1 beaten egg with water; brush potato mounds with egg mixture. Bake for 10 to 12 minutes, or until potatoes are browned and hot.

Sugar Snap Peas

Sugar snap peas are a nice change from shelled peas and an eye-catching addition to any plate.

1 pound sugar snap peas
2 tablespoons butter
salt and pepper
splash lemon juice

Clean peas, removing any tough strings. Steam for 10 minutes over salted boiling water, or boil for 5 or 6 minutes until tender. Season with butter, salt and pepper, and a spritz of lemon juice.

Blueberry Mousse Pie

1 graham cracker crumb pie shell

Blueberry Sauce
2 cups fresh or frozen blueberries, thawed
¼ cup orange juice
¼ cup water
¼ cup sugar
1 tablespoon cornstarch

Mousse Base
1 envelope unflavored gelatin
½ cup cold water
**1 cup blueberry sauce (or 1 can blueberry
    pie filling)**
1 cup heavy cream
½ cup confectioners' sugar
1 teaspoon vanilla extract
mint leaves for garnish

For the blueberry sauce: Combine all ingredients in a medium saucepan. Cook and stir over medium heat 4 to 5 minutes, or until thickened and clear. Set aside and let cool.

For the mousse: In a small saucepan, soften gelatin in cold water; wait 5 minutes. Heat until gelatin is dissolved. Stir in blueberry sauce and let cool. Meanwhile, in a large mixing bowl, whip heavy cream, sugar, and vanilla until soft peaks form. Gently fold in blueberry sauce mixture, reserving a few tablespoons for garnish. Pour into pie shell, and refrigerate until thoroughly chilled. To serve, spread with reserved blueberry sauce, and top with additional whipped cream if desired. Garnish with mint leaves.

Planked Salmon

The Native Americans of the Pacific Northwest—no strangers to salmon—devised a technique of cooking fish on cedar planks. Today, grilling on a plank is easy, and it makes quite a spectacular presentation. Planks can be purchased online in kitchen specialty shops, or you can make your own. Simply visit your local lumberyard and have planks cut ½ to 1 inch thick, about 14 inches long and 10 inches wide (use only nontreated wood). With this method of cooking, the wood is the primary seasoning, and you can use cedar, alder, apple, or other wood of your choice. Just make sure to soak the wood and toast it until hot before adding the fish. Wood conducts heat slowly, so planked foods are moist and flavorful. The fish is cooked skin-side down, and there's no need to turn it.

menu

Appetizer:	*Pear, Walnut, and Endive Salad*
Entrée:	*Planked Salmon with Lemon Dill Butter*
Sides:	*Potato Pancakes; Asparagus Bundles*
Dessert:	*Lemon Ice*

Pear, Walnut, and Endive Salad

4 heads Belgian endive or 1 head frisée lettuce
   or curly chicory
2 bunches watercress
1 large pear, cored, cut once crosswise, then sliced
8 ounces Gorgonzola, Roquefort, or feta cheese
½ cup walnut halves

Dressing
   ¼ cup cider or white wine vinegar
   ¼ cup water
   ¼ cup vegetable oil
   ¼ cup walnut oil

Cut endive or tear lettuce into 1-inch strips or bite-size pieces. Remove tough stems from watercress and break into small pieces. Mix salad greens with pears. Top with crumbled cheese and garnish with walnuts. Combine dressing ingredients, and drizzle salad with dressing.

Planked Salmon with Lemon Dill Butter

4 salmon fillets
1 stick butter, softened
2 tablespoons fresh dill
1 tablespoon grated lemon peel
salt and pepper

Soak 4 cedar or alder planks in water for at least 15 minutes. Remove scales from the salmon's outer skin. Blend butter, dill, and lemon peel. Heat the planks on the grill rack until hot. Oil the planks and place the fillets on the boards. You can also cook the fish on a bed of dill weed or other herbs on the planks, if desired. Season fish with salt and pepper and spread 1 table-spoon lemon dill butter on top of each fillet. Close the grill cover and cook for about 15 minutes, depending on the thickness of the fillets. The wood will begin to smolder and imbue the fish with a smoky taste. Cook until salmon is opaque. Do not turn over. Serve right from the plank, adding another tablespoon of lemon dill butter.

Potato Pancakes

These fluffy potato pancakes are called boxty in Ireland, and they're an inventive way to use leftover mashed potatoes. The mix of shredded and mashed potatoes gives these golden patties more texture than those made with mashed potatoes alone.

1 pound potatoes (about 3 medium), grated
    or shredded
1 cup mashed potatoes (may be leftovers)
½ cup flour
1 egg, beaten
salt and pepper
2 tablespoons minced chives, onion, or scallion
    (optional)
milk
oil or butter (or a combination) for frying

Mix raw shredded potatoes with the mashed potatoes. Mix in flour, egg, salt and pepper, and onion; add just enough milk to make a stiff batter that will drop from a spoon. Drop a heaping tablespoon of potato mixture onto a hot griddle or frying pan that has been coated with oil or butter. Spread with the back of a spoon, or flatten with a spatula. Cook over medium heat until crisp and golden brown. Turn and cook the other side. Serve hot.

Asparagus Bundles

Asparagus bundles can also be served as an appetizer or a first course. Here, they add another level of flavor to the meal without overpowering the salmon.

24 asparagus spears, woody part of stem removed
2 to 3 tablespoons olive oil
2 cloves garlic, crushed
3 to 4 tablespoons lemon juice or juice of 1 fresh
lemon
salt and pepper
6 thin slices prosciutto
fresh chives or scallion greens, cut into long, thin strips

Blanch asparagus spears in boiling salted water for about 3 minutes; asparagus should be bright green and crisp. Drain. In a skillet, heat oil and sauté garlic over medium heat until soft. Add asparagus, lemon juice, salt, and pepper and sauté until coated and tender-crisp. Remove from heat. Place 4 spears of asparagus on the edge of a slice of prosciutto, roll up spears in meat, and tie with a piece of chive or strip of scallion green. Serve warm or cold.

Lemon Ice

On a hot day, nothing tops off a meal better than homemade lemon ice. The secret is the fresh lemon juice. If you don't have fresh lemons, you might as well buy lemon ice or sherbet in the supermarket. To extract as much juice from the lemons as possible, roll them on the counter or microwave them for 1 minute before squeezing. For this recipe, you'll need 4 to 5 lemons. The average yield from 1 lemon is 2 to 3 tablespoons of juice, depending on size (4 tablespoons = ¼ cup).

3½ cups water
1¼ cups sugar
¾ cup fresh lemon juice
2 tablespoons grated fresh lemon zest
mint leaves for garnish (optional)

Boil water in a saucepan and stir in sugar, mixing until it is completely dissolved. Remove from heat and let cool. Add lemon juice and zest. Pour mixture into a plastic bowl (one that will accommodate your mixer) and freeze. When ready to serve, remove the ice from the freezer, let it sit for 15 to 20 minutes, and beat with a mixer until light and fluffy. Garnish with mint leaves. Adults may want to top it off with a splash of Chambord.

Snappy Snapper Fillets

Snappers are gifts from the sea and are found in all of the world's tropical and subtropical oceans. They can grow to be 3 feet in length and make great eating, especially the famed red snapper.

---

menu

Appetizer: Tricolored Pepper Salad

Entrée: Snappy Snapper Fillets

Sides: Red and Blue Potatoes; Sugar Snap Peas and Asparagus Medley

Dessert: Chocolate Chunk Banana Bread with Chocolate Butter

Tricolored Pepper Salad

½ **cup olive oil**
2 **tablespoons lemon juice**
2 **tablespoons red wine vinegar**
1 **tablespoon water**
1 **teaspoon chopped parsley**
1 **tablespoon chopped fresh oregano or** ½ **teaspoon dried**
1 **red, 1 green, and 1 yellow or orange bell peppers**
½ **cup pitted kalamata olives**

For the dressing: Mix the first 6 ingredients in a glass jar. Shake well. For the salad: Slice peppers into thin strips lengthwise. Toss peppers with half the dressing, and let marinate for at least 30 minutes. To serve, arrange peppers on a lettuce leaf on a salad plate. Top with olives and drizzle with extra dressing if desired.

Snappy Snapper Fillets

Cooking *en papillote* (a French term meaning "in an envelope") is an easy way to imbue tender snapper with the delicate flavors of spices. Traditionally, the envelope is a parchment paper packet that keeps delicate foods from flaking apart or from sticking and burning (but paper burns at 451 degrees, so you have to keep your cooking temperature no higher than 425). Here, the packet is made of aluminum foil, which allows you to prepare this dish outdoors on the grill or right in the oven. The packet also holds in flavor and moisture and makes cooking and cleanup easy.

> **4 snapper fillets, about 8 ounces each**
> **salt and freshly ground black pepper**
> **2 tablespoons butter**
> **2 tablespoons olive oil**
> **2 cloves garlic, minced**
> **½ cup white wine**
> **2 tablespoons finely chopped fresh parsley**
> **4 slices fresh lemon**

If using the oven, preheat to 425 degrees. Salt and pepper the fillets, and place each fillet on a large square of heavy-duty aluminum foil. Melt butter and oil in a small skillet. Add garlic and cook for 2 minutes on medium heat; do not brown. Add wine and cook until the sauce reduces and thickens a bit. Remove from heat and stir in parsley. Place a tablespoon of sauce on each fillet, and top with a lemon slice. Fold up and seal each packet completely, with the seam on top. Grill over medium-high heat for about 5 minutes per side, depending on the thickness of the fish, or bake for 8 to 10 minutes or until done, without flipping. Be careful of escaping steam.

Red and Blue Potatoes

The size of the potatoes determines how many you need for this recipe. If the potatoes are large, I use 6, assuming 1 potato per serving. If the potatoes are small, I usually figure on 4 per serving, or a total of 24 small potatoes to feed 6 people. These potatoes are also great served at room temperature.

> **Red Bliss potatoes**
> **4 ounces blue cheese, crumbled**
> **salt and pepper**

Wash the potatoes and cut them in half. Place in a pot with salted cold water and bring to a boil. Boil until tender. If some are done earlier than others, remove them so they don't fall apart. Place hot potatoes on a baking sheet cut side up. If they don't stand level, trim a thin slice off the bottom to make a base. Sprinkle with salt, pepper, and crumbled blue cheese. Pop under the broiler or into a 400-degree oven until the cheese melts.

Sugar Snap Peas and Asparagus Medley

½ pound fresh asparagus spears
½ pound fresh sugar snap peas or Asian-style
    pea pods
2 tablespoons butter
2 tablespoons olive oil
1 clove garlic, crushed
salt and pepper

Remove the woody portion of the asparagus stems, and cut spears in half on the diagonal. Remove strings from the pea pods. Sauté the garlic in butter and oil for 1 minute over medium heat until fragrant. Remove garlic from the pan and sauté asparagus and peas in butter and oil mixture until just tender. Season with salt and pepper and remove to a serving dish.

Chocolate Chunk Banana Bread with Chocolate Butter

2 eggs, beaten
1 cup mashed ripe banana (2 or 3 bananas,
    depending on size)
⅓ cup oil
¼ cup milk
1 teaspoon vanilla extract
2 cups flour
1 cup sugar
2 teaspoons baking powder
½ teaspoon salt
4 ounces semisweet or milk chocolate bar,
    coarsely chopped
¾ cup chopped walnuts

Chocolate Butter
 ½ **stick butter, softened**
 2 tablespoons chocolate syrup

Preheat oven to 350 degrees. Grease and flour a 9- by 5-inch loaf pan. In a bowl, mix together eggs, bananas, oil, milk, and vanilla. In a separate bowl, stir together flour, sugar, baking powder, and salt. Add the dry ingredients to the banana mixture, stirring until just moistened. Stir in chocolate chunks and walnuts. Spread in the loaf pan and bake for about 50 minutes, checking for doneness with a toothpick. Cool in the pan for 10 minutes; then remove and cool on a wire rack.

For the chocolate butter: Mix the butter and chocolate syrup until well incorporated. Fill a small dish with the butter and serve with the bread.

Baked Stuffed Striped Bass

For many anglers, the ultimate sport fish is the striped bass—a saltwater fish that spawns in freshwater. One can fish for these beauties from a boat, but there is something magical about watching an angler surf-cast for a striper along the shoreline. And it's a good thing that the sand and surf are so enjoyable, because devotees of striper fishing must be patient and tireless in their seemingly endless rhythm of casting and recasting.

menu

Appetizer:	*Smoked Trout Spread*
Salad:	*Avocado and Endive Salad*
Entrée:	*Baked Stuffed Striper*
Sides:	*Mashed Potatoes with Bacon, Spinach, and Fontina Cheese; Peas and Mushrooms with Tomatoes*
Dessert:	*Peach Crisp*

Smoked Trout Spread

This spread is an excellent way to use up leftover smoked fish. It you don't have any trout, you can substitute smoked salmon.

>**8-ounce package cream cheese, softened**
>**¼ to ½ pound smoked trout, skinned, boned,**
>   **and flaked**
>**2 tablespoons minced green onion**
>**1 tablespoon fresh dill**
>**1 teaspoon lemon juice**
>**pepper**

Beat the cream cheese until smooth. Add the fish, green onion, dill, lemon juice, and pepper, and mix well until blended. Refrigerate until serving time. Spread on cocktail rye bread, crackers, or crisp bread. Garnish with dill sprigs.

Avocado and Endive Salad

>**4 heads Belgian endive or 1 large head romaine**
>   **lettuce**
>**4 ripe Hass avocados**
>**¼ cup fresh lemon juice plus the juice of ½ lemon**
>**1 tablespoon Dijon mustard**
>**¼ cup olive oil**
>**salt and pepper**

Cut 1 inch off the ends of the endive or romaine. Wash and dry and cut into 1-inch strips. Remove the pits from the avocados, peel, and cut into wedges; squeeze the juice from ½ lemon over the pieces and toss to coat to prevent discoloration. Mix mustard, ¼ cup lemon juice, olive oil, and salt and pepper together for the dressing. In a large salad bowl, mix endive and avocado pieces. Pour dressing over all and gently toss to coat.

Baked Stuffed Striper

Striper is an excellent candidate for stuffing, poaching, grilling, baking, or broiling. Don't be afraid to substitute it in other recipes that call for a moderately fatty, firm, mild fish (such as grouper).

>**4 to 6 pounds dressed striper**
>**6 slices bacon**

Stuffing
>   ½ **stick butter**
>   2 **shallots, finely chopped**
>   1 **small onion, chopped**
>   1 **celery stalk, chopped**
>   ½ **green pepper, diced (about ½ cup)**
>   ½ **pint oysters, including liquor**
>   1 **cup seasoned stuffing cubes, crushed; or buttery**
>   **crackers, crushed, to make 1 cup crumbs with**
>   1 **teaspoon dried sage**
>   **salt and pepper**

Preheat oven to 400 degrees. For the stuffing: Melt butter in a skillet and sauté shallots, onion, celery, and green pepper until celery and pepper are soft. Add oysters and their liquid and cook until the oysters' edges are frilled. Stir in stuffing cubes or cracker crumbs and mix well. If the stuffing is too dry, add more butter or a bit of hot water. Check for seasoning, and add salt and pepper. Fill the cavity of the fish with the stuffing. Place the fish in a buttered baking pan (or buttered foil for easy cleanup), and cover the top of the fish with bacon slices. Bake for about 30 to 40 minutes, until the fish flakes easily when tested with a fork.

Mashed Potatoes with Bacon, Spinach, and Fontina Cheese

>   4 **slices bacon, cut crosswise into ½-inch pieces**
>   2 **to 3 pounds Idaho or russet potatoes, peeled and**
>   **cut into ½-inch-thick slices**
>   6 **ounces spinach**
>   ¼ **cup milk**
>   3 **tablespoons butter**
>   4 **ounces grated fontina cheese**
>   **salt and pepper**

In a skillet, cook the bacon pieces over medium-low heat until crisp. Using a slotted spoon, transfer to a paper towel to drain.

In a large pot, cover the potatoes with cold salted water. Bring to a boil over medium-high heat. Reduce to a simmer and cook until the potatoes are tender, 20 to 30 minutes. Drain.

Meanwhile, remove the stems from the spinach, rinse, and lightly shake. Put the spinach in a steamer over boiling water and cook until wilted, 2 to 3 minutes (or cover and microwave until wilted). Drain well. Cool slightly and squeeze out as much moisture as possible. Chop and set aside.

Mash potatoes in a large bowl; add milk and butter and stir until smooth. Add the cheese, spinach, and bacon, and stir until the cheese melts. Season with salt and pepper and serve.

Peas and Mushrooms with Tomatoes

10-ounce package frozen peas
2 tablespoons butter
8 ounces sliced fresh mushrooms
1 cup cherry tomatoes, halved; or 1 cup grape
    tomatoes, whole
2 scallions, sliced
1 tablespoon lemon juice
salt and pepper

Cook peas in boiling salted water until tender. Drain and set aside. Melt butter in a skillet and cook mushrooms until tender; add peas, tomatoes, scallions, and lemon juice. Heat thoroughly and season with salt and pepper. Serve.

Peach Crisp

No peaches? Just substitute firm apples or pears, and use cinnamon instead of allspice.

Filling

4 pounds peaches, peeled, pitted, and sliced (enough
    to fill your baking dish)
¼ cup firmly packed brown sugar
2 tablespoons butter, cut into small pieces
1 tablespoon lemon juice
2 tablespoons flour
½ teaspoon ground allspice

Topping

1 cup flour
1 cup sugar
½ cup chopped walnuts or pecans
½ cup quick-cooking rolled oats
6 tablespoons butter, cut into bits
½ teaspoon cinnamon
¼ teaspoon salt

Preheat oven to 375 degrees. For the filling: Toss peaches with brown sugar, butter pieces, lemon juice, flour, and allspice. Pour peach mixture into a 9- by 13-inch baking pan.

For the topping: Using a pastry blender or a fork, combine all ingredients until the mixture resembles coarse crumbs. Sprinkle topping over peach filling. Bake for 50 to 60 minutes until bubbling and golden. Serve warm or at room temperature with vanilla ice cream.

Spinach-Stuffed Citrus Trout

What better way to celebrate spring than with an explosion of flavors from your favorite trout stream? Here, the delicate citrus flavor enhances the lightness of the trout, which nicely balances the earthy taste of the wild rice and barley pilaf. Enjoy the meal with a glass of chilled white wine, a chardonnay perhaps.

menu

Appetizer:	*Fruity Salad*
Entrée:	*Spinach-Stuffed Citrus Trout*
Sides:	*Wild Rice and Barley with Mushrooms; Fiddleheads*
Dessert:	*Rhubarb Crumble*

Fruity Salad

2 Granny Smith apples, cored and thinly sliced
½ head curly endive, torn into bite-size pieces
1 bunch watercress
1 head radicchio, quartered, cored, and thinly sliced
1 fennel bulb, trimmed and cut into strips
shredded Romano cheese for garnish

Dressing
> 1 tablespoon Dijon mustard
> 3 tablespoons balsamic vinegar
> ¼ cup cider vinegar
> ½ cup olive oil
> salt and pepper

Combine dressing ingredients in a glass jar and shake until blended. Toss apple slices in dressing, cover, and chill. The salad can be prepared up to 3 hours in advance. Finish the salad by combining endive, watercress, radicchio, and fennel in a large bowl. Add apple slices and dressing. Toss before serving. Garnish with Romano cheese.

Spinach-Stuffed Citrus Trout

> 2 small trout (about 8 ounces each), boned
> 6 tablespoons butter, divided
> 2 tablespoons olive oil, divided
> 2 shallots, minced
> ½ cup sliced fresh mushrooms
> 10-ounce package fresh spinach, torn into bite-size
>   pieces
> ⅛ teaspoon tarragon
> salt and pepper to taste
> ¼ cup fresh orange juice
> 1 tablespoon lemon juice
> fresh minced parsley

In a skillet, melt 2 tablespoons butter with 1 tablespoon olive oil. Add shallots and mushrooms and sauté for 1 minute. Add spinach and tarragon. Cook until most of the liquid has evaporated. Season with salt and pepper. Stuff each trout with half the spinach mixture.

Melt remaining butter and remaining olive oil in the skillet over medium heat. Sauté trout until golden brown, about 5 minutes on each side. Remove from pan and keep warm.

Add orange and lemon juices to skillet. Cook over high heat, stirring constantly, until sauce has reduced and thickened. Add a sprinkle of minced parsley. Pour sauce over fish and serve.

Wild Rice and Barley with Mushrooms

½ **stick butter**
1 small onion, finely chopped
1 10-ounce package fresh mushrooms, sliced
1 cup wild rice
2 tablespoons pearl barley
4 cups chicken stock
salt and pepper

Melt butter in a small skillet, and sauté onion and mushrooms until translucent. Set aside. Simmer wild rice and barley with chicken stock in a covered saucepan until most liquid is absorbed and the grains are tender. Stir occasionally. Add onion and mushrooms and mix. Cook until heated through. Season with salt and pepper.

If bulk wild rice is unavailable, use a wild rice mix and follow the instructions on the package, cooking the rice in chicken broth. Boil the barley separately in water until tender, add to the cooked rice mixture, then add vegetables.

Fiddleheads

Where I live in the Northeast, 'round about May, ferns that grow along stream banks are sending up their curled fiddleheads. These tender green shoots are a delicacy that you can easily gather when you're out angling for the main course. They can also be found in the produce section of larger grocery chains. They taste very much like asparagus and need only the lightest hint of seasoning. If fiddleheads are unavailable, substitute asparagus or tender green beans.

1 pound fiddlehead ferns
½ **stick butter**
1 tablespoon fresh lemon juice
1 teaspoon fresh grated lemon zest
salt and pepper to taste

Wash the fiddleheads carefully, because sand can easily be trapped in the tightly curled heads. Add the fiddleheads to a pot of boiling salted water, and boil until just crisp-tender. Melt butter in a skillet, add fiddleheads, and toss to coat. Sprinkle with lemon juice and lemon zest. Add salt and pepper to taste.

Rhubarb Crumble

Capture the flavors of spring with this delicious old-fashioned dessert. It's easy to prepare and a wonderful way to end your meal.

> **5 cups rhubarb, cut into chunky slices**
> **1 cup sugar**
> **water**

Topping
> **¾ cup flour**
> **5 tablespoons butter**
> **½ cup brown sugar**
> **1 cup quick-cooking rolled oats**
> **1 teaspoon salt**
> **1 teaspoon ginger (or cinnamon)**

Put the rhubarb, sugar, and a little water in a saucepan. Simmer until the rhubarb is almost tender (you can cook the rhubarb while making the crumble). For the crumble topping: Put the flour in a large bowl and cut in butter with a pastry cutter or your fingers. Mix in the sugar, salt, and oats, and finally the ginger. Pour the rhubarb into an 8-inch-square baking dish. Sprinkle the crumble mixture evenly over the fruit. Bake at 350 degrees for approximately 30 minutes, or until topping is lightly browned. Serve warm with vanilla ice cream or whipped cream.

Classic Pan-Fried Trout

Trout, which are related to salmon, are found in the clearest and cleanest streams and lakes. Their flesh is a light-flavored delicacy. Just add a little coating to crisp them up and enjoy them hot from the sizzling pan.

---

menu

Appetizer:	*Clam Cakes*
Salad:	*Oil and Vinegar Slaw*
Entrée:	*Pan-Fried Trout*
Sides:	*Rice Pilaf with Peppers and Onions; Spinach Artichoke Gratin*
Dessert:	*Strawberry Mousse*

Clam Cakes

As a finger food or on a plate, clam cakes (or fritters) are a New England favorite. Whip up a batch to pass around while the trout are sizzling.

1 cup flour
1 teaspoon baking powder
1 egg, beaten
**1 to 1 ½ cups finely chopped canned clams and
    their juice**
1 teaspoon salt

Mix all ingredients to form a thick batter. You may need to add more clam juice to thin the batter or more flour to thicken it. Fry in hot oil (350 degrees) by dropping tablespoonfuls in a fryer or deep skillet. Do not crowd. Fry until golden brown. Drain well on paper towels; sprinkle with additional salt if desired.

Oil and Vinegar Slaw

This slaw is sweet and sour and has no mayonnaise in it.

> **1 head cabbage, finely shredded, or 1-pound bag**
>   **precut slaw mix**
> **1 carrot, shredded**
> **1 small onion, chopped**
> **salt and pepper**

Dressing
> **1 cup sugar**
> **1 teaspoon salt**
> **½ teaspoon pepper**
> **1 teaspoon dry mustard**
> **1 teaspoon celery seed**
> **1 cup vinegar**
> **⅔ cup vegetable oil**

In a large bowl, toss cabbage, carrot, and onion with salt and pepper. In a saucepan, heat dressing ingredients until sugar has dissolved. Let dressing cool a bit, pour over vegetables, and toss. Refrigerate until serving time. Dressing should be tangy but not too sour.

Pan-Fried Trout

It doesn't get much better than pan-fried trout cooked brookside. This simple dish can be sizzling in minutes in an iron skillet over a campfire or cookstove, but it's just as delicious cooked in your kitchen.

> **4 small whole trout**
> **salt and pepper**
> **1 cup cornmeal, seasoned with salt and pepper**
> **2 to 4 tablespoons butter**
> **1 tablespoon oil**
> **parsley for garnish**
> **fresh lemon wedges**

Clean trout and remove heads. Sprinkle trout inside and out with salt and pepper. Coat trout with cornmeal and shake by the tail end to remove excess. Fry in hot butter and oil (the oil prevents burning). Cook for 3 to 5 minutes per side, depending on the size of the fish. The fish should be golden brown and flake easily with a fork. Serve with lemon wedges and a sprinkling of fresh parsley.

Rice Pilaf with Peppers and Onions

½ stick butter
2 cups converted rice
½ cup orzo (rice-shaped pasta)
1 onion, diced
1 red or green bell pepper, diced (or a combination
   of both)
4 cups chicken stock or broth (homemade is best)
1 teaspoon salt
½ teaspoon pepper

In a large skillet or saucepan, melt butter and cook rice and orzo over low heat until just beginning to brown. Add onion and pepper and sauté on low heat for 2 to 3 minutes, until just softening. Add chicken stock, salt, and pepper, and bring to a boil. Cover tightly, reduce to very low heat, and simmer 15 to 20 minutes until rice is cooked but still firm. Fluff with a fork before serving.

Spinach Artichoke Gratin

1 can artichoke hearts, drained and chopped
10-ounce package frozen spinach, thawed, chopped,
   and squeezed dry
1 cup shredded Monterey Jack cheese
½ cup grated Parmesan cheese, plus 2 tablespoons
½ cup mayonnaise
1 clove garlic, minced

Preheat oven to 300 degrees. Combine artichoke hearts, spinach, Monterey Jack cheese, ½ cup Parmesan, mayonnaise, and garlic in a bowl. Mix well. Spoon mixture into a shallow ovenproof dish and bake until hot and bubbly. Sprinkle 2 tablespoons grated Parmesan on top and return to the oven until golden brown.

To serve as an appetizer or party fare: Spray the inside of miniature muffin cups with cooking spray. Press a wonton wrapper into each cup (you'll need 36). Brush lightly with melted butter. Bake 10 minutes until light golden brown. Remove shells from pan immediately and let cool while you prepare the filling. Spoon about 2 teaspoons filling in each wonton cup. Place on a cookie sheet and bake about 7 to 8 minutes at 300 degrees until heated through. Serve hot.

Strawberry Mousse

Nothing says spring like fresh strawberries. Here, they are whipped into a white chocolate mousse and served with whipped cream.

> **1 quart fresh strawberries (about 2 pounds)**
> **1 tablespoon lemon juice**
> **8 ounces white chocolate chips or white chocolate bar, finely chopped**
> **½ packet unflavored gelatin (about 1 teaspoon)**
> **¼ cup cold water**
> **2 cups heavy cream**
> **2 tablespoons confectioners' sugar**
> **1 teaspoon vanilla extract**

Clean and hull the strawberries. Puree enough of the berries (start with 1 pound) in a blender or food processor to make 1 cup of puree. Press the puree through a fine sieve into a bowl; discard the seeds. Process more berries if needed. Add lemon juice, stir, and set aside. Slice the remaining berries and set aside.

Melt white chocolate in a double boiler or a stainless steel bowl set over simmering water (make sure the water doesn't touch the bottom of the bowl). Stir until smooth, and set aside. Melting white chocolate can be trickier than melting regular chocolate, so be careful.

Soften gelatin in a small bowl by sprinkling it over the cold water. Let it sit until softened, about 5 minutes.

In a small saucepan, mix ½ cup cream and confectioners' sugar, and bring to a simmer over medium heat. Add the gelatin mixture and stir until the gelatin has completely dissolved. Pour the cream mixture into the bowl of melted chocolate, stirring until smooth. Mix in ¾ cup strawberry puree and vanilla. Reserve the remaining ¼ cup puree.

Whip the remaining cream with an electric mixer, beating until medium peaks form. Lighten the chocolate mixture by beating in ⅓ of the whipped cream. Using a large rubber spatula, gently fold the remaining whipped cream into the chocolate mixture. Refrigerate for 1 hour. Gently fold the reserved sliced strawberries into the mousse. Spoon mousse into individual serving dishes or a large glass serving bowl. Cover with plastic wrap and refrigerate several hours or overnight. To serve, top with the remaining puree, additional whipped cream, and additional sliced strawberries, if desired.

Rainbow Trout with Pecan Butter

My grandfather loved fishing, but unfortunately for him, he usually had a grandchild or two along, which meant that we learned to love trout fishing and he lost a lot of opportunities because of our antics. We also learned how to take advantage of the wild berries and edible greens in the wilderness. And of course, we got to bring home our catch and eat it. That's quite a legacy—thanks, Grandpa!

---

menu

Appetizer: *Eggplant Rollatini with Tomato Sauce*

Salad: *Grandpa Parrott's Watercress Salad with Warm Bacon Dressing*

Entrée: *Rainbow Trout with Pecan Butter*

Sides: *Parsley Potatoes; Dilled Vegetable Medley*

Dessert: *Raspberry Bars*

Eggplant Rollatini with Tomato Sauce

These cheese-stuffed rolls make an excellent starter or appetizer. Increase the portion size, and they also make a great vegetarian meal when served with a green salad and a loaf of warm Italian bread.

1 or 2 medium eggplants
salt and pepper
olive oil
1 jar marinara sauce or homemade
    (see recipe below)

Filling
> **1 pint ricotta cheese**
> **1 cup shredded mozzarella cheese, divided**
> **½ cup shredded Parmesan cheese, plus 2 tablespoons**
> **½ teaspoon garlic powder**
> **¼ cup chopped fresh parsley, or 3 tablespoons dried parsley flakes**
> **2 eggs**
> **salt and pepper**

Remove the woody stem from the top of the eggplant; peel and cut into ¼-inch slices lengthwise. You need at least 8 of the largest slices. Sprinkle both sides with salt, place in a colander, and let drain for at least 15 minutes. While the eggplant slices are standing, mix the filling ingredients together, reserving ½ cup mozzarella and 2 tablespoons Parmesan to top the finished dish. Rinse eggplant slices and pat dry. Arrange slices on a hot oiled grill rack or on a cookie sheet, drizzle with olive oil, and season with salt and pepper. Broil until softened, carefully turn over, and broil the other side for a minute or two. Cool slices on brown paper bags or paper towels to absorb the excess oil. Alternatively, the slices can be dipped in egg wash, lightly coated with bread crumbs, and fried until golden in a small amount of oil.

Fill each of the eggplant slices with 1 to 2 tablespoons of filling. Roll up lengthwise, and place in a baking dish with the seam side down. (Rolls can be held together with toothpicks, but remove them before serving.) Cover with foil and bake in a 400-degree oven for about 20 minutes, or until the cheese is melted and hot throughout. Remove the foil and sprinkle with the reserved cheeses. Spread some marinara sauce on a serving dish, and top with 1 or 2 rollatini for an appetizer serving. Pass additional sauce if desired.

Basic Marinara Sauce
> **1 small onion, finely chopped**
> **2 cloves garlic, minced**
> **¼ cup olive oil**
> **2 large cans crushed tomatoes**
> **½ cup red wine or water**
> **2 teaspoons dried basil**
> **2 teaspoons dried oregano**
> **1 teaspoon sugar**
> **salt and pepper**

In a large saucepan, sauté onion and garlic over medium heat until soft. Add all other ingredients and bring to a boil; reduce heat and simmer on low until sauce has thickened and flavors have blended.

Grandpa Parrott's Watercress Salad with Warm Bacon Dressing

My grandfather often went in search of wild watercress while trout fishing, and sometimes I would wade in the clear brook with him, searching for this spicy little green found in only the clearest and coldest water. Today, watercress is available in supermarkets, but it's not nearly as good as what we foraged with Grandpa.

8 cups tender watercress (or enough to fill your
favorite salad bowl)
8 strips bacon
½ cup cider vinegar
1 tablespoon sugar
2 hard-boiled eggs
salt and pepper

Clean the watercress, break it into bite-size pieces, and spin or air-dry. Fry bacon over medium heat until very crisp. Remove the bacon from the pan, let cool, and crumble. In the warm pan drippings, mix vinegar, salt, pepper, and sugar until the sugar has dissolved. Chop the eggs, sprinkle them over the watercress, and top with bacon pieces. Pour warm dressing over the salad, and toss to distribute. Serve immediately.

Rainbow Trout with Pecan Butter

6 tablespoons butter, softened and divided
½ cup chopped toasted pecans
2 tablespoons minced shallot
1 teaspoon fresh lemon juice
pinch cayenne pepper
4 trout fillets (1 ½ pounds)
1 tablespoon oil
1 egg beaten with 2 tablespoons water
½ cup bread crumbs, seasoned with salt and pepper

Place 4 tablespoons butter, pecans, and shallots in the bowl of a food processor, and pulse until well combined. Remove from the processor, stir in lemon juice and cayenne pepper, and set aside. Dredge the trout fillets in the egg wash and then the bread crumbs to coat. Melt the remaining 2 tablespoons butter with 1 tablespoon oil in a large skillet and fry the fish until golden brown, about 2 to 3 minutes on each side. Transfer to a serving plate and top each fillet with pecan butter.

Parsley Potatoes

2 pounds small, new, thin-skinned potatoes
½ stick butter
2 tablespoons chopped fresh parsley
salt and pepper

The potatoes can be peeled or not. If they're small enough, just cut them into ¼-inch slices. If they're large, cut them in half before slicing. Cover potato slices with cold water and add a generous teaspoon of salt. Bring to a boil. Reduce heat to medium and simmer for about 15 minutes or until tender. Drain. Return potatoes to the pan, top with butter, cover, and let the butter melt. Season with salt, pepper, and parsley; gently stir. Spoon into a serving bowl and serve immediately.

Dilled Vegetable Medley

1 head cauliflower
1 bunch broccoli crowns
1 cup baby carrots, peeled
2 tablespoons butter, softened
1 teaspoon fresh dill leaves
juice of 1 lemon

Break cauliflower and broccoli into similar-size florets. Steam or boil vegetables in salted water until just tender, about 5 minutes. Drain well. Mix in butter and dill. Sprinkle with lemon juice and serve.

Raspberry Bars

2 cups flour (or use 1 cup all-purpose flour and
   1 cup almond flour)
1 cup sugar
1 cup finely chopped walnuts or pecans
2 sticks butter, softened
1 egg
½ teaspoon vanilla extract
10-ounce jar raspberry preserves

Preheat oven to 350 degrees. In a mixing bowl, combine flour, sugar, nuts, butter, egg, and vanilla until the mixture is crumbly. Reserve 1½ cups of the crumb mixture. Press the remaining crumb mixture in the bottom only of a buttered 8-inch-square pan. Spread with raspberry preserves, stopping ½ inch from the edge of the pan. Sprinkle the reserved crumb mixture over the top of the preserves. Bake for 45 minutes or until golden brown. Cool completely before cutting into 2-inch squares.

Walleye Almandine

The walleye is native to the northern United States and Canada. It is a light-avoiding fish and is best caught in low-light conditions. This great game fish usually comes to the table from the end of a fishing rod, because few markets or fishmongers sell walleye. It is a shame that so few people get the chance to sample this treat. The snow-white flesh is firm and delicately flavored. You can substitute flounder, sole, cod, or rainbow or brook trout for walleye.

menu

Appetizer: Pasta e Fagioli

Salad: Fennel Salad

Entrée: Walleye Almandine

Side: Pasta and Vegetables

Dessert: Brasadella

Pasta e Fagioli

I always loved this soup whenever I ordered it in an Italian restaurant, but no matter which recipe I followed, mine came out too saucy and too red. My husband obligingly ate his way through many pots of soup that were okay but not quite pasta e fagioli. I finally learned the secret from my friend Kim, and now it really is the bean soup with "little thimbles" pasta. Mange bene!

olive oil
2 ounces pancetta, bacon, or salt pork, finely diced
1 cup chopped celery
6 cloves garlic, minced
1 large onion, chopped
8 cups water
3 15.5-ounce cans cannelini beans, 1 can reserved
1 15.5-ounce can red kidney beans, ½ cup reserved
28-ounce can tomatoes packed in juice (not puree)
8 ounces small pasta (e.g., ditalini, elbows), cooked al dente

Cover the bottom of a large, heavy soup pot with olive oil. Sauté the pancetta or bacon until brown and the fat has been rendered. Remove from the pan and set aside. Lower heat and add celery, garlic, and onion to the pan and cook until celery and onion have begun to soften; do not brown. Add water, 2 cans cannelini, ½ can kidney beans, their liquid, and tomatoes. (You can substitute dry beans that have been presoaked and cooked according to the package directions.) If you use whole tomatoes, puree them in a blender. At this point, the soup will be very pale and watery. Bring to a boil and simmer until thickened. Near the end of the cooking time, mash the beans in the pot with a potato masher to thicken the soup. Stir in the reserved whole beans, and cook for 15 or 20 minutes more. Remove from heat and stir in the cooked pasta. The soup will thicken as it stands. This soup is best made a day in advance. You can also keep the pasta separate until serving time. Serve with crushed red pepper flakes, grated cheese, and crusty bread.

Fennel Salad

2 to 3 fennel bulbs, trimmed and halved
1 red onion, thinly sliced
½ cup pitted black olives, halved
2 carrots, cut into matchsticks
1 small shallot, finely minced

Dressing
4 tablespoons extra virgin olive oil
2 tablespoons fresh lemon juice or white wine vinegar
salt and pepper to taste

Shave 2 or 3 fennel bulbs (depending on size) into very thin slices using a mandoline or a very sharp knife. In a mixing bowl, combine fennel, onion slices, olives, carrots, and shallot. Mix dressing ingredients in a small bowl and pour over fennel salad. Toss to coat.

Walleye Almandine

2 to 3 pounds walleye fillets
¼ cup flour
1 teaspoon seasoned salt
1 teaspoon paprika
1 stick butter
¼ cup sliced almonds
¼ cup white wine
2 shallots, minced
1 clove garlic, minced
4 tablespoons fresh lemon juice
4 to 5 drops hot pepper sauce
1 teaspoon chopped fresh parsley (optional)

Cut fillets into serving-size pieces. Mix flour, seasoned salt, and paprika. Dredge fish in seasoned flour. Melt butter in a large skillet over medium heat. Brown fish on both sides, 2 to 4 minutes per side, or until fish flakes when prodded with a fork. Reduce heat, remove fish to heated serving plates, and tent with foil to keep warm. Sauté almonds in the same skillet until lightly golden, stirring constantly. Add wine, shallot, and garlic and cook for 2 to 3 minutes over medium-low heat. Remove from heat and add lemon juice, pepper sauce, and parsley; stir. Pour over fish and serve at once.

Pasta and Vegetables

This vegetable-laden pasta dish can also be a stand-alone vegetarian entrée.

8 ounces linguine
2 tablespoons olive oil
2 cloves garlic, minced
½ sweet red pepper, sliced
1 medium zucchini, sliced
1 medium onion, sliced from top to bottom
½ cup sliced mushrooms
4 Roma or plum tomatoes, seeded and chopped
1 tablespoon finely chopped fresh basil leaves
    (do not use dried basil)
1 tablespoon chopped fresh oregano or 1 teaspoon
    dried
salt and pepper
¼ cup grated or finely shredded Parmesan cheese

Cook linguine according to package directions until al dente. Keep warm. Add oil to a skillet and stir-fry garlic for 1 minute. Add red pepper, zucchini, onion, and mushrooms and cook until crisp-tender. Add tomatoes, basil, oregano, and salt and pepper. Gently stir 2 minutes until thoroughly heated. Remove from heat; stir in warm pasta and cheese. Remove to a serving bowl.

Brasadella

My Aunt Sugar makes this Italian coffee cake every year for Easter and Christmas. The holiday version is slightly different, consisting of a big free-form cake baked on a cookie sheet and decorated with colored sprinkles for the season. Here, the cake is baked in a tube pan, but it's every bit as delicious. Brasadella is great dunked in coffee; it has the flavor of biscotti but is more cake than cookie.

>   3 cups flour
>   1 cup sugar
>   3 teaspoons baking powder
>   ½ teaspoon salt
>   1 stick butter, melted
>   2 eggs
>   ¾ cup milk
>   2 teaspoons anise extract
>   1 teaspoon lemon extract
>   sprinkles or colored sugar

Preheat oven to 375 degrees. Grease and flour a 10-cup tube pan. Mix all dry ingredients in a large bowl. Add butter, eggs, milk, and flavorings and stir until well mixed. Spoon into the tube pan; the batter will be thick. Brush the top with milk and sprinkle with multicolored sprinkles or colored sugar. Bake for 40 to 45 minutes, until a toothpick comes out clean.

part 4

OTHER GAME RECIPES

RUBS AND MARINADES FOR GRILLING

Grilling game meat is easy, and the results can be excellent if you follow some simple guidelines. Remember that dry rubs imbue rich flavor, whereas wet marinades tenderize and moisturize game meat, as well as enhancing its flavor.

Meat can be marinated for several hours or even overnight. Just keep in mind that thin cuts such as steaks or chops absorb the marinade much more quickly than large roasts, so adjust the time accordingly. Keep meat refrigerated when marinating for long periods, and use a plastic (not metal) bowl or a plastic bag. You can soak your meat in buttermilk, evaporated milk, salt water, or any number of marinades. Acidic liquids such as vinegar, lemon juice, pineapple juice, and papaya juice, or even a mustard paste, will tenderize the meat. You can also add a shake or two of commercial tenderizer. Bottled marinades and salad dressings can also be used to marinate before cooking and for basting while grilling.

Even though dry rubs don't add any moisture to the meat, they seal in meat juices. To help prevent those juices from escaping, use tongs to turn the meat rather than poking holes with a fork. And keep thermometer testing to a minimum to retain the juices inside the meat. Grilling at high temperatures also sears the meat and traps the juices. Because game meat doesn't have the fat content of commercial varieties, fire flare-ups are seldom a problem. If the weather isn't cooperating and you can't grill outdoors, you can always use your broiler.

South of the Border Rub

1 tablespoon mild chili powder
2 teaspoons salt
2 teaspoons light brown sugar
1 teaspoon pepper
1 teaspoon ground cumin
½ teaspoon garlic powder
¼ teaspoon ground red pepper (or more to taste)

Tex-Mex Grill Rub

1 teaspoon onion powder
1 teaspoon garlic salt
1 teaspoon crushed dried oregano
1 teaspoon ground cumin

Dry Barbecue Rub

1 teaspoon dry mustard
1 teaspoon chili powder
¼ to ½ teaspoon cayenne pepper (adjust to taste)
3 tablespoons brown sugar
1 teaspoon orange zest or dried orange peel
1 teaspoon garlic powder
1 teaspoon onion powder
½ teaspoon salt
½ teaspoon black pepper

Choose any of these three dry rubs. Mix all ingredients in a small bowl. Brush meat lightly with oil or mayonnaise, and rub the marinade on both sides of the meat. Set aside for 10 to 15 minutes. Grill several inches from the heat source to the desired degree of doneness.

Easy All-Purpose Marinade

½ cup olive oil
¼ cup wine or cider vinegar
¼ cup water
1 beaten egg
1 teaspoon garlic powder
1 teaspoon onion powder
1 teaspoon sage
1 teaspoon oregano
salt and pepper to taste

Combine all ingredients. Place meat in a plastic zipper-style bag or nonreactive bowl, pour marinade over meat, mix to coat, cover, and refrigerate for several hours or overnight.

Sweet and Spicy Glaze

1 cup soy sauce
1 cup sweet sherry, apple juice, or rice wine vinegar
1 teaspoon dried red pepper flakes
¼ cup honey
1 teaspoon ground ginger
2 teaspoons minced garlic or 1 teaspoon garlic
    powder
¼ cup vegetable oil
2 tablespoons sesame oil (optional)

Mix all ingredients, pour over meat, coat on all sides, and refrigerate several hours or overnight, turning several times.

Balsamic Marinade

2 cloves garlic, minced
1 onion, sliced in rings
8 black peppercorns, crushed
2 bay leaves
¾ cup balsamic vinegar
½ cup water
¼ cup vegetable or olive oil
2 tablespoons sugar
½ teaspoon salt

Mix all ingredients in a small saucepan. Heat to boiling, reduce heat, and simmer for 5 minutes. Let cool, then pour over meat. Marinate for several hours or overnight. For garlic lovers, additional slivers of garlic can be inserted into the meat with the tip of a knife before grilling.

Dijon Mustard Marinade

½ cup Dijon mustard
2 tablespoons red wine vinegar
¼ cup oil
1 clove garlic, minced, or ½ teaspoon garlic powder
1 shallot, finely minced
1 teaspoon crushed dried oregano
1 tablespoon Worcestershire sauce
¼ teaspoon black pepper

Mix all ingredients. Marinate meat for several hours or overnight in the refrigerator. Grill, basting occasionally with leftover marinade.

Teriyaki Marinade

½ cup soy sauce
½ cup pineapple juice
2 tablespoons oil
2 tablespoons brown sugar
2 cloves garlic, minced
½ teaspoon ground ginger
1 tablespoon Worcestershire sauce

Mix all ingredients. Marinate meat for several hours or overnight in the refrigerator. Grill, basting occasionally with leftover marinade.

Raspberry Orange Marinade for Wild Birds

2 cups fresh or frozen raspberries
½ cup raspberry, balsamic, or cider vinegar
½ cup orange marmalade
¾ cup olive oil
1 tablespoon fresh thyme or 1 teaspoon dried
½ teaspoon ground sage

Combine the raspberries, vinegar, and marmalade in a saucepan. Boil for 1 minute, and remove from heat. Stir in the remaining ingredients. Cool to room temperature. Pour the marinade over game birds or breast meat. Marinate overnight in the refrigerator, turning a few times. During grilling, baste occasionally with the marinade.

Barbecue Sauce Marinade

1 small onion, finely minced
1 clove garlic, finely minced
2 tablespoons oil
2 tablespoons maple syrup
½ cup ketchup
2 tablespoons Worcestershire sauce or steak sauce
1 teaspoon Dijon-style mustard

Mix all ingredients. Let meat marinate for several hours. Baste with marinade several times during grilling.

Honey Mustard Marinade

1 cup Dijon mustard
1 cup dry white wine
½ cup olive oil
¼ cup honey
1 teaspoon garlic powder
2 tablespoons steak sauce or Worcestershire sauce

Mix all ingredients. Marinate meat for several hours or overnight. Grill, basting meat occasionally with marinade.

PARTY-TIME HORS D'OEUVRES AND APPETIZERS

Nibbling on an hors d'oeuvre is a great way to get your uninitiated guests to sample wild meat. They may find it less intimidating than sitting down to an entrée-sized portion. Using game meat for appetizers is also an excellent idea when you don't have enough for a main course. Be flexible, substitute and experiment, and, above all, have fun.

Caribou Crostini with Roasted Red Pepper Mayonnaise

Looking for hors d'oeuvres that are easy to prepare but out of the ordinary? Caribou crostini fit the bill. They can be made from leftover caribou roast or from a roast that is too small to serve as a meal. Your guests are sure to enjoy them.

> **36 slices thin French baguette, ½ inch thick**
> **4 tablespoons extra virgin olive oil**
> **½ cup roasted red pepper**
> **⅓ cup mayonnaise**
> **salt and pepper**
> **dash cayenne pepper or crushed red pepper (optional)**
> **1 tablespoon butter**
> **1 ½- to 2-pound piece caribou tenderloin**
> **Montreal steak seasoning or seasoned salt**
> **coarsely ground black pepper**
> **2 tablespoons capers, chopped**
> **2 tablespoons pitted black olives, sliced in rings**

Preheat oven to 375 degrees. Arrange bread slices on 2 cookie sheets and drizzle with 3 tablespoons olive oil. Bake until crostini are lightly golden and crispy, about 10 minutes.

Blend the roasted red peppers and mayonnaise in a food processor until smooth. Season to taste with salt and pepper. Add a dash of cayenne pepper or crushed red pepper if you want a spicy dressing. Cover and refrigerate.

Melt butter in a skillet large enough to accommodate the tenderloin roast. Sprinkle the outside of the roast with seasoned salt and coarsely ground black pepper. Brown meat on all sides. Finish roasting in a 400-degree oven until rare or medium rare, about 20 minutes. Cool completely. Slice caribou tenderloin in very thin slices.

To serve, spread each slice of bread with red pepper mayonnaise, top with sliced caribou tenderloin, and garnish with chopped capers and black olive rings.

Cocktail Meatballs with Mushroom Sauce

1 pound ground game meat
½ pound ground pork
½ cup flavored bread crumbs
⅓ to ½ cup milk
1 large egg
1 tablespoon instant minced onion
1 tablespoon Worcestershire sauce
salt and pepper

Sauce
2 tablespoons butter
½ pound mushrooms, quartered
1 small onion, chopped
1 cup beef stock
½ cup dry red wine
2 tablespoons ketchup
1 small bay leaf
1 clove garlic, minced
4 teaspoons cornstarch dissolved in 4 teaspoons
water

Combine meat, bread crumbs, ⅓ cup milk, egg, onion, Worcestershire sauce, and salt and pepper. The mixture should be moist and soft but firm enough to be shaped into balls; if it's too dry, add a bit more milk. Roll the meat mixture into balls, about 1 inch in diameter for hors d'oeuvres or 1 ½ inch in diameter if you want to serve them over noodles as a main dish.

Set the meatballs about ½ inch apart in a nonstick, shallow-rimmed baking pan coated with a light spray of oil. Bake in a 425-degree oven until no longer pink in the center and lightly browned—about 10 to 12 minutes for 1-inch size; 15 to 18 minutes for larger meatballs. Cut one meatball in half to test for doneness. During cooking, use a wide spatula to turn the meatballs after they have browned where they touch the pan, or carefully shake the pan to roll the meatballs.

For the sauce: Melt the butter in a skillet and sauté the mushrooms and onion until soft, about 7 minutes. Add the stock, wine, kethcup, bay leaf, and garlic. Cook 5 minutes. In a small bowl, blend cornstarch with water; stir into sauce. Cook, stirring constantly, until mixture boils and thickens and looks clear. Remove bay leaf. Add meatballs to the sauce and reheat. Serve from a chafing dish to keep the meatballs warm, and supply toothpicks or cocktail forks.

Baked Olives

This is a simple but unusual way of serving olives. The scent will fill the house, and the olives will melt in your mouth. A heavy baking dish or cast-iron skillet is a must.

> **4 cups mixed imported-style olives**
> **½ cup dry white wine**
> **6 cloves garlic, minced**
> **2 tablespoons olive oil**
> **2 sprigs fresh thyme**
> **2 tablespoons snipped flat-leaf parsley**
> **2 teaspoons finely chopped orange zest**
> **¼ teaspoon crushed red pepper flakes (optional)**

Preheat oven to 375 degrees. Pour olives into a heavy baking dish or iron skillet. Mix in wine, garlic, olive oil, and thyme. Bake uncovered for 15 minutes, stirring once. Remove from oven. Discard thyme sprigs. Stir in parsley and orange zest and crushed red pepper if desired. Serve warm with warm French bread and a mild goat cheese, such as a moist and creamy chèvre.

Duck Pastrami

For the bird hunter who likes to present duck in a unique way, this delicious make-ahead duck pastrami is sure to please friends and family alike. Serve it as an hors d'oeuvre or appetizer at your next cocktail party.

> **1 whole boneless duck breast, split in half**
> **¼ cup coarsely ground black pepper**
> **¼ cup coarsely ground juniper berries**

> *Brining Liquid*
> **1 tablespoon black peppercorns**
> **2 teaspoons dried thyme**
> **2 large bay leaves, crumbled**
> **½ teaspoon whole cloves**
> **2 tablespoons minced garlic**
> **1 teaspoon whole juniper berries**
> **½ cup firmly packed light brown sugar**
> **½ cup kosher salt**
> **4 cups water**

For the brine: In a saucepan, combine all the ingredients. Mix and bring to a boil, stirring until the sugar and salt have dissolved. Let steep and cool for 1 hour.

Place the duck breasts in a glass or plastic bowl or in a zipper-style plastic bag, and pour the brine over the duck, making sure that it is covered completely. Cover the bowl and refrigerate for 48 hours, turning the breasts several times. Remove the duck breasts from the brining liquid, rinse well, and dry with paper toweling.

In a small bowl, mix the crushed juniper berries and black pepper. Press about two-thirds of the pepper mixture into the underside of the breast. Press the remaining portion into the skin side of the breast. Cook on a rack in a roasting pan, skin side down, in a slow, 250-degree oven for 60 to 90 minutes. Remove from the oven and let cool. Tightly wrap the breasts in plastic wrap and place in an airtight container. Refrigerate for at least 1 week before using.

Slice thinly and serve with sliced French bread, rye crackers, or other breads or crackers. Serve with Dijon-style mustard and pickled vegetables.

Savory Cheesecake

This is an impressive dish for a wine tasting, and it makes an elegant statement when served with crackers or thin slices of artisan bread. For a first course, serve over a bed of greens sprinkled with a vinaigrette dressing.

> 2 tablespoons butter
> ½ cup dry bread crumbs
> ½ cup finely chopped walnuts, toasted
> 2 shallots, minced
> 1 teaspoon butter or olive oil
> 12 ounces blue or Roquefort cheese
> 2½ 8-ounce packages cream cheese
> 1 tablespoon flour
> 4 eggs
> ¼ cup heavy cream
> 1 tablespoon minced dill

Preheat oven to 300 degrees. Melt butter in a skillet and toast bread crumbs until brown. Add toasted walnuts, mix well, and cool. Press the crumb mixture into the bottom of a 9-inch springform pan that has been sprayed with nonstick cooking spray. Line the pan with a 4-inch paper collar.

In a small skillet, cook shallots in a teaspoon of butter or olive oil, until soft. Set aside. In a food processor or mixer, blend cheeses until smooth. Add shallots, flour, eggs, and cream. Mix well. Blend in dill. Pour into the prepared pan. Place the springform pan in a larger pan in the oven, and pour hot water into the larger pan until it reaches halfway up the sides of the springform pan. Bake for 40 to 50 minutes, or until set and firm in the center. Let cool in the refrigerator overnight.

Cut into 24 serving slices. Serve with assorted crackers, crisp breads, or artisan bread slices.

Venison Kielbasa Bites

If you are lucky enough to have a smokehouse nearby, you can make your own venison kielbasa. These little circles of smoked meat make a great party food. I mix the ingredients in a small Crock-Pot, let the sauce come together, and add the meat just before the guests arrive.

1 smoked venison sausage (kielbasa style)
1 12-ounce jar grape or currant jelly
1 bottle chili sauce
2 tablespoons red hamburger relish
1 tablespoon mustard
dash Worcestershire sauce
dash hot pepper sauce (optional)

Mix sauce ingredients in a small saucepan or Crock-Pot. Stir until melted. Add kielbasa pieces and stir. Let simmer until warm. If you're not serving from a Crock-Pot, heat in the saucepan and then pour into a chafing dish. Pass cocktail forks or toothpicks.

Whiskey Shrimp

30 large shrimp, cooked, peeled, and deveined
1 shallot, minced
2 cloves garlic, minced
6 tablespoons olive oil
3 tablespoons whiskey, bourbon, or rye
juice of 2 limes
¼ cup balsamic vinegar
2 tablespoons honey
½ cup fresh tomatoes, peeled, seeded, and coarsely
    chopped
1 tablespoon minced cilantro
salt and pepper
Tabasco sauce to taste

Peel and clean the cooked shrimp; chill while preparing the sauce. In a skillet, sauté shallot and garlic in 1 tablespoon olive oil. Add whiskey and let the liquor evaporate. Stir in lime juice, vinegar, honey, and remaining olive oil, and simmer gently until all ingredients are mixed; let boil gently for a minute or two. Stir in tomatoes. Remove from heat. Add cilantro, salt and pepper, and Tabasco sauce to taste. Pour over shrimp and marinate for 2 to 4 hours. Drain excess marinade. Serve on a bed of lettuce leaves with lemon or lime wedges.

Duck Breast Pot Stickers

1 pound duck breast meat, ground, minced, or finely
  chopped in a food processor
2 bok choy or Chinese cabbage leaves, finely minced
½ cup finely minced water chestnuts
2 scallions, white and light green parts only, minced
1 clove garlic, finely minced
4 fresh button mushrooms, finely chopped
1 tablespoon cornstarch
1 teaspoon soy sauce
1 teaspoon rice wine or sherry
1 12-ounce package pot sticker or wonton wrappers,
  or dumpling dough (see recipe below)
2 tablespoons oil
½ cup water

The filling ingredients should be of the same size and texture, so chopping the meat and vegetables in a food processor or with the large blade of a meat grinder works just fine. To the meat and vegetables, add cornstarch and mix well. Stir in soy sauce and sherry, and mix well.

Working with 4 to 6 wrappers at a time, arrange them on a work surface. If they are not circular, you can cut the corners with a biscuit cutter or an inverted glass. Brush edges with water and place 1 teaspoon duck mixture near the center. Fold over to look like a turnover, and press out any trapped air, making small pleats around the edge. Turn the pleated side up and tap the bottom to form a base so that the pot sticker will stand up. Place on a piece of waxed paper that has been dusted with cornstarch, and continue until all the filling has been used. At this point, the pot stickers can be frozen on cookie sheets and then placed in an airtight container. Do not thaw to cook.

To cook, heat 2 tablespoons oil in a large skillet with a cover. Set pot stickers in the skillet flat side down, pleats up. You may be able to fit up to 20 in the pan, depending on its size, but don't overcrowd. Cook uncovered over medium heat until bottoms are golden brown. Pour in ½ cup water, cover, and simmer for 10 minutes more. Remove from pan, keep warm, and repeat with remaining dumplings. Serve with dipping sauces (several recipes follow).

If you want to make your own dumpling dough, read on.

Dumpling Dough
2 cups flour
1 cup boiling water

In a bowl, mix the flour and boiling water until a soft dough forms. Knead the dough on a lightly floured work surface about 5 minutes, or until smooth; alternatively, you can use a mixer for this. Split the dough in half. Shape each half into a roll 12 inches long, and cut each roll into ½-inch slices. Roll each slice into a thin circle. Trim with a cutter to a round shape, add filling, and pleat as above.

Hot Mustard for Dipping
¼ cup dry mustard
water

Mix mustard with enough cold water to form a smooth paste. Add more water to thin to the consistency of yellow mustard, as the sauce will thicken upon standing.

Ginger-Soy Dipping Sauce
4 tablespoons soy sauce
1 teaspoon sesame oil
1 tablespoon rice wine vinegar
1 teaspoon fresh minced ginger
1 teaspoon chopped green onion

Mix all ingredients and let stand for at least 1 hour to allow flavors to develop.

Hot Ginger and Soy Dumpling Sauce
3 teaspoons light soy sauce
3 teaspoons dark soy sauce
3 teaspoons rice wine vinegar
1 teaspoon hot chili oil (more to taste)
½ teaspoon sugar
1 clove garlic, crushed
1 teaspoon minced fresh ginger

Mix all ingredients and let stand to allow flavors to blend. Remove garlic before serving.

Goose Breast Morsels

These tender, tasty treats are easy to make and sure to please, so be prepared to watch them disappear quickly.

> **2 to 3 goose breasts cut into thin strips, ¼ by 2
>   inches**
> **2 tablespoons butter**
> **lemon pepper, Mrs. Dash, Montreal steak spice, or
>   your favorite seasoning mix**
> **¼ cup dry white wine**

Melt butter in a skillet over medium-high heat. Add goose pieces and season liberally with lemon pepper or other seasonings. When browned, turn and season the second side. Brown for 1 minute, pour in wine, stir, and simmer for 1 minute. Remove from the pan with a slotted spoon, and serve on a bed of lettuce leaves with toothpicks.

Four-Cheese Ball

> **8-ounce package cream cheese, softened**
> **4 ounces Gouda cheese, finely shredded**
> **4 ounces cheddar cheese, finely shredded**
> **4 ounces blue cheese, crumbled**
> **¼ onion, finely minced**
> **4 slices dried beef, shredded into fine pieces**
> **½ cup finely chopped walnuts**

Mix all cheeses, onion, and beef together. Place on a piece of plastic wrap and shape into a ball. Chill. Before serving, spread nuts on a paper plate or in a plastic bag. Roll the cheese ball in the nuts, pressing them into the cheese. Arrange on a platter surrounded by an assortment of crackers.

Duck Rumaki

1 cup red wine
2 cloves garlic, minced
1 shallot, minced
3 tablespoons soy sauce
1 tablespoon sugar
6 to 8 duck breasts, or 3 to 4 young goose breasts
1 can sliced water chestnuts (or substitute pineapple
    chunks)
1 pound thinly sliced bacon strips, cut in half

Mix wine, garlic, shallot, soy sauce, and sugar in a glass bowl or zipper-style plastic bag. Cut duck breasts into bite-size pieces and add to the wine mixture. Marinate in the refrigerator overnight, stirring or squeezing the bag several times to redistribute the liquid. To assemble, remove the duck meat from the marinade. Wrap one chunk of breast meat with one slice of water chestnut in a half strip of bacon. Secure with a toothpick. Arrange on a baking sheet. Rumaki can be refrigerated at this point and cooked just before serving.

Preheat oven to 350 degrees. Bake for approximately 20 minutes, until bacon is crispy. Turn once if necessary to crisp bacon on all sides. Serve hot.

Drunken Bear Bites

This is a Crock-Pot recipe. Just add all the ingredients and let them cook.

2 pounds bear meat, cut into 1-inch cubes
14-ounce bottle ketchup
1 cup dark brown sugar
2 tablespoons soy sauce
½ cup bourbon
crushed red pepper flakes (optional)

Combine ketchup, brown sugar, soy sauce, and bourbon in a small Crock-Pot. Stir in meat cubes, coating evenly. Cover and cook on high for 4 to 5 hours or on low for 8 hours, until tender. For extra zip, add some crushed red pepper flakes. Serve hot or cold with toothpicks or on cocktail bread slices to catch the sauce.

RECIPE LIST